ON THE
SEMICIVILIZED

ON THE
SEMICIVILIZED

Coloniality, Finance, and
Embodied Sovereignty in Cairo

Julia Elyachar

DUKE UNIVERSITY PRESS
Durham and London
2025

© 2025 DUKE UNIVERSITY PRESS
Project Editor: Livia Tenzer
Designed by A. Mattson Gallagher
Typeset in Minion Pro, Source Sans 3, and Adobe Arabic by
Westchester Publishing Services

Library of Congress Cataloging-in-Publication Data
Names: Elyachar, Julia, [date] author.
Title: On the semicivilized : coloniality, finance, and embodied
sovereignty in Cairo / Julia Elyachar.
Description: Durham : Duke University Press, 2025. | Includes
bibliographical references and index.
Identifiers: LCCN 2024044722 (print)
LCCN 2024044723 (ebook)
ISBN 9781478031901 (paperback)
ISBN 9781478028635 (hardcover)
ISBN 9781478060857 (ebook)
Subjects: LCSH: Cairo (Egypt)—History. | Cairo (Egypt)—
Social conditions. | Egypt—Civilization—638–1798. |
Egypt—Civilization—1798– | Egypt—History—1517–1882. |
Turkey—History—Ottoman Empire, 1288–1918. | Islamic
Empire—History.
Classification: LCC DT143 .E48 2025 (print) | LCC DT143
(ebook) | DDC 962/.16—dc23/eng/20241213
LC record available at https://lccn.loc.gov/2024044722
LC ebook record available at https://lccn.loc.gov/2024044723

Cover art: Geometric brass decoration on an ancient door,
Cairo. Photograph by Khaled El-Adawi / Adobe Stock.

For Tomaž, Elijan, and Martin

CONTENTS

ACKNOWLEDGMENTS

Like all books, this one is a collective endeavor that only authorial fiction puts under my name alone. My debts are of a length and depth impossible to capture here. I am first and foremost indebted to my ancestors who kept records of their life in Palestine as far back as 1500. I owe special thanks to my great-uncle Hai Elyachar for his work as archivist and family historian, and to my grandfather for the stories he passed on to me.

I began work on the sections of this book related to the Ottoman Empire and the Ottoman Public Debt Administration when I was a graduate student at Harvard University in the early 1990s. There, I worked with Tosun Aricanli at the Center for Middle Eastern Studies on two projects that bear directly on this book. The first was a project to develop conceptual vocabulary for comparative analysis of the Ottoman, Mughal, and Saffavid Empires; the second was a research project on the Ottoman Public Debt Administration. Many of the questions raised by the groups Tosun brought together animate my work to this day. Among my colleagues at Harvard, I thank Rosemarie Bernard, Kristen Brustad, Mara Thomas, Paula Russo, Steven Pincus, and Eve Troutt Powell for their engagement, friendship, and critical feedback on my writing and my studies more generally. Also at Harvard, I am indebted to Cemal Kafadar, Roger Owen, Michael Herzfeld, and especially Sally Falk Moore for their support and mentorship. In recent years, I returned to my student work on the Ottoman Public Debt Administration and have had the honor of meeting and learning from Nora Elizabeth Barakat, Aviv Derri, and Ellen Nye. I wish I could have known them as a young woman.

Over the years, I have been lucky to be supported in my research by many institutions. I am grateful to the Fulbright Commission; the Institution of International Exchange, Egypt; the Sheldon Fellowship of Harvard University; the Social Science Research Council and MacArthur Foundation Program in International Peace and Security in a Changing World; the Center for Middle Eastern Studies, Harvard University; the University Committee on Research in the Humanities and Social Sciences (UCRHSS), Princeton University; and the Princeton Institute for International and Regional Studies (PIIRS), Princeton University, for their support of various phases of research that went into this book.

I began something close to the shape of the current book in March 2020 while living in Ljubljana, Slovenia, during the COVID-19 pandemic and have been working on it ever since, in Cairo, Irvine, and Princeton. I had the great privilege and joy in 2020, between Ljubljana and Princeton, of participating in a writing group led by Therí Pickens, whose brilliant mentorship reshaped me in profound ways. Working in the group she led, together with Edward Jones-Imhotep, Chrystal Lucky, and Lora Levett in particular, changed the way I worked and inspired me on a weekly basis. As a draft and then drafts of this book came together, a number of friends and colleagues were generous with their time and critical feedback. For their engagement and contributions to my thinking, I am immensely grateful to Talal Asad, Étienne Balibar, Rana Barakat, Rosie Bsheer, Muna El Shorbagi, Will Hanley, Omnia El Shakry, Noura Erakat, Agustín Fuentes, Julia Gearhart, Behrooz Ghamari-Tabrizi, Onur Günay, Martin Kornberger, Huda Lutfi, Timothy Mitchell, Laila Hussein Moustafa, Joanne Randa Nucho, Janet Roitman, Danilyn Rutherford, Hanan Sabea, Gabriele Schwab, AbdouMaliq Simone, and Neferti Tadiar. For crucial feedback on my writing about family history and Palestine, I am indebted to Lila Abu-Lughod, Gabriele Schwab, Sherene Seikaly, Ngugi wa-Thiong'o, and Chandra Bozelko and the staff of the OpEd Project. My thanks as well to Nick Seaver for sending an article of mine to the novelist Robin Sloan. It was a boost in a difficult period of writing to read his characterization of my writing as "novelistic" and to learn that he had based a character in a new book on my depiction of Mr. Amir, the public sector banker. Work with an incredible editorial collective led by Martin Kornberger, with Geoffrey C. Bowker, Andrea Mennicken, Peter Miller, Joanne Randa Nucho, and Neil Pollock, on our book project *Thinking Infrastructures*, pushed forward my thinking about infrastructure in a way that is directly reflected in this book. Reading Rocío Zambrana's book *Colonial Debts* for my class" Empires of Debt" taught me the importance of literature on coloniality for my work.

Some colleagues went so far as to read the entire manuscript, sometimes twice. Muhammad Addakhakhny, Gil Anidjar, Naor Ben-Yehuyada, Brenna Bhandar, Rosie Bsheer, Essam Fawzi, Ashraf Ghani, Paul Kockelman, Zachary Lockman, Tomaž Mastnak, Umut Özsu, and Sherene Seikaly read various versions of the manuscript, as did two anonymous readers for Duke University Press. They all took me to task in ways for which I am endlessly grateful, offering advice, critique, and wisdom from which I could only partially benefit in the course of completely redoing the book more than once. I am grateful to Ashraf Ghani for reminding me that I am an anthropologist and ethnographer first and for giving me crucial advice about structure; to Paul Kockelman for his many contributions to my thinking and for coining the phrase *phatic labor* in the course of an email exchange about my work; to Tomaž Mastnak for his constant encouragement, feedback, and learned suggestions; to Laila Hussein Moustafa for her support and expert wisdom over many years; to Joanne Randa Nucho for comments and encouragement along the way; to Sherene Seikaly for her capacity to combine uncompromising critical feedback with exemplary collegial generosity and unshakeable trust. Muhammad Addakhakhny read a final version of this book, correcting mistakes I made in transliteration and providing erudite commentary along the way. My debts to Essam Fawzi are immense and beyond measure. I describe our friendship, collaboration, and conversations over the course of thirty years in the body of this book and note here his centrality to all my work in and thinking about Egypt and beyond. Without him, this book would not exist. For their crucial work on proposals for preserving and digitizing Essam Fawzi's "archives from the dust," I thank Laila Hussein Moustafa and Muna el Shorbagi.

In early years of writing material that went into this book, I was lucky to be employed at UC Irvine (2008–2017), where I held appointments in the Departments of Anthropology and Economics and served as the director of the Center for Global Peace and Security. Conversations and engagement with a number of my colleagues there were essential for the development of my thinking. I am grateful to all my colleagues from that time, in particular Geoffrey Bowker, Paul Dourish, George Marcus, Valerie Olson, Leo Chavez, Kris Peterson, Gabrielle Schwab, David Theo Goldberg, and especially Bill Maurer and Tom Boellstorff, for their support and engagement. Teaching graduate and undergraduate students at UCI was inspiring and engaging, and I am grateful to all my students for giving me the opportunity to learn from and with them.

I moved to Princeton in 2017, where I am based in the Department of Anthropology and at the Princeton Institute for International and Regional Studies (PIIRS). I am grateful to my colleagues in Anthropology for their collegiality, engagement, and support. Thank you João Biehl, Elizabeth Davis, Agustín Fuentes, Hanna Garth, Carol Greenhouse, Onur Günay, Abdellah Hammoudi, Jeffrey Himpele, Rena Lederman, Ryo Morimoto, Serguei Oushakine, Laurence Ralph, Ikaika Ramones, Carolyn Rouse, Beth Semel, Aniruddhan Vasudevan, and Jerry Zee. Teaching together with Onur Günay was a masterclass in pedagogy and reworking the anthropological canon. Many students in my classes at Princeton over the past five years inspired and provoked me to articulate my thinking much more clearly on many points that went into this book. I am so grateful. Carol Zanca, Patricia Lieb, and Mo Lin Yee in the Department of Anthropology made everything so much easier and more pleasant with their incredible skills and kindness. At PIIRS, I am grateful for the opportunity to have worked with and learn from Mark Bessinger, Steve Kotkin, and Deborah Yashar; and thank you to Karen Koller and Rachel Golden for making everything work so much more easily. Elsewhere in Princeton, I am grateful to Michael Gordin, Lara Harb, Cornelia Huellstrunk, Behrooz Ghamari-Tabrizi, and Beate Witzler for their friendship, support, and advice, and to Julia Gearhart for inspiring collaboration. Among my amazing graduate students, Omar Abdelqader, Adhip Amin, JahAsia Jacobs, Navjit Kaur, Moad Musbahi, and Jamie Pelling read parts of the manuscript in various forms and gave me important comments for which I am grateful.

Numerous times and at multiple institutions too many to list here, I presented talks on strands of thought in this book, and I am grateful to all the audiences for their questions and feedback, and for indulging my many attempts over the years to draw on lessons from Ottoman history in my work as an ethnographer of post-Ottoman Egypt and Palestine, and to bring together the many strands of my work with some semblance of coherence. I wish I could name everyone who asked questions and pushed back in multiple fora over the years. To all those whose names I have forgotten to mention here, I voice my gratitude and acknowledge my debts.

I had the luck and honor of working with incredible editors in the process of writing this book. Without Hollianna Bryan, this book might not have come together. Finding her after years of struggle with what had become an undoable project was a life-changing experience. She worked with me in figuring out what I wanted to say, how to say it, and how to put things together from start to finish, over multiple reworkings of this book in the course of more than four years. As an editor and writing coach, her range of skills is remarkable, and my gratitude knows no bounds. Here I also want to mark my good luck in having landed at Princeton, an institution with the resources to provide research funds for such essential editorial support. I wish every writer were so lucky as to have such an opportunity.

I began talking to Ken Wissoker, senior executive editor at Duke University Press, about something resembling this book more than ten years ago. He was critical and honest with me the many times my efforts failed, while always leaving the door open for ongoing discussion and exchanges. This combination is precious, and I am so grateful. His contributions to the introduction in particular were essential. I also had the privilege of working with two other wonderful professionals at Duke University Press: Kate Mullen through the second phase of the peer review process and Livia Tenzer, who masterfully oversaw the production editing process. Outside of Duke, Ben Platt gave me important feedback and help in a difficult phase of work.

Without the love and support of my family in the United States and Slovenia over the the many years that went into writing this book, nothing would have been possible. My sisters Liz Botwin and Kate Dvorkin believed in me through a process that mysteriously seemed to go on forever. My mother, Ruth Turner, passed away in the early phases of preparation for writing this book. Her support of my obsessions, my projects, and my writing carry me always. My brother-in-law Matjaž Mastnak and sister-in-law Cvetka Sokolov always made me feel at home in Slovenia, as did my nephews, Peter and Oskar Mastnak-Sokolov, and the late Manca Košir. Also in Slovenia, Vlasta Jalušič has been both sister and intellectual companion for thirty years. In New York, Tania Cypriano took me in, gave me a home, and restored my spirits when we were flooded out of our house. In Cairo and New York, Laila Hussein Moustafa made everything so much easier and kept me laughing. In Cairo, Ljubljana, Sarajevo, and Split, Milijana Vučičević-Salama was the angel and sister who restored my life and gave me hope for the future.

This book is dedicated to Tomaž Mastnak, Elijan Mastnak, and Martin Mastnak. My intellectual companion for more than thirty years, Tomaž supported me in countless ways through the writing of and research for this book, in matters both domestic and intellectual. He read multiple versions of my writing that laid the groundwork for this book and multiple drafts of the manuscript itself, always sharing the bounty of his remarkable scholarship and editorial eye. The appearance in our lives of our sons, Elijan and Martin Mastnak, twenty-six and twenty-two years ago respectively, remains a source of endless wonder and joy. Elijan has been my companion and then coach for more than twelve years of training in fitness biomechanics as taught by the brilliant Ricky Rivera in Irvine, California. Besides allowing me to live injury free, that work with Elijan and Ricky gave me the inspiration for my writing in this book on proprioception. Martin is a companion in some of the obsessions that shape this book, including all matters post-Ottoman, which is another source of joy. My love for Tomaž, Elijan, and Martin sustains me and the writing of every word that follows.

INTRODUCTION

On the Move

I first heard stories about Cairo from my grandfather, who was born and raised in Jerusalem, Palestine. The son and grandson of an Ottoman *sarraf* (usually translated as banker or broker) and grandson of the Chief Rabbi of Palestine, my grandfather grew up moving with his male siblings and cousins around cities of the Arab world and Ottoman Empire for education and for commerce. They were educated in Beirut, Damascus, Cairo, and Istanbul. Cairo was not his home, but it was a place where he was at home.

This history shaped my approach to study of the region in ways I understood only much later. My grandfather brought his young family to New York from Palestine in 1930, after conflicts with the British government of Mandatory Palestine over his refusal to comply with orders from the Jewish Agency for Palestine to fire all the "Arabs" (as they are called in the documents) working under his supervision. As an engineer trained at the French University in Beirut, my grandfather had been hired by the Mandate government to supervise the construction of a road from Jerusalem to Bethlehem. With threats and fines, the Mandate government and the Jewish Agency were pressuring him to hire European Jewish settlers in place of the Palestinian workers. Apparently technical matters about road construction, the labor force, and engineering became grounds for threats, angry memos, and litigation.

The road from Jerusalem to Bethlehem that my grandfather worked on just after World War I was just one of many infrastructure projects underway in Palestine and the region at the time (Al-Saleh and Arefin 2020; Nucho 2018). Roads, railroads, and canals forged connections among different regions of the Ottoman Empire and, as such, were a key terrain of contestation that only intensified with the end of the Ottoman Empire in 1924. In fact, conflicts for control over roads, canals, and railroads across Palestine, Egypt, and the Ottoman Empire were nothing new. Flows of commerce, people, moneys, commodities, and armies across the region had been a prime interest of governance in the Ottoman Empire. With the end of the Ottoman Empire and imposition of new kinds of imperial power, infrastructures of mobility and communicative infrastructures, as I call them in this book, were refigured as well. Control over channels through Egypt remained the object of imperial contestation and even wars, as in the 1956 Suez Crisis or "Tripartite Aggression" of Great Britain, France, and Israel against Egypt, when President Gamal Abdel Nasser nationalized the Suez Canal.

I first encountered traces of these infrastructures of global mobility and sovereign affiliations in pieces of paper I found in a small, maroon leather suitcase in a corner of the dusty attic of my grandfather's home in New York after his death. I opened the lid of that suitcase and found papers my grandfather had clipped together and tied with string. Each piece of paper told a detail of his young life in Palestine: certificates of his training as apprentice to the Greek Orthodox architect Spyro Houris, notes from the Imperial Ottoman Bank, letters from brother to brother across oceans and time, and exit documents from Jerusalem under the Ottoman Empire, the British Mandate, and the state of Israel.

My great-great grandfather's Ottoman exit document from Jerusalem is written in Ottoman Turkish calligraphy (figure I.1). It states his "place of birth" as "al-Quds al-Sherif," the Arabic name for Jerusalem, and his occupation as *sarraf*. My great-uncle's application for "Permission to leave Occupied Enemy Territory," issued by the British Occupied Enemy Territory Administration in Palestine after 1917, is typed in English (figure I.2). It has a new category, "nationality," which my great-uncle filled in as "local." By the time the government of British Mandatory Palestine was established in 1920, official exit documents were printed in English, Arabic, and Hebrew. They included that same query about "nationality," which my great-uncle again enters as "local." This category made sense to me only years later, after I learned about the institution of *local* as a category in British-occupied Egypt (Hanley 2017), which was contrasted to that of *beratlis*—those exempt from local law and taxation.

I.1   Ottoman exit document granting departure from Jerusalem in Islamic-
calendar year 1323 (Gregorian calendar, 1905–6). Collection of the author.

Nº 3822

Local Form O Q. 6 A.

APPLICATION FOR PERMISSION TO LEAVE OCCUPIED
ENEMY TERRITORY.

1. Family Name (in Capitals) ~~HAY~~ ELYACHAR
2. First Name (in Capitals) HAY
3. Description : — Height 5'6'' Build ordinary
   Colour of Hair black Moustache Beard
   Colour of Eyes dark brown Complexion dark
4. Nationality LOCAL
5. Father's Nationality and Occupation Local, merchant
6. Place of Birth Jerusalem 7. Age
8. Occupation and Residence before July, 1914
9. Present Occupation merchant
10. Present Address Jerusalem P. O. B. 130
11. Length of residence at present address 1 year months
12. Destination and Address Salonique
    Haim S. Arovti & prères
13. Previous address there (if any)
14. Reason for travelling business
15. Route of journey fee
16. If self supporting Yess
17. If a Merchant, class of goods trading in Artistic Goods of
    Palestine Trade reference
18. Date of return (if not returning state so) 3 Mounthes
19. Have you previously applied for permission to travel to or from OCCUPIED ENEMY
    TERRITORY? Yess
    If so, when? 29/4/19 (Nº Passer, 1253) From where? from Jerusalem
    To what destination? to Cairo
    Signature (in full) of applicant
    Date

[P.T.O.

Categories such as *local* or *beratli* were part of much broader systems of mobility, commerce, and finance that specialists discuss in terms of the "Ottoman capitulations." The capitulations were treaties organized along principles of extraterritoriality, in which one state (usually an imperial state) allowed another state to exercise jurisdiction over its own nationals within the first state's territory. Exterritoriality, in turn, was a logical extension of the personality of law, a principle usually associated with the Roman Empire, according to which a subject's attachment to the sovereign is embodied—that is, linked to the physical person, rather than to territory and borders—so that it moves through space with the extraterritorial subject, even, crucially, in the domains of another polity.[1] Such systems promoted the free flow of commerce across the domains of empire, wherein goods, money, and transactions carried out by these subjects were free from the constraints of local law as well.

The Ottoman capitulations were not restricted to the East. They were nothing exotic or oriental. On the contrary: the Ottoman capitulations were essential to the organization of global commerce for centuries. They brought extraterritoriality into the core of the international legal system of Westphalian territorial sovereign states (Özsu 2016a). And yet the capitulations, extraterritoriality, and personal law remain remarkably absent in Western social and political theory, as well as political economy and anthropology, up to the present day.

Over the centuries, relations between the Ottoman Empire and (what became) the capitalist West were mediated through these commercial and financial infrastructures and in private international law along the fluid and incorporative boundaries of empire (Burbank and Cooper 2011). Sojourners and travelers through Ottoman domains thus kept their sovereign affiliation with their place of birth. They moved through space along channels of extraterritorial belonging across domains of empire, rather than crossing with a passport the borders of nation-states in which the rule of law was (theoretically) homogeneously applied to all residents of the state. They might have carried with them an exit document of the kind carried by my great-great grandfather when he traveled out of Palestine.

Such exit documents marked the bearer's tie to his sovereign while traveling in distant lands. This attachment of people to their sovereign moved with them through space according to principles of personal law and was respected inside the domain of another sovereign. Subjects of an empire or state, meanwhile, might have multiple forms of sovereign affiliation. These principles were essential to global infrastructures of commerce and finance that ran through the Ottoman Empire for centuries. I will unpack the implications of this global infrastructure of mobility and commerce for the making of what I call in this book the "semicivilized condition."

I came to think about the notion of the semicivilized through a set of problems that preoccupied me first as an ethnographer and student of both the history of thought and the former Ottoman Empire and then as a historical anthropologist of the region and ethnographer of Cairo from the vantage point of the former Ottoman Empire. I had questions: How did the vast literatures on colonialism and postcolonialism pertain to lands of the former Ottoman Empire, which was never (fully) colonized in a traditional sense? Why were the extraterritorial treaties in private international law—known in English as the capitulations, in Ottoman Turkish as *ahdname*, and in Arabic as *imtiyazat* (pledges, or privileges)—that provided essential infrastructure for global commerce through World War I so overlooked in political theory and political economy? Why were essential categories of social class in Egypt linked to that legal infrastructure absent in works of political economy and social science? Why were novels, films, and poetry so much better than the social sciences at capturing the essential dynamics of social change and political economy? And how could understanding such connections in relation to Egypt help us make sense of the world more broadly?

The concept of the semicivilized also gave me a vantage point from which to rethink a whole set of concepts in social sciences and critical theory such as sovereignty, territory, colonialism, and postcolonialism.[2] These foundational concepts had come to seem increasingly problematic in the years I worked on this book, as the twentieth-century global order they no longer adequately described came crashing down. Thinking from the standpoint of the semicivilized allowed me to better understand the ethnographic research I conducted in Cairo, Egypt, over many years and to consider how a set of problems long considered unique to the Middle East were in fact essential for understanding the world taking shape in the twenty-first century.

Literatures on colonialism, postcolonialism, and sovereignty did not do justice to this history or to the global scale, import, and effects of the institutions and infrastructures it generated. I turned to different kinds of literature to find analytic language that could help me make sense of what I saw. To make sense of that problem space, I began to use a concept cluster that cohered around the notion of the semicivilized. To clarify: by drawing on this language, I in no way mean to imply that Ottomans or Egyptians or Palestinians were somehow "semicivilized beings." That said, it is my contention that it is a mistake to dismiss the semicivilized as an obscure and perhaps laughable contortion of civilizational discourse. After all, in the months when I finished this book, Israeli leaders were calling Palestinians "barbarians," a category linked to the semicivilized, to justify their dehumanization and attempted eradication through genocidal violence.

After decades of critique, the primitive/civilized divide remains a constitutive and unstable binary of twentieth-century Western thought. Inserting the semicivilized into that unstable binary can help destabilize the entire edifice of civilizational thinking. In any case, the so-called civilized world to which the semicivilized were so long denied entry is collapsing upon itself. Bringing this undercurrent of the barbarian and the semicivilized into sharper focus is an essential step of any project to imagine things differently in the bloody aftermath of civilizational thinking and colonizing orders.

Most of the ethnographic research for this book took place in Cairo. But to arrive at the core of those stories about Cairo over the many years I conducted research there, I travel in a circuitous path through this introduction to set the groundwork for the Cairo-based account that follows. Over the years, I have pursued parallel tracks of ethnographic and archival research in Cairo while continuing to read in Ottoman and Egyptian history, international law, the history of political thought, Middle Eastern studies, and coloniality studies. In what follows, I weave together these strands of inquiry to tell stories that emerged through both ethnography and the archives in which I was immersed.

Reintroducing in this way the concept of the semicivilized, which is absent in political economy, social theory, and studies of colonialism, shifts the meaning of conventionally used concepts and leads us to question the meaning they have in today's usage. It calls for the introduction of concepts such as personal law, dividual sovereignty, and extraterritoriality. These concepts help me make sense of my materials, such as my forebears' exit documents from Jerusalem with which I opened this book. That is not all. They mesh incredibly well with concepts I have previously developed to theorize my long-term ethnographic research in Cairo, such as embodied infrastructure, social infrastructures, and communicative channels (Elyachar 2010, 2011, 2012b). Through this cohesion, we can see that longer temporal dynamics and patterns are at play.

That said, this book is not about "the Ottoman exception." It is not a case study. It does more than increase awareness, I hope, of an important region neglected in many analytic frameworks. I do not want to add to the list of exceptions to "classic colonialism" or to grant the semicivilized its rightful (if shameful) place in the middle of the primitive/civilized divide, thus inadvertently bolstering civilizational logics.[3] The point is not to develop a new subaltern category or "minoritizing view" (Sedgwick 2008, 1). It is to unsettle the entire organizing logic of how we think about colonialism, postcolonialism, and the primitive/civilized divide. I do so in this book by elucidating how dynamics of power, mobility, and sovereignty have often worked differently than dominant accounts of colonialism lead us to believe.

Arrangements of belonging, mobility, and transacting with others across space look quite different in empire-states around the world from China to the Ottoman Empire. Scholars have tried for decades to theorize these arrangements outside the constraints of area studies. Jane Burbank and Frederick Cooper (2011) built on many of those efforts in their masterful study called *Empires in World History*. But there is more to do. So much has been modeled on understanding the state, colonialism, and postcolonialism as territorial. In this book I present another model of how relations of subjects to states, bodies to rulers, residents to land, commoners to their cities, might be organized. The semicivilized is one element of this model, and the one I have chosen to signify its logics. The semicivilized is linked in my account to other important concepts that were set aside in the making of classical social theory, political economy, and theories of colonialism, such as the concept of extraterritoriality.

As a concept, extraterritoriality is tied to territoriality and to the system of territorial nation-states that shaped twentieth-century global order.[4] But there is nothing "extra" about extraterritoriality.[5] The term indexes this global regime of mobility that predates territoriality and never disappeared. The fact that extraterritoriality never went away highlights another reality: in modern territorial states, as in empires, sovereign power does not in fact map uniformly onto territory or citizenry. True enough, as a global infrastructure regulating the movement of people, finance, and commerce around inter-imperial worlds, extraterritoriality was largely dismantled in the early twentieth century with the dissolution of the Ottoman Empire at the end of World War I. But extraterritoriality continued as a practice of international law: Legal extraterritoriality became known as "the assertion and exercise of jurisdictional powers beyond a specific territorial framework" (Margolies et al. 2019, 8).

Despite these continuities, extraterritoriality somehow sits ill at ease with contemporary notions of sovereignty and global order. Zones of exception for those who enjoy the benefits of extraterritoriality provoke outrage among locals in cases large and small, from crimes committed off base by

US military stationed abroad to cases of unpaid parking tickets accumulated by diplomats and their children in New York City. Sometimes people mix up extraterritoriality with the notion of cosmopolitanism. It is important to note that these two concepts operate on different levels. One is legal, jurisprudential; the other is an ideological construct, fashionable among the men of letters during the Enlightenment and then among early socialists in the nineteenth century. Cosmopolitanism often refers to the notion that we are citizens of the world rather than of a particular nation or state. Sometimes cosmopolitanism refers to the ability of some people to use multiple passports and to feel at home in different countries. Extraterritoriality is different. It refers to a global legal order.[6]

The new world order that took shape after World War I, formalized at the Paris Peace Conference and in the resulting Treaty of Versailles, abolished the Ottoman Empire and many provisions of the extraterritorial treaties, or capitulations. But despite declarations from the post-Versailles League of Nations about self-determination for all countries, only some would be allowed to enjoy rights of sovereignty and self-determination. Many countries had to wait until after World War II, or even later, to gain independence from colonial powers. Others enjoyed formal sovereignty but, in practice, held only partial power over their territory and inhabitants thanks to the continued salience of these extraterritorial treaties and the notion of the semicivilized to which they were linked.

The capitulations and the principles of extraterritoriality and personal law that they reflect and helped shape are not only absent in texts on political economy, social theory, and colonialism. They are more generally ignored in universalizing theories in the West, even though they are a global infrastructure of commerce and finance in Europe as well. There are exceptions; a few scholars have discussed capitulations as a kind of colonialism or imperialism, but they often get things wrong. In such formulations, the capitulations become but another example of imperialism or colonialism moving unidirectionally from the West onto an external East or Global South (Anghie 2012; Hindess 2005; Fidler 2000). Rosa Luxemburg wrote about Egyptian debt in *The Accumulation of Capital* ([1913] 1951), but in her analysis, Egyptian and Ottoman debt expressed a crisis of capital accumulation in Europe, exported to the East, rather than being part of an intertwined system of finance and banking.[7]

My grandfather's documents were part of this legacy. Those travel documents and papers, I would later realize, were ghostly traces of this global infrastructure of mobility based on principles of embodied sovereignty, personal law, and extraterritorial belonging. As such, it became clear to me, the former Ottoman Empire—the region of the semicivilized—was a good place from which to rethink sovereignty, territory/ground, infrastructure, and embodiment more broadly. Thinking from here, different logics come into view. But as I will stress throughout this book, paying attention to these different logics is not about respecting cultural or regional difference. It is not a matter of the supposed exceptionalism of the Middle East or Arabs or Muslims or Orientals. Ottoman logics of sovereignty, territory, and international law, once again, are at least as universal and systemic as are cognate concepts in Western political theory.

Some matters at play are general to empires. Empires, to repeat, generally do not have fixed boundaries. They do not have territory; they have "domains." Power in empire can hop and skip along channels and across gaps of land and water. Such connecting channels across domains, lands, waters, and shores are a thread that moves through this book. I draw on these ideas to portray a world (and soon enough, a more general situation) that was labeled in Western international law and civilizational discourse as "the semicivilized."

Stories I will recount in this book are not exotic stories from the Middle East. They recount neglected infrastructures of the global order we live with today. Making my case entails a deep dive into history. Throughout this book, it is not the events of history I am after but rather "the processes that underlie and shape such events" (Wolf 1999, 8). Making sense of historical processes, in turn, demands engagement with concepts to help make sense of what is going on. But use of concepts "without attention to the theoretical assumptions and historical contexts that underlie them can lead us to adopt unanalyzed concepts and drag along their mystifying connotations into further work" (21). This is why I look to the semicivilized to unsettle established concepts in the social sciences and turn to other concepts to help me in that endeavor, such as dividual sovereignty, embodied infrastructures, global commerce, and communicative channels.

In thinking through this material, I also found it helpful to work with the concept of coloniality, which is delinked from the concept of territory that lurks behind the most common usages of *colonialism*.[8] Like the semicivilized of the former Ottoman Empire, many peoples have been unable to gain effective sovereignty over their land and resources or to escape the bonds of structural debt. Accounts of nonsovereign futures (Bonilla 2015), remaindered lives (Tadiar 2022), and "in between spaces that disturb the certainties of territory and mapping" (Thomas 2022, 250) felt strangely familiar to me, as did Rocío Zambrana's (2021) work on coloniality and indebtedness without end. These kinds of conditions grouped together in the body of literature surrounding the concept of coloniality resonated with what I analyze in this book in terms of the semicivilized condition.

While semicivilized is a historical category, and one out of use today, the semicivilized remains with us as a condition of the present as well. This most obviously pertains to the Middle East, a region left to cope with violent legacies of extraterritoriality, the semicivilized, and the barbarian—even though these conditions are in no way unique to Egypt or the former Ottoman Empire. The war on terror launched after September 11, 2001, brought these concepts back to center stage. One hundred and more years after Versailles, the semicivilized, as a condition and a concept, continued to shape our world in ways that could no longer be overlooked, as twentieth-century institutions and certainties came unraveled in turn.

But that is not all. I will also shed light on practices that could be considered a kind of subaltern politics of the commons of the semicivilized. Such a politics includes, I suggest, potentiating forgotten pathways of moving, thinking, and acting in common on shaken grounds. I will explore the politics of movement and grounds by reading stories centered on Cairo. I will do so with the help of the concepts of personal law, embodied infrastructure, semiotic commons, and proprioception (the way we know where we are in space and how parts of our bodies relate to one another).

I wrote this book motivated by questions formed in the ethnographic present across my career, from my family archive in Palestine to thirty years of work in Cairo, and in my final year of work on this book, in the killing fields of Gaza. My experience living and working part time in former Yugoslavia (Slovenia and Croatia) since 2013, including living at a remove through the wars of succession and the genocide in Bosnia, also shaped my thinking about the semicivilized and the ways I learn from the semicivilized about pathways that move, however tenuously, toward different futures.

Inventing the Semicivilized

Ultimately, my grandfather decided to leave Palestine and emigrate to the United States. My grandfather's fight with the Chief Engineer of the British Mandate, refusing dictates to build infrastructure for a Jewish state with Jewish labor alone and to cede expert control to outsiders over details of how to build a road, pushed him to leave Palestine. But it was just a small moment in the hundred-year struggle for Palestine (Khalidi 2020), in the story of the semicivilized as a category of international law, and in the designation of peoples of the region as uncivilized and undeserving of sovereignty.

The term *semicivilized* was also used in discussions of Japan, China, and the Philippines as well as the Mayan and Aztec Empires in the face of Spanish conquest (Brinton 1885; Hawkins 2020). These polities had recognizable sovereigns but were seen as fatally marked by extraterritoriality and uncivilized cultural practices. But the term *semicivilized* was coined by writers on international law who were attempting to make sense of the power of the Ottoman Empire and its extensive treaties with "Christian nations" of Western Europe. Many texts written in the nineteenth and early twentieth century took the Ottoman Empire as an exemplar of this "'semicivilized' status," which came to be "intimately associated with a host of perceived similarities between sovereign but politically and economically weak extra-European states" (Özsu 2016a, 124–25). The semicivilized were not deemed civilized enough to forgo extraterritoriality, which was "an exceptional mechanism best suited to circumstances in which existing laws were held inapplicable to western subjects" (125).

The term *semicivilized* is entangled in discourses about civilization that came into usage in the second half of the eighteenth century. *Civilization* was first used in France by Comte de Mirabeau (1756) and then across the Channel by Adam Ferguson in *An Essay on the History of Civil Society* (1767).[9] By then, historians and philosophers had developed the "stadial theory" of the progress of human societies, according to which human society progresses through a sequence of stages, from the "rude" to ever more complex, and finally to a "civilized" state. When *civilization* entered usage, it was slotted as the adjective "civilized" into the pinnacle of stadial theory. This pinnacle of civilizational status was also called "commercial society" or (in Ferguson's *Essay*) "civil society" (Pocock 2009, 2). Another part of this schema was the much older concept of "the barbarian" or "barbarism," usually slotted into the second of four stages of civilizational progress.

Barbarian was Greek in origin. With the Roman conquest of ancient Greece, the concept was incorporated into Roman law and transmitted through the Middle Ages to early modern and modern Europe (Pocock 2009). Originally, barbarians were those who did not speak Greek, but soon the term came to denote the differences between Greek and Persian ways of life, and thus the kind of "civilizational differences" that would later be invoked to mark the semicivilized as other.[10] Barbarians were first "spatialized" as part of an ontologically different world and later "temporalized" as belonging to the remote past, at the beginning of history, even though they might live close by. In Reinhart Koselleck's view, the barbarian was an "asymmetric counterconcept" to the civilized world, essential to the very definition of the civilized as its negative and dehumanized counterpart (Koselleck [1975] 2004, 155–91, as cited in Vogt 2015, 126).[11]

Over time, the imaginary geography of barbarians shifted. For the Romans, barbarians were said to reside north of the Danube River. By the Crusades, barbarians were relocated to the south of the Danube (Pocock 2009, 2), to regions that, by the end of the Middle Ages, were known as the Balkans (Mastnak 2008). These lands would be incorporated into the Ottoman Empire over the course of the fourteenth and fifteenth centuries. In this geographic imaginary, barbarism was further associated with shepherds, who sometimes stood in for the second "barbarian" stage of stadial theory (as in Adam Smith's four stages theory; see Smith [1796] 1982). Barbarian shepherds were "nomadic." They moved around, resisting the civilizing virtues of commerce and settled cultivation. They were not productive, countable, and taxable, a dilemma faced as well by the Ottomans (N. E. Barakat 2023).

This was not all. Backward societies could, according to stadial theory, progress to higher stages of civilization. After 1492, those dubbed "primitive" in the Americas and Africa were usually seen by Westerners as being "stuck" on the civilizational ladder. Those dubbed "barbarian," in contrast, were often seen as capable of "receiving" civilization, of becoming civilized. Barbarism was a condition from which some people could advance. Those in the higher stages of development could—and must—take on the mission of transmitting civilization to those in the lower stages. This was the theory behind the post–World War I system of Mandates for regions of the former Ottoman Empire; it was the logic that underlies what would become "development" in the twentieth century as well as the wars on the region in the early twenty-first century. This is a logic I will take up further in chapter 2.

Semicivilized never entered anthropological discourse. Instead, it is associated with international law. But the concept carries the stain of the concept of the barbarian and thus lies at the heart of the notion of Western civilization. The concept of the barbarian played an important place in the field of "comparative ethnology" that was influential at the University of Chicago, in particular (Camic 2020; Stocking 1987), and in the writings of many ethnologists, anthropologists, and economist/sociologists at the turn of the twentieth century, including those of Thorstein Veblen, who regularly drew on the concept of the barbarian to analyze what was wrong with the parasitic and nonproductive "leisure class" of the United States (Camic 2020; Veblen 1899). Soon enough, the paired concepts of the "primitive" and the "civilized" became central to anthropology instead. Anthropology put aside the category of barbarian in favor of the primitive.

In comparison with the wholesale critique of colonialism and the notion of the primitive in anthropology and postcolonial studies, the barbarian has been relatively ignored. That is, until it erupted in the first half of the twenty-first century. The discourse of the war on terror declared by US president George Bush in 2003, and most recently seen with the war on Gaza and the Palestinians in 2023, overtly used the language of the barbarian to justify carpet bombing, genocidal violence, urbicide, and ethnic cleansing in former Ottoman regions of the semicivilized such as Iraq, Bosnia, Syria, and Palestine. This book provides conceptual language to understand why this dehumanizing language of the barbarian has such continued power and how it relates to the semicivilized in Egypt and places much farther afield.[12]

But this dehumanizing language is not totalizing. Associating the semicivilized with the barbarian and the nomad points to submerged potentialities and pathways of mobility that escape territorialization and totalizing control. Nomadic pathways of mobility exceed frameworks of territory and territorial coloniality. In the second half of this book, I move from the hinterlands of the so-called shepherds and barbarians of stadial theory to focus on the embodied infrastructures and communicative channels forged by and tended to by commoners of the semicivilized. I call these the "commons of the semicivilized," which I analyze in conversation with the work of Fred Moten and Stefano Harney (2013) on the undercommons, AbdouMaliq Simone's (2022) concept of the surrounds, and Neferti Tadiar's (2022) analysis of remaindered life. Such embodied infrastructures exceed the fictions of homogeneous territory at the core of classic concepts of sovereignty in Western political thought. The commons of the semicivilized, I argue, give other grounds for the constitution of collective life on shaken grounds than those that were lionized in the 2010s by Western political theorists of the commons, and which rest on problematic entanglements of the concept of the commons with Christian moral philosophy and British colonial practice.

Archives from the Dust

As an anthropologist, I find my questions in ethnography and in the archives, which I read together with the silences and aporia of theory. Ethnography is an unparalleled approach to revealing emergent phenomena taking shape in times of vast social and political transformation. This kind of approach was described by Eric Wolf (1999) in his posthumous collection, *Envisioning*

Power. Beginning with problems emerging in the ethnographic present, he says, ethnographers also "locate the object of our study in time" (8). This gives us the capacity to identify the conjuncture of forces acting on a particular field in overlapping circles or frames. Throughout these chapters, I tell stories of people making their way through moments of conjuncture and flux at national and global levels. This helps us see, in Cairo and elsewhere, how dismantled institutions and political arrangements of the semicivilized, personal law, and extraterritoriality wield their influence in the present and, in turn, how we can more consciously respond to their influence. Those stories sometimes appear in archives from the street, or of the kind collected by my friend and colleague Essam Fawzi over the years.

I met Essam after the first year of my dissertation fieldwork in Cairo in 1994. My research was still focused on the circular migration of Egyptian men to the Gulf States and the impacts of that migration on the remaking of identity and urban space in Cairo. We began to have regular conversations, went on to work together in key parts of my dissertation fieldwork that shifted over the year to come, and have remained friends ever since. Over the course of two years in the mid-1990s, and then whenever possible in the years that followed, we talked and walked down streets, jumped on buses, walked into cafés, visited friends, debated theory among ourselves in Arabic and in conversations with friends—sometimes in three languages, English, Arabic, and Russian.

In those early years, we worked and thought on the move. We might jump in an instant down from a microbus and up onto a public-sector bus, only to step down again and glide into the rhythm and pace of the neighborhood in which we landed. In the immediate aftermath of the 2011 Egyptian Revolution, and then with the momentous changes and our own aging that followed, our movement around Cairo became more constrained. Our pathways moved through only specific neighborhoods and streets. We began to spend more time with Essam's interlocutors in the archives piled up around him in endless files and papers and posters along the walls.

One mild day in February 2019, I stepped out of a taxi on Qasr el-Aini Street in Cairo. I was spending time in Cairo, visiting friends and talking together over various projects of which we had dreamed and still dreamed, even as the years possible for their achievement and the scope of possibilities for life itself had constricted so drastically over time. I stepped into the dark, shadowed lobby of a once glorious building. The *bawab*, or doorman, waved me on toward the hand-worked iron open elevator that had served the building for over fifty years. Upstairs, Essam opened the door with a

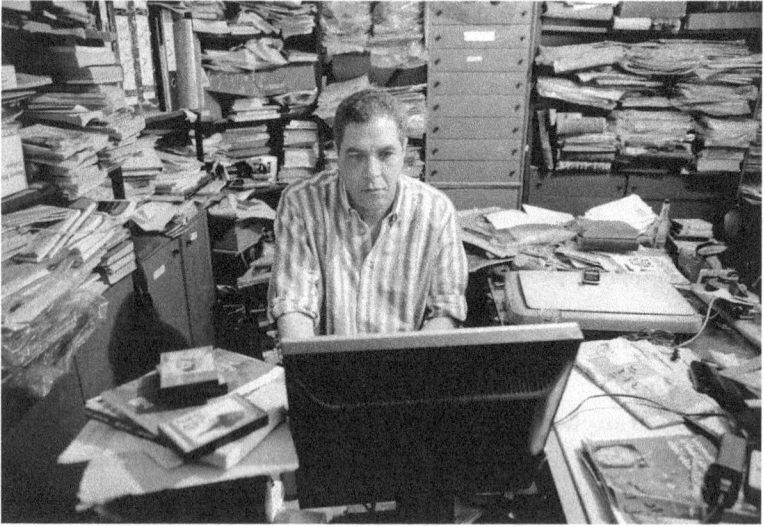

I.3   Essam Fawzi at work with his collection, "archives from the dust," Cairo, 2009. Photograph by Hossam el-Hamalawy.

smile and welcomed me in. Two years ago, this apartment had been little more than a warehouse of paper overflowing from boxes, files, and shelves. The apartment was a collection of paper, posters, records, and files that we had come to call "archives from the dust" (figure I.3). That was the name we had given to the project in our grant applications seeking funds to digitize Essam's collection. The COVID-19 pandemic interrupted that project just a year later.

Essam has supplied help to generations of researchers in Cairo, both Egyptian and foreign. We were meeting with our friends Laila, who had become an archivist in the intervening years, and Muna, who was also working on the archive. In calling it "archives from the dust," we were not thinking then of historian Carolyn Steedman's (2002) book *Dust*, in which archival work emerges as a kind of embodied practice, and we did not know of the emergent work of anthropologist Aya Nassar (2017) on dust and archival method in Cairo. It was simply the embodied experience over two decades of pulling paper out of the dust of basements and boxes and garbage and of working with the dusty piles of paper in Cairo apartments that gave us the idea for the name in our early applications and writings.

This time, however, things looked neater and more organized than they had been a few years ago, when the paper and dust had really been out of control. I remembered one visit when the stacks of boxes of paper were piled up on the apartment's small balcony and there was barely any room to walk. Now, some folders were even labeled. That said, paper was still climbing up the walls. Files and papers and photos peeked out from shelves lining the hallway, amid dusty images of an Egypt supposedly gone. Framed movie posters from the 1960s, an old gramophone, and photographs of 'Umm Kulthum and President Nasser marked the walls. Essam's archives from the dust were living archives, in endless bits of knowledge shared for free, sometimes for a living wage, and sometimes in precious interviews that can be found on YouTube. Our shared archives were kinetic and formative for my work on gesture, embodied commons, and social infrastructure at the core of this book.

Essam's living archives were also material culture: turn on an old gramophone from Cairo and play some of the old 33s with the music of 'Umm Kulthum and Abdel Wahab, and a different Cairo comes alive, channeling its power into the present. For a time, in the years after the January 25 Revolution of 2011, Essam had shared his living archive of Cairo in a short-lived television show called *al-Arshevgi*, or *The Archivist*.

Archives are never neutral; violence is often intertwined with the making, destruction, abandonment, and theft of archives. In her book *Archive Wars*, Rosie Bsheer (2020) shows the centrality of archives to the ideological work of politics and state-making anywhere. What is gathered, what is forgotten, and what is destroyed? These foundational questions of the archives pertain to my movement through archives in this book as well. In Egypt and around the region in the eighteenth and nineteenth centuries, books and files from the Arab and Islamic worlds were gathered up and appropriated for petty cash by greedy collectors who turned local knowledge into raw materials and archives of the "civilized West."

Most of the documents in Essam's collection were literally reclaimed from the trash. During a 1990s real estate boom in Cairo, investors bought up villas in upper class sections of Cairo and destroyed them in order to redevelop the land for more lucrative purposes. Before tearing down the buildings, they had emptied out storehouses of papers and boxes from the basements. All of it had been thrown out. From the basements of a villa here and a villa there, built by and lived in by the cultural and political elite of Cairo from the 1880s through the 1980s, a treasure trove of materials was discarded.

But nothing ended there: disentangled from the people and lives that gave meaning and value to those archives from different moments of Egypt's dramatic history, moments of conjuncture, and times of flux, the paper entered a vast Cairene recycling system. The paper moved through layers of garbage sorters and traders and merchants who were experts in sorting out its value. These *zabaleen* are experts in revaluation: they turn back into value any trash with a potential market. They were central to the making of this archive from the dust.

Each piece of paper recounts a moment of life amid revolutions, coups, invasions, commerce, opera, and war sweeping through the region and this city cursed and blessed with being 'Umm el-Dunya, center of the world. There were personal letters, official transcripts, scripts, musical scores, letters of passion and distress, faded pages of Coca-Cola ads, movie posters from the 1910s to the 1940s, transcripts of meetings made historic only over time. Stacks of paper, the records of lifetimes lived in quite different historic conjunctures—documents from the British Occupation after the 'Urabi Revolt of 1882, the Khedivate, from 1853 to the beginning of World War I, and the British protectorate from 1914 to 1922; political parties' pamphlets and magazines of popular culture; letters of love and the scripts of plays; accounts of commerce and the founding of companies—multiple worlds and lifetimes went into the trash as speculative real estate took off in the 1980s and 1990s. But that was not the end of the story.

We followed the trails of some of these stories and pieces of paper in Essam's archive to see how traces of these pasts were manifest in the distributed collective practices of the common people of Cairo. The many archives of Cairo cohere as a kaleidoscope, bringing together accounts from different institutional actors that administered, governed, and exercised (degrees of) sovereignty over Cairo and Egypt. In this way, extant imperial and inter-imperial formations leave ethnographically tractable traces in archives of urban space.

Everywhere were the embodied archives of Cairo, or the history we carry on our backs, as the great Egyptian sociologist Sayyid 'Uways put it in the 1970s, in collectives practices, patterns of movement on the street, and the embodied infrastructures that supported (for a time) the political economy of survival in Cairo and which attracted the attention of investors, bankers, development officials, and revolutionaries across Cairo's many circles. This "embodied archive," "carried on our back[s],"[13] will be an important focus of this book, where I weave together accounts of personal law in which travelers and sojourners (Benton 2002) carry with them their sovereign affiliations as they move through space, infrastructures of extraterritoriality that promoted flows of commerce through inter-imperial worlds, and embodied infrastructures as a collective resource, or commons, of the "locals," or commoners, of Cairo. This embodied archive helps bring to light many other collective resources of the common people of Cairo.

The notion of carrying history in movement down the street is part of what I call "embodied infrastructure" (despite the problems with the concept embodiment).[14] We will see this through analyses of gestural commons, social infrastructures of communicative channels, and proprioception. The history of the urban commons is an archive—an embodied archive—of Cairo, a great city founded in and continuously inhabited since 646 CE. History is nothing abstract, 'Uways made clear. Those blessed and cursed to be born, live, and die in a "living encyclopedia" like Cairo carry that history with them. This is another legacy of the semicivilized.

Some neighborhoods and people of Cairo are (or perhaps were) called sha'bi. The word is usually translated to English as "popular," or part of the urban masses. In recent years the word sha'bi has become known globally through associations with the mahraganat or sha'bi music used by Egyptian director Mohamed Diab in the blockbuster Marvel Studios/Disney film Moon Nights. The term sha'bi is central to Cairene culture and life and yet is generally missing from social science analytics. The word is used descriptively in wonderful ethnographic work on Cairo (e.g., El-Messiri 1978). But it is possible and in fact urgent to approach sha'bi as a concept and to locate its meaning in a broader discursive and political field that may no longer have legal efficacy but that leaves ineffable traces, nonetheless.

Lives of the popular urban masses of Cairo, according to 'Uways, are deeply rooted in the built space of their neighborhoods, or hara. The past is present here in the most visceral of fashion.[15] It lives on through communicative channels built into the historic structures of Cairo, such as the messages 'Uways studied, which were written on paper and stuffed into the porous walls of the Mausoleum of Imam Shafi'i, which dates back to 1176 and is located in the City of the Dead. This is an inhabited district of Cairo and also a UNESCO World Heritage Site with historic mausoleums in a cemetery that has been in use since the Arab conquest of Cairo in 646. Key parts of this neighborhood were bulldozed in the early 2020s to make room for superhighways connecting Cairo to the New Administrative Capital, located twenty-six kilometers to the east of Cairo, which we will discuss further across this book. Those messages stuffed into the walls of a shrine are also calls for intervention in the most difficult and sensitive aspects of life.

All this could be quite vivid for someone born, like many of my interlocutors in the 1990s, right after the Free Officers Movement of 1952 that overturned the lingering monarchy carved out of the Ottoman order by Mehmet Ali and his heirs. They lived through the rise of Nasser, the one president of Egypt with the power and legitimacy to make movement on streets and in marketplaces around the Arab world come to a complete standstill through the mere sound of his voice over the radio (Salem 2020). They lived through the assassination of Nasser, the rise of President Anwar Sadat and the *infitah*, or the economic "opening" of the national economy, during a period of politics and time with many of a generation in jail. The assassination, in turn, of Sadat in 1981 and the rise of President Hosni Mubarak, who was forced to resign by the January 25 Revolution, centered around Cairo's Tahrir Square, was part of their lived experience, as was the making and deconstruction of Egypt's "socialist" face and the country's move away from the its location at the center of the "three circles of Egypt," in the Middle East, Asia Minor (Turkey), and Africa, toward the West, with the financing and military aid of the United States, since the signing of the Camp David Accords in 1976.

The archives of Egypt were long read as unfolding toward a territorial nation-state sovereignty—a perspective on Egypt's history that took precedence after the 1952 coup that brought Nasser and the other "Free Officers" into power. Nationalist historiography of Egypt marginalized its Ottoman past, most famously through the rewriting of the name of the governor and then founder of a ruling dynasty, Mehmet Ali, as Mohammed Ali (Fahmy 2009, 2010). The historiography of Egypt, focused on the territory of Egypt within its national borders, hides its complex entanglements with the Sudan, Syria, Hijaz, and the eastern Mediterranean, or Levant. All this gives too unitary a picture of the archive and of power and sovereignty. When we expand our vision of the archive, the grip of territorialism on our imagination can loosen.

Semicivilized Infrastructures

The Middle East was global in orientation long before globalization; circuits of mobility for pilgrimage, commerce, and labor inscribed the region even before the rise of Islam; and markets have been highly monetized for millennia. The region not only had some of the oldest and most sophisticated market, political, and military systems in the world. It also had written language, states, and religions that were recognizable to both Crusaders and colonizers. Global flows of people, goods, and moneys moved across transimperial spaces and global cities in different kinds of arrangements without nation-states, fixed borders, passports, or territorial colonialism.

From this perspective we can ask: How are global flows of mobility of people, goods, and moneys regulated without the assumed role of territory, borders, and passports? What happens when we drop the assumptions of territory and territoriality that form a shared discursive space in debates about colonialism and postcolonialism?

Territoriality indeed tends to be taken for granted in many discussions of sovereignty in the social sciences (Elden 2013; Philpott 2020). In such discussions, the relation of citizen/subject to the sovereign is set by a person's location inside a fixed geographic location (Philpott 2020). This approach to sovereignty emphasizes the unitary relation of citizen to sovereign in a bounded area of land. Land and individual are related here in a way that echoes definitions of unitary ownership of private property in land (Bhandar 2018; Philpott 2020).

A common definition of *sovereignty* is supreme authority within a territory (Philpott 2020). Sovereignty is unitary in classic approaches to the topic and in the constitution of the European political system of states (Philpott 2020), which evolved in the process of reworking relations among rulers rather than relations between rulers and the ruled (Hinsley 1966).[16] Despite an endless series of exceptions to unitary sovereignty cited in the literature— including arrangements made in all sorts of colonial ventures—unitary sovereignty remains the default case. And yet, there is another tradition of thinking about sovereignty from within the Western tradition, referred to as "dividual sovereignty."[17] Neither exceptional nor a marker of failed sovereign projects within these threads of Western political thought, dividual sovereignty is a key part of the semicivilized condition.

Dividual sovereignty can be found in writings of Hugo Grotius (1583– 1645), such as his classic analysis of public authority, *De jure belli ac pacis* (*On the Law of War and Peace*, [1625] 1925). In this book, Grotius explicitly endorsed the theory of unitary sovereignty that had recently been advanced by Jean Bodin (1530–96), agreeing that "sovereignty (*summum imperium*) is a unity, in itself indivisible" (Keene 2004, 44, citing Grotius [1625] 1925, 123). But even while endorsing Bodin's conception of sovereignty as indivisible, Grotius "proceeded to offer a series of exceptions to the general definition that, to all intents and purposes, nullified it." In both theory and practice, according to Grotius, sovereignty was often divided. This was neither exceptional nor problematic (Keene 2004, 44).

Arrangements of dividual sovereignty are at least as common as unitary sovereignty and formed the empirical material for classic political and social theory from Grotius to Henry Sumner Maine (1822–1888). British rule in

India and in North America was pragmatic and situational (Keene 2004, 93). Imperial rulers had no interest in the arrangements of settler colonialism or in controlling a territory when they could reach their aims by incorporating local systems of rule or through legal commercial arrangements. Even the commons were an essential part of these modes of colonial rule, as Maine made clear in his work theorizing British practices of dividual sovereignty in India, where the British state inserted itself into polities of the Mughal Empire, first via the "company state" of the East India Company. Maine put things very simply: "Sovereignty has always been regarded as divisible" (Keene 2004, 78).[18] Maine wrote of sovereignty as a "bundle of powers" that could be divvied up and separated from one another (Maine 1915; Keene 2004, 108).[19]

Given the many problems with unitary sovereignty in both theory and practice, many anthropologists and critical theorists have challenged the relevance of sovereignty and statehood altogether. But when thinking from the semicivilized in the Middle East, things look different. So many lives have been lost in the endlessly denied struggle for sovereignty and viable collective futures that it becomes harder simply to dismiss the question of sovereignty as a false dream. What pathways of thought and politics emerge when we linger more with concepts of dividual sovereignty and the semicivilized?[20]

Rather than promoting or dismissing sovereignty, I draw on concepts that cohere around the semicivilized. Here I refer, first, to the concept I mentioned earlier, personal law—the notion that law is linked not to territory but to individuals in their place of birth and, crucially, moves with the body through channels of imperial space. Linked to this notion of bodies moving through channels is, of course, the concept of extraterritoriality, which puts into a spatial framework the implications of personal law and highlights the stark reality that in modern territorial states, as in empires, sovereign power does not map uniformly onto territory. From this framework, I turn in the second half of the book to what I call "embodied infrastructures," which coexist with more traditionally conceived kinds of physical infrastructure such as roads, railroads, or telephone lines, and which anthropologists, among others, have extensively studied.[21]

This starting point allows me to focus on channels rather than on unitary infrastructures within a territory and to shift away from assumptions of territory and stable ground that underlie concepts of sovereignty, political economy, and economic growth. Thinking from the semicivilized, I focus on contests for dominance over the channels through which commerce, military, and value flow. Both territory and solid ground are, in fact, unsettled as assumptions in the background of social theory and political economy. Cultivating capacities for awareness of collectivity on shaken grounds becomes a starting point for theory and politics alike (Elyachar 2022; Morimoto 2012).[22]

To consider other possibilities for collectivity on shaken grounds, it is important to note arrangements linking body, ground, and sovereignty in the Ottoman and other empires. We know by now that empires such as the Ottoman, Safavid, and Mughal had no passports or fixed borders.[23] Instead, such empires had a different logic, a "spotty" (Burbank and Cooper 2011) relation to their "domains." They had no "territory" and were not "territorial states." Being part of an empire was regulated in large part through relations of tax and tribute. Political belonging was thus linked to finance, which was a mode of rule, a language of political power, and a channel of ongoing interaction and mobility with Western Christian nations (Derri 2021b). This is a very different ecosystem of finance and politics than what is often taken for granted in discussions about colonialism or postcolonialism and will thus also be at the heart of this book. Such an ecosystem brings together questions of finance and mobility that are unfamiliar in most approaches to political economy or colonial studies.

This global infrastructure of commerce was enshrined in international law. Negotiating an end to the capitulations was the "greatest challenge facing US negotiators at Versailles," in the words of one participant in the negotiations ending World War I.[24] The United States was the last "Christian power" of the West to gain an extraterritorial treaty with the Ottoman Empire. The United States fought hard to retain its privileges even as the Ottoman Empire was being dissolved. It retained for itself the right to intervene in the region to this day. US Syria expert Dana Stroul (2019), for example, overtly used this language of the US "owning" parts of (resource-rich) Syria and casually referred to the "right" of the United States to determine the course of events in a state it formally recognizes as sovereign.

Successor states to the Austro-Hungarian Empire, also defeated in World War I, were quickly recognized in international law to block the spread of communism. Regions of the Ottoman Empire had no such luck. The semicivilized states were deemed unworthy of the "gift of sovereignty" (Grant 2009). The very existence of extraterritorial treaties that the United States and other Western powers had refused to renounce was also invoked as a logic for refusing sovereignty. The semicivilized retained the stain of the barbarian, outside the sphere of civilization, in a less-than-human status.

The attribution of semicivilized status would have devastating impact in the century to come, in a fashion that only intensified as I completed this book at the beginning of 2024.

The Three Circles of Egypt (and the Levant)

Archives from the dust, and the long history of archives and archiving in Cairo, reveal other forms of extractive violence. Knowledge contained in Cairo's Arabic books and manuscripts was transformed in the nineteenth century into the raw archival materials of the West and, in the process, revalued and financialized property was transformed into waqf—a form of pious property or trust.[25] Egypt, like the Ottoman Empire as a whole, was put into the box of the semicivilized from which archives could be extracted, debts without end accumulated, and channels through its terrain fought over by multiple players.

This process is not unlike more recent methods of turning national wealth into financialized debt. In the early twenty-first century, the wealth of the Egyptian nation, held as public goods by the state, was securitized by a stroke of an administrative pen and turned into public-private partnerships. Moving land and buildings as "real estate" into Sovereign Wealth Funds generated immense profits for foreign investors and military-owned companies alike. Resources and channels for which so many lives were given in past centuries were handed over for a pittance to new overseers of the semicivilized—sovereign wealth funds of the Arab Gulf States together with Western corporations and the Egyptian military. This is one of the stories we will chart across this book. Citizens of Egypt still have little recourse to determine the fate of their resources and how they are deployed. They remain in the waiting house of history (Chakrabarty 2000; Seikaly 2019).

Cairo has long been experienced as a place of multiple sovereignties and generative identities. It has been a node on circuits of movement across empires, on trade routes across sub-Saharan and North Africa, and around the regions of the Arab world for centuries and even millennia. As such, Cairo has long been integrated into multiple and overlapping circles of belonging. One of those circles is a circle of empire—the Ottoman Empire. Egypt was part of the Ottoman Empire from 1517 to 1914, with various degrees of integration. The Ottoman Empire was dissolved at the Treaty of Lausanne in 1923. And yet, some aspects of this Ottoman order—such as regimes of extraterritoriality and personal law instituted to promote flows of commerce across Ottoman domains—lasted much longer, including in Egypt.

In this book, I write of Cairo from the standpoint of a post-Ottoman, postimperial ethnography with multiple circles of sovereign belonging. This approach grew out of my frustration with concepts that did not help me theorize the worlds in which I was immersed. I had no conceptual language with which to analyze crucial aspects of daily life that attracted my analytic eye—ways of moving, talking, chatting, hanging out, and making markets that I subsequently analyzed in terms of phatic labor (Elyachar 2010) and social infrastructures of communicative channels (Elyachar 2010, 2011, 2012b). Another concept I found helpful was Gamal Abdel Nasser's "three circles of Egypt"—Arab, Islamic, and African—in his *Egypt's Liberation: The Philosophy of the Revolution*, which was published in 1955, one year after consolidating power in Egypt following the Free Officers Movement.

This concept is related to political movements of pan-Arabism at the time and to long-standing efforts of Egypt, since Mehmet Ali, to conquer and, under Nasser, to form a union with Syria. The phrase "three circles of Egypt" also had resonance in the global nonaligned movement and in Black internationalist movements of the 1960s. Malcolm X invoked Nasser's concept to theorize "U.S. domestic coloniality in terms of overlapping diasporas" (Alhassen 2015, 1).[26] Cairo became a "Black Atlantic Metropole" in the 1960s that offered a "welcoming stance as a home for African peoples" (3). As adopted by Malcolm X, Nasser's vision of the "three circles of Egypt" gave grounds for an internationalist "geo-racio-religious imaginary" that reconfigured common understandings of "home" delinked from the necessary referent of "a land" (14) or the unified territory of a nation-state.

Nasser's three circles made no mention of the Ottoman Empire. Ottoman pasts were boxed off in nationalist accounts of Egypt's history. And yet, this imperial circle of Egypt's past did not simply disappear with the Ottoman Empire or with Egypt's relative independence achieved by Mehmet Ali from the Ottoman Empire.[27] For example, the "Egyptian Mixed Courts" that grew out of the Ottoman system of extraterritoriality were part of the Egyptian legal system until 1947. Key categories of this order—such as the "local" who is subject to local rule of law, versus the "extraterritorial" who is not subject to local law—leave traces in the present and lie at the heart of this book.

The last circle of Egypt, or of Cairo more specifically, that I draw on in this book is the Levant. The term *Levant* usually pertains to the Ottoman shorelines of the Mediterranean, or the former Ottoman Province of Syria, today's Syria, Lebanon, and Palestine. That would seem to have nothing to do with Cairo, which is not even on the Mediterranean, unlike the Egyptian city of Alexandria. Nor does the Levant as I use it in this book overlap with the geographic concept of the Eastern Mediterranean that is commonly used by historians of the region. And yet, Cairo is regularly mentioned as part of "the Levant" in archival documents about commerce and its flows through the Ottoman Empire. And Cairo is a key location of the world's first lingua franca of commerce in the Levant.

Before *lingua franca* denoted any composite language of trade, it was a specific commercial dialect of the Levant, spoken among all those engaged in commerce around the Mediterranean and the Levant. The Levant and its lingua franca make explicit two archaic meanings of commerce crucial to this book: communication and the exchange of goods with others in different locations. *Franca* or *Frank* eventually became the signifier of all Western non-Muslims in the Ottoman Empire. The lingua franca of the Levant was a communicative channel for all who engaged in commerce.

This lingua franca referred to both a language and an identity. The Levantini, as they were called in Venice, were responsible for moving key commodities of urban life around the region. They differed from locals, or commoners, who stayed in one place and were linked only to one sovereign ruler. Sometimes *Levantini* had the dual meaning of being "shifty, even sketchy men" from the region who could easily shift from one language and location to another (Rothman 2012, 2013). By the early eighteenth century, *Levantine* had become a headword in an Italian-English dictionary, meaning "Natives or Inhabitants of the Levant, the Eastern People" (Rothman 2012, 213). It had its own natives. It became meaningful to speak of "Natives of the Levant."

By the nineteenth century, *Levantine* had come to mean "non-Muslim Ottoman subjects, marked by vaguely 'European' habits and sometimes ancestry but corrupted by their surrounding environment into a lifestyle that was not quite European" (Rothman 2012, 214). The Levantine had become something recognizable as a "nation," or "ethnic group." Or else it could mean an "Easterner" from the eastern end of the Mediterranean. Eventually, the notion of Levantine as nation became attached to geography—the eastern shores of the Mediterranean in particular. However, Levantine remained an inter-imperial relational concept as well.

Levantine is not an identity used by anyone in this book. Egypt was, and is, enmeshed in much broader geographies of political economy and attempts at imperial state formation from the Sudan to Syria. But the concept of the Levant appears repeatedly in the archives I draw on. The Levant is a space where infrastructures of commerce crisscrossed the Mediterranean from today's Italy to the eastern Ottoman Empire.[28] It matters further as a space where categories of embodied sovereignty, extraterritorial belonging, and channels of commerce/communication were worked out. Those categories appear over and over in the living archives of so-called popular culture in Cairo. These categories form an extant world of the semicivilized and shape the embodied infrastructures and commons of urban life I am concerned with in this book.

Debts of Improvement

The semicivilized were only exceptionally and temporarily subjected to full territorial colonialism. That said, their fate is deeply marked by the theory that "civilized" peoples with supposedly more "advanced sciences and arts" have a right to settlement in the name of "improvement." This is most clearly visible in the case of Palestine.[29] But everywhere, rendering the lands of the semicivilized "improved" entailed multiple investments and forms of violence (Li 2014). Theories of improvement were also important to the Ottomans, who by the nineteenth century deployed theories of improvement to deem the land of Bedouin communities in Ottoman Syria "empty" and to promote the settlement of groups they considered potentially more productive (N. E. Barakat 2023).

Improvement also entailed the mobilization of huge amounts of credit and debt for the laying of new infrastructural channels by which to move goods to market, to convert fruit into commodities, or to transform the Isthmus of Suez into a primary channel of commerce up to our own times. Responsibility for the credits and debts of building infrastructure fell on the Ottoman Empire and its constituent (and semi-independent) parts. Finance was inseparable from regimes of mobility throughout the domains of empire. Finance did not cause the problems of the semicivilized. But it was a channel through which those problems took shape. One such moment was with consolidation of the theory of "improvement" as a legal basis for settlement. Alberico Gentili (1552–1608), known as a "father of international law," along with Hugo Grotius and Francisco de Vitoria (1483–1546), provides important material to see how this is so.[30] I take a moment to delve into this issue because of how productively it complicates common binaries of colonized/decolonized and provides pathways for rethinking both settler colonialism and a notion of the semicivilized.

Gentili theorized the right of technically advanced, civilized Western Europeans to settle in the Ottoman Empire even though, he emphasized, the sovereignty of the Ottoman sultan was fully legitimate. Gentili was a

Levantine of sorts. He was from the Marches region of central Italy, on the Adriatic. He grew up in a world of commerce flowing across the Adriatic and Mediterranean and regulated by the Venetian and Ottoman Empires. He lived through the move of the English into the Levant trade, initiated by Queen Elizabeth I, and England's establishment of the Levant Company through the merger of the Turkey Company and the Venice Company. He was a refugee from the Inquisition in today's Ljubljana, before he and his father went on to England and he was appointed Regius Professor of Law at Oxford in 1587.[31] Particularly helpful is his focus on the urban as the key site for distinctions between residents categorized as commoners versus extraterritorials.

Gentili wrote at a time of growing maritime struggle for control over global commerce, including Spanish and Ottoman aspirations for "universal monarchy" (Kingsbury 1998, 719). He countered those aspirations in part by drawing on Roman law and the Roman notion of jus gentium (or law of nations) "as a kind of transnational law, applied by custom and on the basis of reason in many different political and legal orders" (Kingsbury 1998, 715). Gentili's legal thinking pertained to the geographic scope of the Roman Empire in a very urban picture of geography, international law, treaties and extraterritoriality (720–21).

In Gentili's view, commerce was part of natural law. Any attempt to ban this new global expansion of commerce led by England and its corporate sovereign entities like the Levant Company and the Royal African Company, he thought, would be contrary to natural law and, as such, not only futile but also an invitation to war (Kingsbury 1998, 714). Gentili was fully aware of the power of the Ottoman sultan and granted, without reservation, the legitimacy of his sovereignty. He included the Ottoman Empire and the exterritorial treaties of the Ottoman capitulations (those extraterritorial treaties established by the Ottomans to promote and regulate commerce in Ottoman domains that I discussed above) in his loose framework of the international law of nations.

Gentili's use of the concepts of "nations" and "law of nations" took the Ottomans and their extraterritorial legal infrastructure fully into account.[32] Each nation had its own culture and legal system that was accorded respect and legitimacy in treaties and agreements with other sovereigns. In this legal ecosystem, the customs and traditions of each nation (before the era of the territorial nation-state) were recognized as valid.[33] At the same time, Gentili conceded "extensive rights to Europeans over non-Europeans to settle in the lands of the Ottoman Empire on the grounds of their greater technical capacities, [and he] was certain that such occupation would be licit" (Pagden 2015, 139). Such settlers were "bound to accept the sovereignty of the Sultan" even as they had rights according to natural law to settle (139).

Gentili helped formulate the deeply consequential theory of "improvement,"[34] which became the key and supposedly objective grounds for declaring land terra nullius, even lands of the sovereign Ottoman sultan (Gentili 1877, 131). "Improvements" allowed Gentili both to recognize that the sultan had sovereign authority and to argue that it was legal for Western settlers, who supposedly had the capacity (due to their being Western Christians) for "improvements," to take up residence on "unimproved" land. Large tracts of territory of the Ottoman Empire were effectively "unused," jurists stated (Kingsbury 1998, 713–23, 723n, as cited in Pagden 2003, 196n34).

That "unimproved" land—which was, in fact, used and owned in ways the jurists could not see—could be claimed by Europeans as terra nullius, and thus "settlement" to "improve the land" was legitimate. But it would be illegitimate for Western civilized nations to ignore the sultan's rule or to set aside the multiple treaties that supplicant Western nations had signed with him. Terra nullius, in short, was decoupled from territorial and settler colonialism. The sultan's sovereignty was legitimate, but he had no sovereignty over his domains. Nor would aspiring nations emerging from regions of the Ottoman Empire. This decoupling of territory from sovereignty, together with the granting of rights for outsiders to settle under the name of improvement, is another hallmark of the semicivilized.

Close attention must also be paid to finance and its workings in the case of the semicivilized. In the Ottoman Empire, finance was directly linked to the internal politics of the Ottoman Empire even when the power of the empire was at its apex (Kafadar 1986). The Ottoman Empire was an "Empire of Debt" (Yaycıoğlu 2022). This does not mean that the empire was indebted to the West, although the structure of finance would flip that way in the second half of the nineteenth century. Rather, it means that political, kin, and commercial relationships were interwoven through a medium of debt (and credit). Looking at these multiple functions of finance, credit, and debt can help us make sense of a common situation of structural indebtedness in which the ongoing flows of credit-debt relations were locked into systemic extraction, immobility, and nonsovereignty—whether in Egypt or Puerto Rico, or in intergenerational unpayable debt in the United States.

This system was fully financialized in ways that seem familiar to a twenty-first century eye. Finance was linked to the ongoing mobility of humans carrying letters of credit and specie across space. Brokers mediated nodes of commerce across multiple levels of social, kin, and political worlds and conducted with different kinds of currencies and financial instruments. Part of this credit-debt nexus faced inward, mediating relations of power in the most direct of ways. Finance was the "lifeblood of bureaucracy," of the state bureaucracy managed by the grand vizier. Finance was also an engine of growth in state capacity (Clay 2000, 86). Finance mediated power struggles between the Porte, the seat of the imperial bureaucracy, and the palace and its own distinct sources of wealth (Eldem 1999). In Egypt as well, relations of credit and debt were at the center of politics long before the nineteenth century. After years of growing indebtedness, territorial losses, and the military defeats of the Ottoman Empire, matters took a more decisive turn in 1875, when the Ottomans suspended payment on a portion of their external debt.

In 1881, the Ottoman Public Debt Administration (OPDA) was established.[35] Unlike previous ad hoc schemes, from the beginning, the OPDA rendered official the final disentanglement of credits and debts that underlay the Empire of Debt. It stripped away as well the specific link of a financial instrument to a particular project. Debt now stood for the collective interests of the (mostly foreign) bondholders of Ottoman debt, who gained the right to interfere—without the benefits and costs of occupation—in the workings of the local economy. The situation resembles the "dollar diplomacy" in the Americas after the United States lost interest in the powers and liabilities of territorial conquest (Rosenberg 2003). Here, too, fiscal powers of the state are devolved to an outside, more powerful country that assumes the right to revalue debt.

Ontologies of debt in the Ottoman Empire offer important lessons for considering the politics of the semicivilized today. The semicivilized were a "great social laboratory" of the social sciences (El Shakry 2007) and coloniality. Global commerce moved through channels of the Ottoman Empire long before any theory of capitalism or imperialism was penned. Finance in the Ottoman Empire contradicts classic models of imperialism, in which excess capital from overproduction in core capitalist countries is the source of "finance" elsewhere. From this perspective, it is not finance or debt per se that locked Egypt and the region into the straitjacket of the "semicivilized." The politics of valuation and revaluation must be considered as well. "Finance is composed of processes that make debt valuable" (Poon and Wosnitzer 2012, 253). The work entailed in making debts of all kinds valuable—and disvalued—is the underbelly of finance. Employees of banks, the OPDA, or Egyptian banks or debt overseers are sometimes stuck with the labor of sorting things out and deciding what has value and what does not. When valuation schemas rapidly change, the consequences can be severe.

Sometimes the messy and bloody business of revaluation is framed as necessary and objective "austerity." Sometimes, like in Egypt during the 2020s, it appears like inflation and exchange-rate collapse, even as assets quietly change hands behind the scenes. "Financial relationships," economist Perry Mehrling (2017) has said, are not about "mediating something else on the 'real' side of the economy." Rather, they are "the constitutive relationships of the whole system" (1). In times of mass revaluation, investors can end up penniless and die by suicide; mistakes can ruin the lives of countless invisible others. Radical upheaval in valuation schemes can take on the neutral attributes of finance. But the political is never fully cleansed away. This is well known by the "semicivilized" who suffer the indignities of structural indebtedness without end, whether in Egypt, Puerto Rico, or the United States.

On Shaky Grounds

Egypt's geographic location has long attracted the interest of powers trying to control global flows of commerce, militaries, and value. The Suez Canal is but the most famous and consequential channel through Egypt. Plans to transform the Isthmus of Suez into the Suez Canal date back to pharaonic times. Those early plans were revived by French Saint-Simonian engineers in the 1830s, and as we will see in chapter 2, the canal remains important in Egypt's performance of sovereignty. Engineering of all kinds of channels for the movement of people, goods, and armies along railways, roads, and canals entailed associated and interlinked innovations of finance and engineering. Chapter 1 demonstrates the continued strategic place of control over channels of mobility in Cairo today as part of urban planning for counterinsurgency, international tourism, and state power. Passageways and channels were important in the provisioning and governing of the Ottoman Empire and in the making of all kinds of social infrastructures and commons in Cairo that are another focus of this book.

But Egypt itself was also a channel—to the "crown jewel" of British Empire in the Indian subcontinent. Since the Ottoman Empire was not colonized, other arrangements and innovations in finance, international law, and engineering were found and imposed. Building infrastructure is a key part of this story, and thus appeared with the very opening of this book in a story about conflicts over building the road from Jerusalem to Jericho in which my grandfather played a small part. But as important as the literature on infrastructure from the Middle East has been, the now over-extended concept cannot explain everything. In this book, I foreground channels over infrastructure, drawing as well on debates in Great Britain in the sixteenth century about the rise of commerce. Such concepts may seem far removed from Egypt in the twenty-first century, but they are not. After all, the oldest faculty of economics and accounting in Egypt is still named the "Faculty of Commerce" (*tijara*).

Commerce denotes more than what we think of as "business." It was theorized long before the notion of "economics" came into being. Commerce encompassed communication and transformation. Commerce meant the "affayres of business" (T. Thomas 1587). It was also a form of liberty: "an entercourse or libertie to cary marchandyse from one place to another" and to sell it (Elyot 1538, 1542). Moving from one place to another was a central part of commerce. Commerce was a spatial relation and a form of communication. Commerce was "communication for buying and selling, entercourse of merchandise from one place to another" (T. Thomas 1587).

As a dual human imperative to exchange merchandise and communicate with others, commerce was enshrined in natural law. Commerce was an agentive force, driving men and corporations to ends divine and terrible. Commerce was also central to life in the Ottoman Empire; but this kind of commerce was inseparable from violence and the waging of new kinds of war financed by new kinds of debt. Hugo Grotius argued in the early seventeenth century that the oceans were channels for commerce and, as such, a common—in the sense that no one nation or sovereign power should control it. This challenged Portuguese claims to vast sweeps of the New World under the papal bull *Inter caetera*, issued by Alexander VI in 1493.

The concept of channels reappears in the theory I draw on in this book. It is central to communication theory and features prominently in the classic writings of Roman Jakobson ([1960] 1990) that I draw on in my analysis of social infrastructures of communicative channels among the urban masses of the semicivilized. This notion of channels of commerce and communication will reappear in the chapters that follow and in my analysis of the social infrastructures of communicative channels and the urban commons of the semicivilized. This adds other dimensions to discussions of infrastructure that focus more on roads, bridges, telegraph lines, electric and water meters, and more. Such infrastructures appear across our story, inseparable from systems of communication, commerce, and commonalities that create the commons: as resource, concept, people, and platform of revolt.

Twice colonized by European powers—by France for three years in 1798, and by Great Britain for much longer in variable arrangements after 1881—Egypt is no doubt a postcolonial country. But the concept of postcolonialism is not sufficient to grasp the complexities of Egypt's legal, sovereign, and cultural conditions either in the past or today. Following the French failure to absorb Egypt into its liberal imperialist French Republic of Egypt (Cole 2007), British, French, and Ottoman imperial strategists alike were reluctant to even try to claim sovereignty over it (Genell 2013, 2016). Even so, Egypt's strategic location as a passageway to the East left it vulnerable to incursions by powers seeking to capture the benefits this afforded and made it the object of many fantasies and plans pertaining to channels and infrastructure. This began long before the late nineteenth century, when administrative, financial, and policing responsibilities were coordinated among three imperial powers—the British, the French, and the Ottomans (Genell 2016; Shlala 2018).

In such a context, it was a complex matter to sort out which bodies were associated with which sovereign, to which part of the legal system they belonged, and who was responsible for any debts or credits they had assumed. Here it helps to focus on citizenship as practiced (Hanley 2016, 278) rather than assuming that there is a unitary relation of "the citizen" to "the state," or a singular history moving from territorial colonialism to postcolonialism and the postcolonial state. Chapter 3 looks at multiple forms of citizenship as practiced through workings of the Egyptian Mixed Courts, an Egyptian institution that grew out of the Ottoman capitulations to sort out differently lived sovereignty relationships, within ties both commercial and personal.

But sorting things out denotes more than categorizing who belongs where under the law and deciding who is extraterritorial and who is local. It points to an ongoing, embodied practice of being local, together, and in common. Ethnography can show us how simple, everyday practices create and reproduce what I call social infrastructures of communicative channels that run across and through multiple nodes of distributed agency. Themselves a commons, these channels are an essential infrastructure for political economy writ large as well as for the sustenance of collective life. As we will see across chapters 4 and 5, these social infrastructures that long functioned as a commons of the urban masses became increasingly visible and accessible as a platform for profit at the end of the twentieth century, when different kinds of adventurers roamed the world to civilize and profit from the semicivilized.

Social infrastructures were then integrated into platforms of revolt in the 2010s. At that time, mass revolt spread around the region as life became more precarious, in a trend that has drastically accelerated in the ensuing years. The politics of "resistance everywhere" stood on the same ground as ideologies of productivist labor and endless growth—the ground was seen as something stable and unchanging for people to stand on, feet firmly planted, fists upraised. Yet, that stability was an illusion. As the ground of this political economy that supposedly replaced imperial domains and their exterritorial/commoner divides began to recede, the politics of the commons shifted as well. For me, the notion of the isthmus as a channel connecting two separate areas of land became a productive metaphor for thinking differently about polity and ground, and the different ways in which they can intersect, a topic I turn to in chapter 6.[36]

This division between extraterritorials and locals is a generative rubric through which to consider politics in regions of the semicivilized. But it is more. In a time of climate catastrophe, assumptions of stable ground, territoriality, and territorial sovereignty that linger in the usual formulations of colonialism, postcolonialism, and the commons have become untenable. What happens to the commons on the shaken grounds of a world in which territorialism cannot be taken for granted and in which climate destruction has upended the notion of stable ground altogether? In such a time, the notion of the commoner, a local, as rooted in place or as part of a polity stretched across the space of a loosely regulated empire, takes on increasing salience. The battle to defend the possibility of life itself in a town, a community, and on earth has never been starker.

FIXING SPACE, MOVING PEOPLE

Laila, Essam, and I met in front of Masrah al-Salam on Qasr el-Aini street one day in February 2018. We stopped by a small self-service "supermarket" to buy a few things for the house. An older man with wire-rimmed glasses and dressed in a tweed suit jacket and a white button-down shirt—open at the bottom to make room for his belly—stood by the cash register; he greeted Essam, and they chatted about this and that. Down the street we went, then turned right, and down another street—this one with a rare, wide sidewalk—to Essam's house. On a low table in the living room, we spread out some small things to eat after putting everything else away in the kitchen, with its neatly organized rows of dishes, drying cloths, silverware, and cups for coffee and tea.

We ate a bit, just to share the moment together. Essam went to the kitchen to make coffee, and we stood by the stove together chatting about coffee, cooking, and our kids. Back in the living room, we sat down on the sofas, put our coffee cups on the table, and caught up on our lives as old friends do who sometimes go months or years without meeting and yet always pick up as if it had been yesterday. Soon, we wandered out to the small balcony to enjoy the breeze and to look at people walking down the streets in this busy lovely neighborhood near the Institut Français (the French culture center in Cairo), El-Mounira Palace and and the Institut Français d'Archéologie Orientale du Caire (usually referred to as the IFAO), founded during the

French occupation of Egypt in 1800. The quiet and calm of the institute, with its white walls enclosing a rare oasis of green and the well-maintained walls of a former palace, kept the bloody entanglement of research and war far from sight.

Not far away, closer to Tahrir Square, was the original site of the French Institute, which had housed the massive libraries and archives Napoleon's army had collected during their brief occupation between 1798 and 1802. There the archives stayed until 2011, when the institute and its eleven thousand volumes were torched during the January 25 Revolution, in murky circumstances surrounding attacks on the Shura Council next door. The government blamed the fire on "revolutionaries." Many witnesses said they saw thugs, or *baltagiyya*, on the government payroll throw a Molotov cocktail at the building. Undercover government troops had been firing on demonstrators from the roof of the library, which made the building a target. This essential archive and store of knowledge about Egypt, gathered by the French aspiring colonizers, was almost fully destroyed, although citizens and experts mobilized to save what they could.

As I stood on the balcony and discussed what was slated to happen in Cairo now, overlooking the IFAO and the zone of green and open space it enclosed, that history and the many accounts of its meaning and implications seemed far away. The IFAO and El-Mounira Palace were lovely, seen from above. From the street, they were but one more place in a bustling neighborhood of stores, offices, and apartments occupied by clerks and employees of state ministries. Now, on that day in February 2018, we looked over that expanse of blocks and talked over what the future was slated to bring.

Entire ministries were to be emptied out. This was part of the long aftermath of the January 25 Revolution of 2011 and the 2013 coup against the government of President Mohamed Morsi, a member of the Muslim Brotherhood, that had installed General Abdel Fatah Sisi into power as president. The decision had been made to move the state administration out of the city center. All the contents of all the ministries in all these buildings and all the employees who worked at these offices were to be moved to a "New Administrative Capital" to the east of Cairo—an area legally speaking part of Greater Cairo.[1] The megaproject was already underway. Cairo had been built and rebuilt so many times and in so many different ways by so many different rulers over the centuries. And so it would be again.

After the 2013 military coup, a total clampdown had ensued. Then came surveillance, or *rikaba*, all around the central neighborhoods of Cairo. The security services worked to better track what was going on. The shock of what had happened was still palpable. How had the streets been taken by the urban masses? Could it have been stopped? And what would ensure that such a thing would never happen again? The streets were the channels through which information flowed, demonstrators marched, and security forces swooped in. Those channels were a strategic object of control. They had to be taken back.

In 2011, a carnival-like atmosphere had prevailed around Tahrir following the January 25 Revolution. But after 2013, street vendors, artistic events, and street theater were shut down. Streets were cleared. Military tanks and troops were everywhere. Coffeehouses and other gathering spots where intellectuals and activists sat and chatted with those they trusted were shut down. When downtown coffeehouses reopened, it was under the watchful eye of cameras mounted on posts all around. One square kilometer of downtown Cairo had been home to eleven ministries. Now, their employees' loyalty could no longer be trusted. Nor could professionals, such as lawyers and doctors, who had also gone down to the street during the revolution to risk and sometimes lose their lives. State employees were deemed even more unpredictable than members of the professional associations, which had at least entered into negotiations with the government in the decade following the revolution.

The continued presence of all of these residents and workers in the downtown was too risky. What if they got angry again and were again willing to risk everything? Moving them all out of the center of Cairo became part of the counterinsurgency strategy to consolidate military rule. Over the years to come, urban planning as counterinsurgency merged with new forms of financialized real estate that ran through military businesses and their corporate partners. Once cordoned off as a key but hidden part of the Egyptian economy, the military economy expanded and spread into all aspects of life.[2]

An internationally recognized symbol of the revolution, Tahrir Square was a big problem. The Egyptian state had its center in Tahrir. There, and around its edges, stood key symbols of the state, ever since the Free Officers Movement of 1952 had brought President Gamal Abdel Nasser into power. Such symbols, built by or associated with Nasser, remained in place long after his death. The buildings in which state ministries were housed had their own legitimacy. President Hosni Mubarak had associated himself with the symbols of the state and "popular sovereignty" as a source of legitimacy for his regime. Those buildings and symbols of the state had been accessible to protestors in central Cairo. The distinction between (legitimate) state and (illegitimate) regime had held up for quite some time. It collapsed in the process of the revolutionary moment. That situation would not be allowed to recur.

The new capital at first seemed a fantasy, another empty plan, like so many new neighborhoods built in the desert by former president Mubarak, only to remain empty, or half empty. Such half-inhabited zones of extra-urban settlements proliferated around the world by the late 2010s (Tadiar 2022; Simone 2022). Would this new capital city just repeat what had come before?

Urban Planning as Counterinsurgency

A few hours later, I walked home. This was a vibrant bustling neighborhood of offices and homes lived in by many state employees. Soon, according to the plan, it would be empty; but, for now, everything seemed restored to normal, on the surface at least. Still, something hard to identify made the very ground under my feet feel unsteady. Here was that feeling of unsettled ground that marked life in Cairo for me and so many of my friends after 2013.

These were years of relative quiet. This was a waiting time. Nothing unfolded per the plan, of course. Soon enough, inflation and debt crises would turn from abstract economic forces into a most personal and collective disaster. My friends' cousins, brothers, and friends started collapsing on the street from heart attacks or dying at home after refusing to step out into the street anymore. A long wave of reduction of energy and life-force and collective possibilities was underway. One friend talked about the new situation with the Sufi concept of *qabd* (contraction): everything that had so recently seemed possible in a time of expansion, or *bast*, was being constricted. It had become hard to breathe.

We were all busy in this first decade after 2013, making a living, going to work, dealing with lingering health issues accelerated after the years of revolution and counterrevolution. By 2018, things had settled into a new unsettled reality. A miasma of uncertainty hung in the air. My friends did not use that word, *miasma*, but everyone I knew spoke of this sense of walking through heavy air, never knowing how to adjust to any sense of a future or even the ground we walked on. Was it a prescient awareness of the next phase of the unthinkable? If Cairo was a "living encyclopedia" ('Uways 1989) of all that had been and all that was to come, then the threads weaving together past with present, the living with those who were gone, were coming undone. This time, it was not the abstract forces of neoliberal development or property speculation unmaking and remaking the city. This was urban development as counterinsurgency.

The January 25 Revolution had radically altered, as Jacques Rancière (2004, 12) has put it, "the very perception of there being a city, what a city is, how it is assembled, who inhabits it." Rancière wrote those words about mid-nineteenth century Paris, but they could have been written about Cairo in 2011. Both revolutionary moments affected a redistribution of "spaces, times, and forms of activity." Urban planning as counterinsurgency strove to eliminate an entire "regime of perception" of the Egyptian people in mass revolt and on the streets of Cairo as well (Douglas 2007, 8).[3]

In counterrevolutionary Cairo, one thing was imperative: never again should the military be prevented by the size or shape or materials of the roadways from moving quickly and decisively against its own people in times of revolt. To draw on Rancière's framing of counterrevolutionary urban planning in Paris, "boulevards"—straight, wide, passages through which armies could pass and along which vision could not be impeded— would make impossible the building of "barricades" by the revolutionary proletariat of Paris (Douglas 2007, 8; Engels [1848] 1994; Rancière 2004, 12). As in Paris after 1853, gaining control over such channels in Cairo was a decisive site of political struggle. But in Cairo, rather than widen the streets, the government decided to empty them.

In 2015, the decision was announced to move the administration of Cairo and of Egypt outside of the city and to leave downtown itself for people to mess around in as they liked. Once the institutions of state had moved, if people revolted again, it would impact nothing. Those people who remained would not be able to cause much trouble even if they dared to try. At the time of writing this chapter, in the early 2020s, that moment of revolt had not yet arrived, although the sense was growing that the situation simply could not continue. Inflation and new kinds of poverty had taken hold with a death grip on so many who had not so long ago been considered middle class. This showed up in the data. It showed up in how people did the simplest of daily life practices like shopping for and cooking food. A new kind of "window shopping" for food had even emerged. Essam and I had started talking about it a few years earlier.

New categories of food had emerged by 2018. The meaning of "chicken" changed. It was sold differently. Earlier, people might have said they were "going to get a chicken." Chicken had never been a luxury good. But now, to get a chicken, a whole chicken, had become a luxury. New markets also emerged. Different parts of the chicken went to different markets. Formal markets got the legs and the breast; the leftover second-rate parts went elsewhere. New pricing technologies emerged. Things that would have been given away to children living on the street, or to poor beggars, now had a price. Bruised vegetables, chicken bones, gristle—all had a price where none had existed before. At first this seemed temporary, an anomaly. By 2022, this was the new world in which everyone lived. One story in the news in late 2022 illustrated the depth of the mess. Scores of young chicks being raised for the market were slaughtered: the grain used for their feed was stuck at the ports because the companies had no access to foreign currency reserves to pay the importers (El Wardany 2022). Chicken prices went up even further. An end was nowhere in sight.

Back in the 1990s, many of the women I worked with mentioned how much they loved window shopping for clothes or appliances with no aim to buy. They missed that pleasure of window shopping with their friends when they were displaced to new neighborhoods on the outskirts of Cairo. Window shopping was different from food shopping, which was a pragmatic task undertaken to get food into the house to cook for the family. But now there was window shopping for food as well. We called it "price shopping." For the first time, we saw people who went to food markets just to look at prices. One day at a market in Saiyda Zaynab, we saw a woman take out her money and count it, over and over, and then over again. And then put it back in her bag. Buying nothing. Not even the one bag of lemons she had been looking at.

These new ways of shopping came with the new poverty. Even those with college degrees and professional jobs were struggling to pay for the basics. Possibilities were constricting. The mood of *qabd*, contraction, took hold of the city as a whole and the lives of everyone I knew. The situation had seemed temporary at first. The contraction of all that had seemed possible and doable had come in dribs and drabs—except for those who spoke out against the government and the military and disappeared in regime prisons.

Life in Cairo was marked in this decade by endless and growing uncertainty under the grinding pressures of endurance (Abaza 2020, 9). But Cairo was not alone here. This situation had become an essential feature of contemporary urbanism (Abaza 2020, 9; Simone 2013, 245). Slow-paced "ambient terror" (Nixon 2019) replaced the dramatic pace of revolution and counterrevolution in the early 2010s. The state's "revolutionary reaction," to use a term invoked to describe the counterrevolutionary regime of Napoleon III (Mundt 1861, 308, as cited in Mastnak 2021), was striking in its slow-moving brutality.

This terror was different from the dramatic scenes of revolt and of retaking the streets in 2011 or from the violence exercised on protestors whose eyes were shot out, whose limbs were destroyed, or whose lives were taken, culminating in the massacre at Rabaa Square in 2013. This was a grinding, personalized terror and contraction of the capacity to be human. Huge swaths of the people of Cairo who had been able to make do and feel middle class were joining the ranks of the "devalued" and the expanding ranks of urban poor left to manage somehow on their own as "remaindered life" (Tadiar 2022). Amid all this, the multibillion dollar New Administrative Capital project took shape.

During the summer of 2022, I was transfixed by commercials running nonstop on state-sponsored television about the megaproject of the New Administrative Capital. I started to think of it as infrastructure porn. Gleaming images of the New Administrative Capital with its green parks and flowing water and modern real estate investment vehicles flowed parallel to the realities of constricting life in Cairo. The contrast was already impossible to miss in the spring of 2021, when the government undertook a spectacle to celebrate this remaking of Cairo and the victories of Egypt over trying circumstances: the Parade of the Mummies.

Museums Living and Dead

The Pharaohs' Golden Parade (or the Parade of the Mummies, as many called it) on April 3, 2021, was an occasion to celebrate this new Cairo and President Sisi's vision of Egypt and Egyptian civilization (figure 1.1). I watched the parade on video stream along with hundreds of millions of other viewers around the world. By order of the Ministry of the Interior, bystanders were banned from the six-kilometer route. Here, too, military/security concerns reigned supreme. The possibility of protests or disruption was thus foreclosed. This parade was to be viewed on television by a passive audience; it was not a shared experience for the public along a parade route in a shared urban space.

The parade began at the Egyptian Museum, located on one side of Tahrir Square, and it ended at the site of the new National Museum of Egyptian Civilization in the Cairo neighborhood of al-Fustat (or just Fustat), the capital of Egypt established with the Islamic conquest in 597. President Sisi urged Egyptians—and the world—to watch the spectacle on television: "With all pride and pleasure, I look forward to receiving the kings and queens of Egypt" (Omar 2021). With this tweet on his official Twitter channel, the president placed himself as legitimate heir of the great pharaonic rulers of Egypt.

1.1 Parade of the Mummies (Pharaohs' Golden Parade), April 3, 2021. Photograph by Khaled Desouki.

The parade opened with operatic songs performed by the singers of the Cairo Opera House. The lyrics were from the Book of the Dead, in the ancient Egyptian hieroglyphic language as Egyptologists imagined it would sound (Tabikha 2021). After the opening opera, gold-plated tanks carried the mummies down the appointed route. Singers and actors moved along with them in choreographed harmony. The opera singers were central to the event and "came in a manner befitting Egypt's position in front of the world," as noted by Egypt's minister of culture and minister of tourism in a ceremony at the Cairo Opera House a few days later (Samir 2021). After about forty-five minutes, the parade ended in front of the new museum with a twenty-one-gun salute. There, singers, actors, and mummies were greeted by President Sisi, who had inaugurated the museum's main hall earlier that day. Just as the people had become the audience watching the parade on television, so too had the government become a performance to be watched: an opera.

The Parade of the Mummies was covered in art and archaeology journals and on global media platforms. *Artnet News* put it like this, with pictures from the event:

Safely moving the millennia-old remains was a multimillion-dollar affair that involved building special shock-absorbent vehicles as well as repaving the roads along the route to ensure a smooth ride. To maintain optimal preservation conditions, the mummies were put into oxygen-free nitrogen capsules for the duration of their journey. Each of the 18 kings and four queens had their own gold and blue car, designed to look like the pharaonic boats used to transport ancient royals to their tombs, and featuring the winged sun symbol used by the pharaohs. . . . The most famous pharaohs in the parade were Ramses II, of the nineteenth dynasty, who led the New Kingdom in the 13th century BC, during its most powerful period, for 67 years, and Queen Hatshepsut, who ruled as the second female pharaoh, during the eighteenth dynasty in the 15th century BC. All the mummies were originally excavated in the nineteenth century from the Valley of Kings and nearby Deir el-Bahri. (Cascone 2021)

The Parade of the Mummies was controversial. Disagreement ran within families. People talked about it for months. My friend Heba told me of her own family's arguments. Most of her (middle-class) family were happy for this moment of pride in Egypt and its history. They were tired of the constant upheaval of the last years and disdained those critical of the return to a modicum of normality. They welcomed a moment of pride and pleasure. Others were disgusted by the expense, the glitter, and the glamour covering over a horrific situation in Egypt. Thousands of critics of the military regime were in prison. Life was getting worse every month. It was bad luck, moreover, to stage such as ostentatious event in the face of widespread suffering. It was against Egyptian ways and would attract the evil eye. Calamities would ensue.

Indeed, bad things did ensue. A passenger train derailed in the southern Egyptian governate of Sohag, killing nineteen Egyptians. The next day, a building collapsed in the Cairo neighborhood Gesr el-Suez, leaving eighteen dead (Amin 2021). Then the giant container ship *Ever Given* ran aground in the Suez Canal, blocking international shipping traffic for days at a cost of billions of dollars. Hundreds of giant container ships were involved. A week's closure of the canal cost the global economy between $6 and $10 billion (US), according to the insurance giant Allianz (Khalili 2021). Popular accounts linked these tragedies to the audacity of the event and the "curse of the mummies" known to fall upon anyone who dared to disturb their resting place (Amin 2021). News and a flood of social media memes about the *Ever Given* and attempts to dislodge it washed away discussion of the Parade of the Mummies. Global commerce was severely impacted, given that 30 percent of global trade moves through the Suez Canal (Khalili 2021).

President Sisi had already undertaken a project to widen the Suez Canal in 2013, setting to work military engineers to draw up the plans. He had called on the Egyptian masses to support this project as a patriotic duty to revive Egypt's international standing after the chaos of the revolution and Muslim Brotherhood rule. The canal's expansion was hoped to increase daily traffic from seventy-eight to ninety-seven ships per day, doubling annual revenues from the canal to $13.5 billion by 2023. Citizens had been encouraged to express their support of the government by purchasing special investment certificates paying 12 percent interest in local currency. The government even instructed preachers in mosques to cite the Prophet Muhammad's digging a trench to defend Medina from attackers on Friday prayer (*Economist* 2015). But the endless images, memes, and stories about the *Ever Given* stuck in the canal, holding up global commerce, erased memories of the lavish New Suez Canal celebrations that had been held in August 2015. The canal would have to be expanded yet again.

The pace of Sisi's megaprojects had started to pick up by 2015. One megaproject lay at the end of the Parade of the Mummies: the new National Museum of Egyptian Civilization, where the mummies would now be housed. This museum was part of another megaproject being built in al-Fustat, including the Al-Fustat Garden Restoration, built in the location of the old Fustat Gardens, established in 641 CE by Arab commander Amr Ibn Al-Aas, and the Ain El-Sira Lake. The project was intended to integrate a public park with views of "several archaeological and historical sites and landmarks" put on display for regional and foreign visitors. Most of those archaeological sites had been uncovered by Egyptian and French archaeologists and engineers in 1912, just before the outbreak of World War I and Britain's declaration of Egypt as a protectorate in 1914 (Mohammed 2022).

The National Museum of Egyptian Civilization was to mark the new branding of Cairo as an "open air museum." Visitors to Cairo (carrying desperately needed hard currency) could see Egypt on display, right in place. This was not the first time that Cairo had been designed for an elusive foreign eye. The 1867 World Exhibition in Paris offered up representations of Egypt for Europeans' consuming gaze (Mitchell 1991). Now, those interested in Egypt and its civilization could gaze at Cairo without worrying about Cairo's people or the pace of Cairo's daily life getting in their way. The new megaprojects, as well as private sector investments bringing together Egyptian and Saudi investors (Addakhakhny 2022), made a sterile, three-dimensional museum out of the living reality of urban Cairo. The new museum and the megaproject of which it was part were not living—at least not for Cairenes. Cairo's living history was being cleansed. Cleaned-up versions of Egypt's archaeological history would be staged as a Disney-like display for the increasingly elusive Western tourist and for Arab visitors from the Gulf, in a death grip of what historian Rana Barakat describes as museumification (R. Barakat 2018a, 11) and what we can call an example of the antimuseum, in the sense of 'Uways's notion of Cairo as a "museum of life" ('Uways 1989).

Lots of work went into the Parade of the Mummies. Some of it was infrastructural, focusing on creating channels for the parade's unimpeded movement. Roads had to be paved and smoothed; neighborhoods cleaned up or torn down. Some residential neighborhoods along the way and at the destination were demolished to make way for the new tourism complex in al-Fustat with its "5-star hotels, cafes, restaurants, and The National Museum of Egyptian Civilization" (Naguib 2021). While spectacular in impact and operatic in scope, this was far from the first time that infrastructures of daily Cairene life were demolished to make way for government's alternate visions, and it would not be the last.

Some areas of Cairo had been destroyed for political reasons in the 1990s as well. This included designating them as "hotbeds of terrorism" or as "slums." Residents had little recourse when the state decided that their homes had to go (see Ghannam 2002; Elyachar 2005). Such residents of Cairo were not deemed full property-rights-bearing subjects. Under the Mubarak regime, especially in the later years, neoliberal consultants were brought in to formalize informal property, ostensibly to make property rights more transferable and to create a mortgage schema that would "unlock," under the tutelage of neoliberal ideologue Hernando de Soto, the hidden value of informal property (Elyachar 2012b; Mitchell 2008). But this was a different kind of siege.

Cairo's popular, or *sha'bi*, neighborhoods had been a stronghold of resistance to the Mubarak regime during the revolution. These central neighborhoods had also housed many government buildings. All this made attacks on the state more feasible and urban planning as counterinsurgency in the aftermath, perhaps, inevitable. Government employment had been the economic base of these neighborhoods. Following completion of the New Administrative Capital, the old central Cairo buildings left standing would, theoretically, be stripped of residents, tax base, and function. Elsewhere, neighborhoods were literally bulldozed to make way for new tourist attractions. What began with the counterinsurgency logic of a military armed against its own people was soon capitalized as an investment vehicle for public-private ventures for which the military served as incubator, broker, and part owner.

Even those with official contracts of property ownership, testified to by state paperwork duly garnered after waiting in long lines at government offices, found themselves stripped of home and property, memory and relations, and even life itself. Some lucky residents were given an "equal trade" for an empty box of walls in a "new neighborhood." Some were offered a small apartment in the Al-Asmarat housing project of Cairo's Muqattam neighborhood (Naguib 2021). That was certainly the case in Fustat, where residents often lacked formal documentation of their ownership or long-term residence in their homes. Such documentation is rare in the vast "informal" neighborhoods of Cairo. But without official documentation, residents could be evicted without compensation (Naguib 2021).

Wealth in property acquired in legitimate, if informal, ways was wiped out as if it had never existed. Property acquired over years of work and investment, from migration (in the form of funds sent home year after year), property accrued from bits of wealth acquired in dribs and drabs from here and there, was wiped out too. For those on the losing side, their property was rendered trash, its value liquefied to become empty space for open air museums. All this was part of the broad project of redistributing wealth and property once again, this time for the benefit of the military and its allies. From those new but dead museums, the hope was, streams of foreign-currency-bearing tourists would come forth, infusing the Egyptian economy with hard currency. This quest for foreign reserves merged with the military remaking of Cairo and the performance of Egypt as a civilized sovereign state in the Parade of the Mummies.

Operatic Infrastructures

With the Parade of the Mummies, President Sisi marked the completion of one phase of the military's reconquest of space in Cairo, celebrating Egypt's history and his new regime as its legitimate heir. This was not the first time that a military political leader deployed opera and other tools of an "operatic state" (Berenson 2002; Mestyan 2014) to conquer political space. Nor was it the first time that operatic events and performers, musicians, and singers were mobilized to celebrate conquest of space in Cairo and Egypt. Napoleon

Bonaparte used pageantry, music, and drama in his attempts to impose French authority in Egypt after the 1798 invasion. So did Ismail Pasha, khedive of Egypt, most famously with the (nearly) simultaneous opening of the Suez Canal in 1869 and Giuseppe Verdi's opera *Aida* in the Khedivial Opera House in 1871 (the story of *Aida* is based in ancient Egypt). Such moments are not particular to Egypt. Nor is this a matter of repetition characteristic of oriental despots. My concern is more general. Such operatic infrastructures are part of global patterns of contestation over space and part of what Nora Barakat and others call building "state space."[4]

By staging *Aida* with the Parade of the Mummies, President Sisi inevitably brought to mind the long history and implications of that opera's production. Verdi's *Aida* was, in the view of Edward Said and others, a paean to imperial domination and the "true cultural invasion of the Egyptian capital from the West" (Said 1987, 1993; Scham 2013). The premiere of Verdi's opera was originally planned to coincide with the opening of the Suez Canal, but the timing did not work out. Instead, the Suez Canal opened two years earlier, in 1869, and was celebrated in multiple locations, in Suez and in Cairo, with opera—lots of opera. The opening itself was operatic in scale: ships of state slowly made their way through the canal, with a carefully determined order of precedence, overturned by the British at the last moment.[5] The new Khedivial Opera House was opened with Verdi's *Rigoletto*. Grand opera merged with celebration of khedivial power.

All this came at a price. Between 1869 and 1875, Khedive Ismail oversaw the expenditure of more than one million French francs in every year on the theaters he constructed in an official capacity. This momentous sum was more than just display of culture; it was also a performance of Egyptian state sovereignty. Thanks to the achievements of Ismail's father, Mehmet Ali, Egypt was already relatively autonomous, possessing the right to pass on hereditary rule. It was still formally a province of the Ottoman Empire. But responsibility for these debts did not move to the imperial capital. Debts stayed with Egypt and sometimes with Khedive Ismail personally (Mestyan 2017, 110). In this system, debts that could otherwise have been matched by other credits within the budgetary flows of the Ottoman Empire were instead localized outside of imperial state budget.

In a similar move, under President Sisi after 2013, the building of the New Administrative Capital and other megaprojects took place outside of the Egyptian state budget, protecting the projects from public scrutiny and review (Kassab 2019; Sayigh 2022). It might seem odd to find such resonances between arrangements of 1870 and 2022 in Egypt, which likewise seem familiar in many places where debts accumulate outside the control or will of the (supposedly) sovereign state.[6] But as we will see, this is a classic condition of the semicivilized, which is characterized by dividual sovereignty and the apportionment of fiscality and the accumulation of debts to institutions outside the control of the (supposedly sovereign) state.

Financing the Suez project outside the Ottoman budget was even more complicated. During the regency of Ismail Pasha (1863–79), Egyptian debt to foreign creditors rose from about three million to one hundred million pounds sterling. The khedive took on debt denominated in British sterling currency, convertible to gold on global markets, which was spent on completing the Suez Canal, training the army, building the Khedivial Opera House, remaking Cairo, and building more railroads and a port in Alexandria.[7]

Building a canal through the desert to unite the Red and Mediterranean Seas had been an aspiration of the rulers of Egypt since pharaonic times. It had been a dream and hope of Napoleon I, for which he commissioned the engineer Jacques-Marie Le Père in 1801 to assess the possibility of constructing the canal (Huber 2012, 143).[8] By the mid-nineteenth century, other people held this dream, too, including French Saint-Simonian socialist engineers, who were an important influence on Mehmed Ali and his projects of industrialization in the 1830s and on Khedive Ismail in the 1860s (Elshakry 2007; Fahmy 2009, 2010).

According to the Saint-Simonians, finance could help build infrastructure that would speed up the circulation time of capital, which would create savings that could be mobilized to reduce poverty and social strife. This vision was essential to the political project of Bonapartism, after the defeat of the revolutionaries in France (Mastnak 2021). In the 1830s, the Saint-Simonian leader and engineer Barthélemy-Prosper Enfantin traveled to Istanbul and then to Cairo with a small group of followers, hoping to instantiate his vision of transcending conflict between East and West, male and female, with a Suez Canal. But the project did not gain the support of Mehmet Ali, who had instead invested resources in overland routes from the Red Sea to the Mediterranean (Huber 2012; Jakes 2020).

It took further innovation in the Saint-Simonian tradition to actualize plans for building the Suez Canal. First, a number of institutional arrangements for managing the financing had to be made. Ferdinand de Lesseps created a joint-stock company in 1858 to excavate and manage the canal in which, through multiple twists and turns, his diplomatic experience was as important as financial innovation.[9] Decisions such as the pledge to de Lesseps's Canal Company to build the canal with unpaid corvée labor, and the later decision to change to a paid labor force had financial implications going forward (Marsot 1975).

In 1875, British Prime Minister Benjamin Disraeli bought shares for the British government from Egypt, as if it really were an independent sovereign state. By 1876, a system of "Dual Control" of Egyptian finances under Anglo-French control had been accepted by the khedive, with two "controllers-general" of audit and public debt and of receipts, respectively.[10] French and British control of Egyptian finances continued until 1882, when there was a massive revolt against foreign influence in Egypt that resulted in full British occupation of Egypt in 1882.

The debts accumulated by Egypt in this period were remarkable. Historiography of this debt tends to go in two directions. One view is that Khedive Ismail was duped and lured into a "debt trap" by unscrupulous foreigners, who got Egypt entangled in debt obligations for projects with no solid economic footing or backing and for wasteful celebrations, thus laying the groundwork for British colonization of Egypt and massive debt that could never be repaid (Marsot 1975, 89). Others see Khedive Ismail as a clever and clearsighted developer of national infrastructure that would provide Egypt with opportunities and strategic wealth for decades to come, even if the finances of this development landed Egypt in trouble (Marsot 1975; Vatikiotis 1980, 73–83; Vatikiotis 1987; Hunter 1999; Mestyan 2017).

Be that as it may, opening the Suez Canal in 1869 "transformed the Mediterranean from a closed sea into a passageway" (Huber 2012, 141), changing the world of capital forever even as it reinforced the semicivilized status of Egypt. Opening this infrastructural channel through Egypt was key to speeding up flows of global capital via the conquest of time through space. The Saint-Simonian dream of increasing turnover time through infrastructure and innovative financing was achieved. Commerce and military imperatives converged when the canal helped to create much-desired faster passageways to India after the mass revolts of 1856 against the East India Company's rule of the subcontinent. Bypassing the long path around the Cape of Good Hope was a world-changing accomplishment. The canal also made visible in its infrastructural splendor the realities of dividual sovereignty and the many different institutions shaping the future of Egypt. As with the Parade of the Mummies, totalizing sovereignty was performed here. But performativity is never totalizing in its effects. And it can come at a cost, sometimes in the shape of unpayable debt obligations stretching into the future.

In itself, taking on unpayable national debt is nothing unique—the US national debt, for example, will never be paid down. More significant is that

Egypt's supposedly sovereign debt was controlled by outsiders. Fiscality here is split off from the "bundle of powers" of a sovereign state. Ultimately in Egypt's case, the conditions of the Ottoman capitulations, and the principles of extraterritoriality and personal law on which they rested, left Egypt without agency over debt contracted in its name. France and Great Britain (as well as any of their subjects) were, according to the capitulations, able to conduct business in Egypt (and all of the Ottoman Empire) without regard for local law. This debt became a kind of extraterritorial person, with a stranglehold on Egypt in a situation of coloniality: Egypt had no agency over its debts, its finances, its budget, or its future. All this turned financial debt into another barrier—as an expression of coloniality—to Egypt's consolidation as a fully sovereign state. Unpayable debt controlled by outsiders was here, as elsewhere in the decades and century and a half to come, a mark of the semicivilized. Financial innovation allowing new kinds of debt of the kind taken on to finance the Suez Canal can reinforce the semicivilized condition, as can be seen in more recent innovations coordinated through Egypt's sovereign wealth fund (The Sovereign Fund of Egypt, TSFE) and its deployment in remaking modern Cairo for new investors.

From National Wealth to "Assets"

What about the place where the Parade of the Mummies began, Tahrir Square? Tahrir was a symbol of the post-1952 modern Egyptian state, and it was the site of revolutionary clashes since the 1919 Revolution, when Egyptians clashed with British soldiers who used the square for their daily parade grounds outside of the former royal barracks of Qasr el-Nil, for which the square was first named (Rabbat 2011). The name was then changed to Midan el-Isamiliyya in honor of Khedive Ismail, until the 1952 coup, when it became Midan el-Tahrir (Rabbat 2011). This square and the buildings that surrounded it were associated not only with the Nasserist post-1952 state but with decolonization itself (Rabbat 2011; Saad 2020). Retaking and remaking Tahrir Square was a central priority of the military government after the 2013 coup.

Remaking Tahrir Square involved different tactics on each of its four sides. The American University in Cairo was moved to a new location near the New Administrative Capital, far to the east. The Museum of Egyptian Antiquities, or the Egyptian Museum as it is usually called, stands at the northern side of the square, just north of the barracks of Qasr el-Nil. The museum had been completed in 1902 to house Egypt's collection of pharaonic antiquities

(Rabbat 2011, 185).[11] It was left standing in place but was marginalized in funding and attention afterward.

On the southern side of the square was the Mogamma (figure 1.2), home of a significant part of the administrative offices of the Interior Ministry of Egypt, which had "come to be universally associated with the labyrinthine and gargantuan Egyptian bureaucracy" (Rabbat 2011). Gifted to Egypt by the Soviet Union and designed in 1951 by Mohamed Kamal Ismail, the fourteen-story modernist center for government offices with 1,356 rooms was constructed in 1953 (El-Din 2021; Saad 2020). Bringing all the government administrative procedures together into one bureaucracy and one building, it had been hoped, would simplify and modernize workings of the state in its interface with its citizens. The Mogamma was then seen as representing "simplicity, centrality, monumentality, and efficiency of the Egyptian social-ist government" (Saad 2020, 39). Until the January 25 Revolution in 2011, it was the workplace of nine thousand government employees (El-Din 2021).

The Mogamma was the face of the state for Egyptian citizens who needed birth or death certificates, passports, permission for free medi-cal treatment, criminal records, identification cards, copies of marriage contracts, or a multitude of other documents (Emam 2021). But it became a symbol of inefficiency and endless waiting in multiple lines. On Febru-ary 7, 2011, demonstrators in Tahrir Square blocked all three entrances to the Mogamma, "leaving thousands of perplexed civil servants waiting out-side" (Rabbat 2011, 188).

At the time of my first visit to Egypt in 1991, the building was seen by many as a black hole in which the horrors of bureaucracy were housed to-gether with bodily horrors of the security police. For resident foreigners like me, it was a place to go to stand in long lines for a renewal of an *iqama*, or residency stamp. It was a place of fear and uncertainty for my Egyptian friends: Would it be possible to extract one of many necessary documents for accessing health care, starting university, or traveling abroad? One never knew if the hours spent waiting would bring forth the urgent document. Other fears were even more visceral. Under Mubarak, young men in Cairo could be picked up by security police and taken for interrogation at the Mogamma; they might be held there without recourse for days at a time. The Mogamma was where my husband was taken for a midnight interview in 1993 by security police concerned by his passport from an unrecognized new state from the former Yugoslavia.

Even after the relocation of the state ministries and offices from the Mogamma to the New Administrative Capital, the building's fate was frozen

1.2   The Mogamma, home of a significant part of the administrative offices of the Interior Ministry of Egypt, viewed from across Tahrir Square, Cairo, during the January 25 Revolution, 2011. Photograph by Ahmed Abd El-Fatah, 2011.

for years. Then, by presidential decree in September 2020, the future of the Mogamma was quietly announced. The building, the land on which it stood, and its surroundings—totaling over three acres—were transferred into Egypt's sovereign wealth fund. Also transferred into the fund were seven other state-owned properties, including the old administrative headquarters of the interior ministry and its land (over 4.6 acres); 3.9 acres of land of the former National Democratic Party building that had been partially damaged during the January 25 Revolution; and four other buildings located in the governorates of Cairo and Gharbiya (Moneim 2020). This was but one small part of a broader process of the capitalization of military companies through the sovereign wealth fund and the private capital it could mobilize on international markets (Sayigh 2022, 1).

In December 2121, it was announced that the Mogamma would be turned into a luxury hotel and shopping center. A development consortium of corporate entities from the United States and the United Arab Emirates won the bid to "redevelop the Mogamma al-Tahrir complex" in "iconic Tahrir Square" (El-Din 2021), together with companies of the military. Once empty, the building could be valued as real estate. Reconceived as real estate, wealth of the Egyptian people that had been seen as public goods became assets that could be financialized on private markets through the sovereign wealth fund. Street vendors, artistic events, and street theater were long gone. Even the military barricades on Tahrir Square had become a memory. Cairo was being taken back in this phase through militarized financialization instead. As a giant sign mounted on the right of the building said in English and Arabic, with a backdrop of tropical flowers and birds, it was a "new beginning."

Sovereign wealth funds are investment funds owned or managed by a state or state institution. Despite their importance in the global economy, the literature on such funds generally does not offer a definition of what exactly they are (Bahoo, Alon, and Paltrinieri 2020, 8).[12] The rise of these funds allows states to take wealth and turn it into financialized assets that generate rents. The range of institutional arrangements under which sovereign wealth funds can be established can make them hard to define. The first state-owned fund of this kind was the Kuwait Investment Authority, created in 1953 to invest oil revenues even before Kuwait gained independence from Great Britain. Egypt's sovereign wealth fund, The Sovereign Fund of Egypt (TSFE), was established in 2018, five years after the coup that put the military and current President Sisi in power and seven years after the January 25 Revolution of 2011.

As a legal semisovereign semicorporate entity, TSFE has its own autonomous sphere of action regarding the national wealth for which it is fiduciary.[13] In a strange echo of dividual sovereignty, now spun off into global financial markets, TSFE's assets and investments can be outside the purview of central banks, although the line between TSFE and the sphere of the Central Bank and the national economy can be hard to define or maintain (Rozanov 2005). In an era of "capitalization" or "assetification" (Birch and Muniesa 2020), the structure of TSFE allows state actors who were charged with preserving the nation's wealth for the citizenry to turn it instead into financial assets that generate more wealth for the few. Wealth held in trust as "public goods" can, once moved into a sovereign wealth fund, become assets or capital invested on financial markets with returns flowing to foreign investors or to members of the military. In Egypt, crucially, assetification via TSFE also makes possible the infusion of capital from global financial markets into balance sheets of military corporations, with returns flowing out to foreign corporate investors as well as to the military. This is a profound if subtle switch, a modern form of *istibdaal*.

In the nineteenth century, *istibdaal* allowed managers of waqf to "change the nature of the endowments" by exchanging the endowed object for another (El Shamsy 2022 19; cf. Moumtaz 2021). One form of wealth held as perpetual trust could be transformed into another, in a form of revaluation. This allowed directors of a waqf to transform the type of property they had originally been mandated to supervise and which was technically held in perpetuity and impossible to sell—like national wealth and public goods held in trust for all the citizens of a state. Books, for example, were a store of value as well as of knowledge. Transformation of the form of value could yield money profit, some of which might be siphoned off by the director or administrator of the waqf. Books and rare manuscripts were relatively easy to convert into money, and thus a frequent target of embezzlement schemes by librarians and waqf supervisors in times of political instability and lax legal supervision (El Shamsy 2022, 19).

This was not so different from how, in 2020, TSFE became a mechanism for the transfer of the collective wealth of the Egyptian people into privatized capital of corporations based in the Gulf and the United States and into capital for Egyptian military companies. In its early days, the Mogamma had been a locus of Egyptians' aspirations for modernity and sovereignty; it had become a symbol of how the aspirations of the "semicivilized" in Cairo and around the region had failed. In this new form of *istibdaal*, transfer of the Mogamma leveraged that history into privatized wealth for stakeholders in the military, in the Gulf States, and in the United States. How had this happened?

In Egypt, the institution of a sovereign wealth fund has allowed for the creation of public-private partnerships to attract foreign investment into Egypt in joint deals, such as the deal for the Mogamma to become an elite hotel complex, signed between TSFE and a consortium including Global Ventures, Oxford Capital Group, and United Arab Emirates–based Al-Otaiba Investment. The chair of TSFE has the power to create subfunds that fall even further out of the public eye (Haroun 2021; Moniem 2020; Sayigh 2022). Such subfunds are another step removed from the long-standing debates over socialism, the public sector, and the private sector that had shaped politics in Egypt and around the postcolonial world for decades.

A presidential decree of September 2020, published in an official state gazette, gave the subfund the authority to function for ninety-nine years with the possibility of renewal, granting it financial and administrative independence (Moniem 2020). Subfund administrators could buy, sell, or rent fixed and transferred state-owned assets. These individuals had the right to borrow, obtain pre-approved and flexible long-term loans or credit facilities, and to issue bonds, and other financial instruments such as fixed-income capital market instruments that were compliant with Islamic law such as *sukuk* (Moniem 2020). One such subfund established in 2020 for the "financial and digital transformation services" had a "registered capital of EGP 30 billion and an issued capital of EGP 500 million" (Moniem 2020). The politics of debt and finance in the region, and in the world of global commerce or global capital, had come full circle. Just like with the Ottoman capitulations, global finance flowed into and out of Egypt without Egyptian state regulation or taxation in a kind of extraterritorial corporate zone.

Moving buildings like the Mogamma into a sovereign wealth fund also whitewashed the building's complicated history. Battles over privatization had shaped the decades of the Mubarak family's rule, both with international financial institutions like the World Bank pushing the regime to privatize the state-owned public sector created under President Nasser in the 1960s and with professional organizations, unions, and political parties that fought against privatization with broad-based public support. Under President Sisi, all that supposedly disappeared. Nasser's regime could be characterized as a regime of industrialization via the nationalized financial industry. In Sisi's regime, the political economy evolved into financialized real estate controlled by the military and formally owned by the state.[14] Such links between commerce, finance, the military, and war are nothing unique to Egypt; they were part of the "financial revolution" in seventeenth-century Great Britain as well.

Using public-private agreements in the sovereign wealth fund to transform the national wealth of the Egyptian people into profit opportunities for corporate interests in the Gulf and the United States was completely new. Yet it escaped public debate or outrage at the time. It bypassed decades of sharp social conflict between advocates of the state-owned public sector and advocates of "free market capitalism." Everything proceeded quietly, by a stroke of the pen under the counsel of experts in global financial markets.

Attempts to privatize public wealth beginning with President Anwar Sadat, under pressure from the United States and international financial institutions such as the International Monetary Fund and the World Bank, had led to massive street demonstrations in the 1970s. President Mubarak had, if sometimes ambivalently, continued this long-term process of privatization of the public sector in the 1980s and 1990s. But these new techniques of financialized bait-and-switch under the regime of President Morsi attracted no such attention until it was too late. Once in the sovereign wealth fund, state wealth became financialized assets valued on global financial markets, outside the sway of Egyptian state institutions for audit and financial control. Urban renewal as counterinsurgency and militarized finance went hand in hand. Together, they reinforced the continuity of the semicivilized condition.

The Cost of Green

By 2022, it was clear that Sisi's megaprojects would cost at least three times as much money as originally budgeted. President Sisi was "a man in a hurry" (Springborg 2022). He repeatedly insisted that projects be completed ahead of schedule, considerably raising costs with no clear benefit.[15] All these megaprojects drained state coffers. And yet, since a military corporation led the construction, the expenditures remained outside the purview of state budgets or auditing agencies, not subject to state audit by the state agencies that still tried to rectify maleficence across all political regimes in Egypt (Kassab 2019; Sayigh 2019, 2022).

These megaprojects aimed to achieve the security imperatives of the military state. Images of the beauty, cleanliness, and dignified futures of the new areas were presented at every opportunity. The new areas were "green," the new operatic imperative. The production of green, smart cities was put forward as a solution to Egypt's and the world's woes. Much was kept behind stage in this production. Where would the water come from? How would the military government mobilize the water needed to keep bright green those lawns and a park "larger than Central Park," as the advertisement running around the clock on state-affiliated Nile TV repeated? Egypt was already enmeshed in regional conflicts with Ethiopia about redirecting the Nile River. While alliances with Israel and the Gulf States made technologies for desalinization available, the ground under the regime still seemed somewhat solid in 2022. But the salt was not so simple to remove, and the fate of grounds all around the New Administrative Capital became increasingly unclear.

Every day I was in Cairo during the summer of 2022, I sat transfixed by Nile TV informercials about President Sisi and the future of Cairo. Clips featured the building of ports, the expansion of the Suez Canal, the free movement of container ships, and the pouring forth of water into a new Cairo, rendering the desert green. The desert would sprout green hydrogen for the region and for Europe. The international conference on climate was being held in Egypt, and messages ran nonstop promoting the government's "green" initiatives. At the same time, the literal and figurative grounds of the urban masses were being destroyed. In their place grew a mythic picture of "real estate" as an undervalued "natural resource" of Egypt. I heard a minister use those words on a television interview one day, saying, "Real estate is a little appreciated natural resource" of Egypt. That which was not turned into marketable real estate had no value.

The wealth built up by working-class men of Egypt during their years spent working as migrant laborers in the Gulf, and the wealth they had been able to create and solidify, they thought, on the streets of Cairo, turned into nothing, a devalued asset. Meanwhile, the states in the Gulf constructed with Egyptian labor, and the infrastructure Egyptian laborers had built, became the platform for the growing wealth, reach, and diversification of the Gulf State economies, which moved decisively into the Egyptian economy after 2013 (Hanieh 2018).

With the continued decimation of public wealth and worsening prospects for the future, despair grew. In the central neighborhoods of Cairo hung the specter of hunger. The future brought promise of more depletion. Those who could make it out were in Germany or in the United States. First, the activists who could leave, left—as did, over the coming decade, many with the resources to do so. Others flocked to areas of the new Cairo, to the New Administrative Capital and its surrounding New Cities being constructed by the military/private companies, in the hope that those areas would hold their value. But this too was a dream. In the new areas, real estate ruled: buyers did not even fully own the land or the building they thought they bought. These were in a "condo" structure. Residents could be forced out at any time.

Friends told me stories of growing despair in their families. My friend Dalia grew up in Shubra. She had left Egypt years before the 2011 Revolution, which took a hard toll on her family. Her nephew had been martyred in the revolution's early days; another relative passed away from sudden death on the street, the strain of life itself having taken a fatal toll. Her father had spent much of her childhood working as a contractor in Saudi Arabia, as had millions of Egyptians in the 1970s and 1980s. His work and effort had paid off: he had purchased apartments in Cairo for his children, guaranteeing their futures, he thought. But now, his own children could not sell their apartments fast enough, in a desperate effort to recoup some value before it all collapsed. There were simply no buyers.

Grounds for a collective life were coming undone. Cairenes of the popular classes were being left to a slow death in the crumbling remains of the once-living museum of Cairo. In case they ever got an itch to revolt and found a way to assemble, no one would be there to listen or pay attention anyway. I saw this vision in maps of Cairo drawn up by a real estate agency set up especially for the "wandering investor."

At this time of state and internationally backed public-private real estate investment deals, these were opportunities for foreign investors in a "contrarian mood" looking for "value opportunities" in undervalued assets with potential to grow. From a perspective that viewed real estate as a natural resource, all properties in historic Cairo, including its once upper-class neighborhood of Zamalek, were "poor buys." Hundreds, even thousands, of years of vital urban life of the masses had been completely devalued. This erasure and epistemic violence were a new blow, not quite registered by the public, coming as it did on top of the grinding devastation of the decade just gone by. And yet, not all could be enclosed, contained, sold off, and moved. Something remained; something beyond capture (Simone 2022) was taking shape once again.

2

INFRASTRUCTURES OF THE SEMICIVILIZED

I would have known with my eyes closed that Mr. Amir worked in the public sector when I first met him toward the end of 1995.[1] Neglect was palpable in the smells and the heat in the building where he worked. Air conditioning in Mr. Amir's office groaned more than it cooled: the hot and humid air of Cairo in July could not be cordoned off. Here was the feel of Cairo as lived by the "urban majority" (Simone and Rao 2012) struggling each day to get to work in ancient public buses or furiously beeping microbuses to jobs that barely paid enough for the commute and food for the kids.

The bank that Mr. Amir worked for had garnered millions of dollars in capital from foreign donors for loans to Egypt's working poor, unemployed, and youth. Mr. Amir lent some of those funds to established tradesmen who had grown up learning their trade, and to unemployed college graduates who used the loans to open microenterprises. It was still possible in the 1990s for these young men (*shabab*) to believe in the exemplary life of the "microentrepreneur" who would make his life without any handouts from the state. These were high years of neoliberalism. Empowerment debt and the market would solve their problems (Elyachar 2002, 2005). When things went wrong, they blamed "the bank" rather than the Mubarak regime. This would change by 2010, in the years of the mass revolts that forced President Mubarak to step down from power.

Mr. Amir had a degree in commerce (*tigara*) from Cairo University. He spoke excellent modern standard Arabic, easing into Egyptian Arabic only after a few minutes. He did not sprinkle English phrases into his Arabic like other bankers who worked with USAID did in an interview situation— even when he was talking about banks or business. Rather, he switched to a more "popular" (*sha'bi*) level of Cairene Arabic instead. His language for talking about lending and markets and commerce came from Cairo and its streets and educational institutions, not from English-language economics classes at the American University of Cairo or from Switzerland or the UK.

Mr. Amir conducted his financial business in the flow of conversation, which was punctuated, in turn, by a flow of cigarettes, phone calls, and streams of people coming and going, offering coffee and water, and asking for help. He worked three landlines on his sprawling desk without losing concentration or looking harassed. Doors opened and closed; telephones rang and were answered; requests were considered and addressed; cigarettes were passed across the room and lit. Here, too, commerce was communication. Through these communicative channels, finance flowed—a kind of finance that was neither abstract nor flattening (Simmel 2011). Although Mr. Amir's way of gathering, filtering, and processing information could appear chaotic, he had little problem assessing risk or calculating value. His lending unit was profitable and had an excellent track record. His strongest lending technique and mode of risk assessment, he said, was his sense (*hiss*) of the market, which he had honed over the years.

Mr. Amir was from a central *sha'bi* neighborhood of Cairo and grew up before the Free Officers Movement took power in 1952. Educated both on the streets of a popular neighborhood of Cairo and at Cairo University, Mr. Amir admired the "technocrats," as students of faculties of commerce are often called in the literature (Vitalis 1995), who constructed the Egyptian public sector. His education in a department of commerce (*tigara*), rather than a department of economics, was typical of his generation. After graduating in 1965, he went straight to work for the Industrial Bank of Egypt. His training came on the job, like the craftsmen and small business owners he specialized in funding.

Mr. Amir was an employee of the state (*dawla*) and a defender of the wealth of the Egyptian people, held in the state public sector. The government (*hukuma*), by way of contrast, often stole and privatized that wealth for the benefit of a few. This difference, between the government in power and the legitimate institution of the state as public authority, mattered. Mr. Amir's job was to lend out this part of the state's wealth and to make sure it would be returned. Anyone—including government officials—who tried to steal the state's wealth was immoral. To guard against that eventuality, Mr. Amir had to know the market, as only someone with long experience in the constantly changing rules of the game could. That knowledge was intertwined with his body and his sense of self.

Mr. Amir was, on one level, just really good at his job. He showed the real value of a great middle manager (Jaser 2021). He translated policy effectively, understood those for whom that policy was shaped, and knew how to put that policy to work in the context of public-sector finance. He also had a "sense" of the market, which was hard to explain to outsiders. It was nothing he could have learned from books. It was tacit knowledge— knowledge that came through the senses and experience rather than from book learning (Polanyi 1966).

Mr. Amir's tacit knowledge was a collective affair. It belonged to those who spoke Egyptian Arabic and had access to its semiotic resources. It was a resource of master practitioners of market life. Tacit knowledge was a collective inheritance, embodied in collective subjects. It remained so even if not recognized as a property right. A successful public-sector banker had to be a son of the people, *ibn al-balad*, the exemplary figure of Egyptian *sha'bi* culture. He had to know how to maneuver in any kind of situation, how to talk the language of the educated with the educated, the language of the streets on the street, and the language of the elite with the state. He had to be a master of *fahlawa* (cleverness) (El-Messiri 1978, 49).

A master of *fahlawa* knows with whom he is dealing and how to act in any situation, in the market and in politics. From this point of view, *fahlawa* can be used to advantage in the marketplace or in politics by a weaker group against a stronger group, or to access information that is not available to all. At the same time, *fahlawa* is an embodied collective competence—no one can learn it alone or from books. Its mastery was essential to the success of a charismatic leader such as Gamal Abdel Nasser maneuvering among powerful and arrogant ex-colonial powers, or the success of a public-sector bank operating in a vast sea of commerce. Street smarts of *fahlawa* were needed in the shifting tides of geopolitics and commerce alike.

In Middle Eastern studies, *fahlawa* is usually discussed in the context of "popular Egyptian culture" of the poor urban masses of Cairo. *Fahlawa* "implies such qualities as sharpness, cleverness and alertness" and "a kind of intelligence that springs from experience rather than formal education." It comes "from continuous interaction with all sorts of people, [through which] a person becomes knowledgeable about human behavior" (El-Messiri 1978,

50). *Fahlawa* is a characteristic of the *ibn al-balad*, the young male heroic figure of the popular classes who defends the weak and community property and who watches out for his own (Elyachar 2005, 137–38; El-Messiri 1978, 41). It is a language of the popular *baladi* classes, spoken by leaders with a capacity to activate communicative channels with the masses in a way we call charisma.

President Gamal Abdel Nasser was such a leader. His mastery of communication with the Egyptian and Arab popular masses can be observed on video footage and in radio recordings of his speeches. Accounts of one of Nasser's speeches in July 1956, when he announced nationalization of the Suez Canal, convey that mastery well. In that speech, Nasser switched from his (until then) typical use of modern standard Arabic into popular, *baladi* Arabic.[2] His mastery of communication with the masses did not go unnoticed in the West. According to accounts by the French journalists and (later) biographers of Abdul Nasser, President Nasser adopted the "mocking tone of Egypt's satirical songwriters and the language of the poor" (Lacouture and Lacouture 2002) to take on the arrogant and ignorant United States and its arrogant World Bank president Eugene Black.

Black had been in Egypt to explain why the United States was withdrawing its support for the Egyptian construction of the Aswan Dam. He cited "objective economic and financial reasons" for the decision and traveled back to the United States, certain that President Nasser had understood and accepted his reasoning. But Black had missed everything essential in the conversation (Tignor 2022, 7–8). He had no sense for what his words and logic had conveyed. Nasser and the Egyptian people heard his language differently. The wounds of interlinked powers of finance, infrastructure, and sovereignty went far too deep for Black's language to sound neutral or objective.

Switching to Egyptian popular Arabic, Nasser said that Black reminded him of Ferdinand de Lesseps, the Frenchman who finalized and carried out the Suez Canal plan with Khedive Ismail Pasha of Egypt. De Lesseps had "tricked" Egyptians into accepting terms for construction of the Suez Canal that enriched the French and the British and that left the Egyptians with nothing but humiliation. This take on the Suez Canal's history resonated with the Egyptian masses. Commerce stopped and shopkeepers shut their doors. In fact, everything stopped on the Arab streets whenever Nasser spoke.

Nothing much stopped on the streets for President Hosni Mubarak, however. In turn, *fahlawa* became "clever maneuvering" by negotiators with international lending institutions, according to one economist writing on the period of the 1990s. Links to the popular street and its commerce faded away. *Fahlawa* became a kind of weapon of the weak against international financial institutions. The Mubarak regime would give verbal compliance to orders from the United States and the International Monetary Fund to privatize the economy, even while keeping up practical resistance (Abdel-Malek 2002).

Mr. Amir was, indeed, a master of commerce and *fahlawa*. He could enter different worlds, communicate with everyone, and successfully predict how people would act. He deployed finance to weave together people and projects in places distant and near, mobilizing instruments of credit and debt and promises to pay that would come to terms at different times in the future. He maneuvered through a shifting world of debts and credits with his well-honed arts of improvisation. Finance as *fahlawa* could not be taught through training sessions run by international bodies or development agencies like USAID. Instead, locally embodied knowledge of commerce was needed, even after the nationalization of banks and the financial sector in the decade after the Free Officers coup and the creation of a state-owned public sector that many associate with the beginning of the postcolonial era in Egypt. Mastery of commerce and finance was embodied, both in and out of the public sector.

Planning an Economy and Finding Finance

The state-owned public sector was constructed by a group of men who are often called "technocrats" in the literature.[3] The word *technocrat* is something of a negative concept that comes from literature from the Cold War that drew stark contrasts between socialists and free marketeers. Technocrats in Egypt were neither. They were not driven by socialist ideology. Nor were they anti-socialists. Rather, they worked to improve the resource base of a (sometimes quite tenuous) national economy.[4]

These men grew up in a world of commerce. Like Mr. Amir, their university degrees were often in commerce. The term *commerce* as a field of learning and competence is still relevant in Egypt. While the American University in Cairo might deploy the English word *business* in Arabic to describe what their students study, students at Cairo University study *commerce*.[5] In fact, the Faculty of Commerce traces its history back to 1837, when Mehmed Ali, the Albanian Ottoman governor of Egypt created de facto autonomy for Egypt in part through the arts of *tigara*, including with the establishment of a school of accounting (Cairo University's School of Commerce).[6] A high school for commerce was established in Cairo in 1911, shut down for a time, and then reopened, merged with Cairo University in 1935.

Some of these technocrats studied commerce elsewhere or taught in the Faculty of Commerce in Cairo University. While the Egyptian elite of the 1920s to 1940s had typically studied law, officials and the new elite taking shape after 1952 were more likely to study commerce or engineering (Reid 1990).[7] Abd al-Galil al-Imari, for example, had a degree in commerce from Leeds University. He served in Egyptian administrations before the 1952 coup and was pretty much "left alone" to devise economic policy in the first years after (Tignor 1998, 68). Rashid al-Barrawi had been a professor in the School of Commerce at Cairo University, had socialist credentials, but favored liberalizing laws that restricted the growth of Egypt's potential oil and mining industries.[8] Aziz Sidqi, Egypt's first minister of industry and the chief architect of the public sector, had a first degree in commerce, went to the United States in 1946 to receive two MAs (one in architecture and the other in planning), and then a PhD in regional economic planning from Harvard University in 1951, with the thesis "Industrialization of Egypt: The Case Study of Iron and Steel" (Tignor 1998, 68–69).

Professors in Egyptian universities' departments of economics in the 1940s and 1950s were usually trained in Great Britain or the United States. Others got their economics degrees in France.[9] Through the mid-1970s, classical and Keynesian economics, economic development, economic planning, and public finance were the key subjects they taught their students back in Egypt. The theories they taught had no stance regarding the relative advantages of "free market" versus "socialist" economies.

Like these technocrats, the Free Officers in charge of the Egyptian government after the 1952 coup did not set out to create a socialist economy. Here, the encounter between Eugene Black for the World Bank and President Nasser takes on particular historical meaning. The US retreat on promises for a loan to build the Aswan Dam led to the Suez Canal's nationalization, which, in turn, played a decisive role in the decision of Great Britain and France to join Israel in the "tripartite aggression" against Egypt in 1957. Economic visions for the future changed as well. Technocrats trying to build a strong national economy in Egypt were pushed into the socialist camp.

Such a move had strong grounds for popular approval. Hopes of building Egypt's economy on Western models of the liberal free market had been rebuffed. The Aswan Dam loan refusal had touched on a well of anger about the ways in which Egypt had fallen subject to the actions and machinations of commercial and financial actors with the legal status of "foreign." By the 1960s, Egypt's decisions were made in the context of a global nonaligned movement of postcolonial states who received material aid from the Soviet Union more reliably than from the United States. Late nineteenth-century language of "colonial domination" had been solidified with the British occupation of Egypt in 1882. Anticolonial politics intersected with a global anti-imperialist language that focused on the oppressive role played by foreign finance capital.

The Ottoman capitulations had granted both foreigners residing in the empire and an increasing number of locals extraterritorial exemption from the local rule of law and burdens of taxation. The act of making a "public sector" by nationalizing banks and industrial enterprises, by contrast, created a "national economy," a bounded territory over which the state could exert effective fiscal and monetary policy and something closer to unitary sovereignty. Nationalizing the banks was key to this effort to redirect finance toward a national economy. This built on earlier attempts by local Egyptian industrialists and bankers to build up the core of a "national economy" from the interwar period (Vitalis 1995). In terms of this book, all this moved to upend lingering infrastructures of the semicivilized.

Economic development took on a radical transformative potential. Development offered a language and set of practices to act on "an economy" and to make it "grow." Development also provided a new language for the familiar (if unreachable) goal of finally proving civilizational status (Davis 2022). Nationalizing the banking industry provided a start. It seemed to be a pathway to reorient financial infrastructure away from its legacy role as an accelerator of commerce between the Ottoman Empire and Western Europe, ultimately to the benefit of Western Europe. In other words, Egypt's public-sector technocrats were motivated by a radical commitment to development of a national economy (Tignor 1998) rather than an ideological commitment to socialism.

Before the 1952 coup, there had been little direct governmental involvement in economic activity. The state had owned some shares in the banking sector, such as the Crédit Agricole et Foncier d'Egypte and the Industrial Bank (Wahba 1983, 28). The state owned the main railway lines and telephone and telegraph networks, and it had ownership rights in some of the irrigation canal projects (El Etreby 1968, 16–21, as cited in Wahba 1983, 28). That situation had changed drastically by 1957, when the Free Officers passed Ordinance Number 22, which "stipulated that all banks operating in Egypt were to have only Egyptian shareholders and Egyptian directors" (Tignor 1998, 136).

The Free Officers regime asserted control over finance and banking as well as industry. This move followed similar logics expressed in theories of social advancement through industrial mobilization and financial innovation formulated by the disciples of Henri de Saint-Simon in France from the 1830s through the 1860s. By nationalizing large industry and banks, Nasser aimed to stop the relentless draining of wealth from Egypt to Europe under lingering terms of those commercial treaties, called the capitulations. In 1956, Nasser had nationalized the Suez Canal, which had been built in the 1860s with French financing and engineering and with the labor and sweat of tens of thousands of Egyptians. Banks such as Barclays Bank, the Ottoman Bank, Crédit Lyonnais, and Comptoir Nationale d'Escompte de Paris were made Egyptian by the stroke of a pen. Some of these banks had been present in Egypt for more than one hundred years. Also in 1957, the Free Officers laid the legal groundwork for the public sector and created the Egyptian Economic Organization (al-Mu'assasa al-Iqtisadiya), the legal entity and primary instrument for the public sector's expansion in the years to come (Tignor 1998, 136–37).

Nationalization proper began in July 1961, with the issuance of laws 117, 118, and 119. In December 1961, the Supreme Council for Public Organizations was established to supervise 38 public organizations, themselves comprising 367 companies. By 1964, nationalized firms were controlled by 50 general organizations (Wahba 1983, 28). By 1967, 48 organizations oversaw 382 affiliated companies "in operations ranging from arms production to theatres" (McDermott 1988, 122). By the 1970s, twenty-five Higher Sectoral Councils oversaw the running of public enterprises, with crosscutting involvement of ministers, chairmen of boards, and extensive staffs, the "Technical Secretariat" (Wahba 1983, 30).

These laws (117, 118, and 119) "left the power of the state virtually unchallenged in the corporate sector"; the Nasser regime proclaimed that it would achieve "popular control of economic institutions" via public-sector control (Tignor 1998, 163). Industrial productivity would be drastically increased, even as a more just society was created (Tignor 1998, 163, citing *Al-Ahram Weekly*, July 11, 1961). The public sector turned out to be a vast and sprawling sphere in which decentralization and autonomy, rather than total state control, prevailed (Tignor 1998, 185). As such, the public sector fulfilled neither the hopes of Nasser and his colleagues nor the nightmares of the founders of neoliberalism like Friedrich Hayek and Ludwig von Mises. Rather, state power was "virtually unchallenged in the corporate sector." The Nasser regime proclaimed that it would achieve "popular control of economic institutions" by way of public-sector control (163).

The pervasive antimonopoly stance of the Free Officers (Vitalis 1995, 215–17) was matched by the imperative of development. If capitalists would not invest to grow the national economy, then the state would expropriate their resources and do it for them. And yet, despite this formal power and a powerful aspiration for a national economy constructed through the making of a public sector, at the end of the day, the state would, in fact, exercise little day-to-day control over the sprawling public sector it had created.

At the beginning of the twentieth-century, antisocialist neoliberals like von Mises had argued that any move toward state control of economy would undermine the possibility of rational economy, and rationality itself (von Mises 1920, 121). In his later work, Hayek even claimed that a public-sector economy would lead to "serfdom" and totalitarianism (Hayek 1944). The Egyptian case proves otherwise. Egypt ended up with a loosely regulated public sector, where decentralization and a great deal of freedom of operation reigned (Tignor 1998). The state had absorbed the capacious street smarts of commerce into its bounds. Companies operating in the private sector were subject to more scrutiny and more effective controls. The "free market" private sector—not the public sector—was marked by intense scrutiny and control by state actors (Tignor 1998).

Some bankers left Egypt when the banks were nationalized. Mr. Amir talked about this as a great loss to the national wealth of Egypt. All of those "trained by Barclays" left the country and started to work in the United States, the United Kingdom, or the Gulf States. Barclays was the archetype of a high-class and professional bank with a long presence in Egypt. Those trained by Barclays had an intuitive sense of finance. They were not just stuck into a bank by public-sector bureaucrats who might have sent them anywhere. Whether trained by Barclay's or not, good middle managers in the public sector or private sector carried out their responsibilities as fiduciaries of the national wealth.

By the 1970s, changing global constellations of power impacted debates about the public sector in Egypt. The West was clearly winning the Cold War, the socialist world had entered stagnation and began to succumb to economic pressures from the West, socialist ideology was being undermined, and the neoliberals had crawled out of the basement and asserted ideological hegemony. The balance of political power on the world stage and the global ideological climate had changed. All this played out in Egypt as well, where multiple problems with public-sector enterprises led to efforts at reform and then privatization from the 1970s onward.

Increasingly, managers of enterprises in the public sector saw state ownership as a liability and even a form of "oppression" (Handoussa 1979, 2). One solution in the late 1970s and early 1980s (Wahba 1983, 36–37) was to undertake joint ventures with the private sector. Public-sector firms became at least as important for their "welfare effect" as for their economic viability. They kept workers employed and with benefits, even if at relatively lower rates.

Public-sector privatization began in 1976 with Anwar Sadat's policy of the *infitah*, or economic opening. The push for an open society replaced the struggle for a just society. But privatization was not accepted without resistance; it was vigorously fought and contested in the decades that followed. Privatization in Egypt was a far more drawn-out process than, for example, in the Central and Eastern European countries more commonly studied in the anthropology of postsocialism, where there was a rush into the ecstasies of privatization. In Egypt, it was contested, fought, and staved off by strikes and protests on the part of workers and by delaying tactics on the part of the Mubarak administration when privatization did not suit their interests. Given the importance of finance in the story of the semicivilized, it might not be surprising to hear that Mubarak held onto the banks the longest. As late as 1998, four state-owned banks still accounted for 80 percent of all commercial deposits in the country (Handy 1998, 56).

Banks had been proclaimed a public utility under Nasser, yet even under Nasser, the meaning of "the public" in public utility was unclear. Under Mubarak, banks were clearly an infrastructure for channeling finance to political allies. The shape of privatization changed when Gamal Mubarak, Husni's son who was being groomed as his father's successor, returned from his career as an investment banker in England to take his appointed place in Egypt. From that point on, the pace of the privatization of financial assets sped up, and a close group of friends of the Mubaraks began to quickly acquire new state assets at prices far below market rates.

Gamal Mubarak was first educated at the American University in Cairo, and then went for further study and work in London. Upon his return to Egypt, he appointed advisers who were locally called "neoliberals." They, too, had been educated in neoliberal economics departments in the United Kingdom, the United States, and at the American University in Cairo. Egypt drastically sped up privatization, revamped its stock market (the world's oldest stock market is in Alexandria), and targeted telecommunications, mobile phones, and internet as key areas of investment and reform for the Egyptian economy.

This brand of neoliberalism caused immense offense to Egyptians struggling to survive on pitiful wages whose value was wasting away, who were subject to arbitrary arrest and torture, and for whom the chances for generational reproduction had become an ever-more distant dream. It was also offensive to high members of the military who had fought wars to defend Egypt's national interests and national wealth and who had their own economic interests to watch out for. Even so, international development and lending agencies like the International Monetary Fund (IMF) and the World Bank kept pushing Egypt to privatize more and faster—especially the banks. At the same time, they funded and established a parallel training program called "education" that was linked to the provision of debt. Many of Mr. Amir's peers attended such training sessions. I attended a number of these training sessions myself during my dissertation fieldwork.

Many such training programs were funded by development agencies in Egypt in the 1990s. Development agencies and multilateral lenders required that employees attend these programs before they would provide infusions of foreign exchange–denominated bank capital (FOREX) in banks or in the Bank of Egypt. Compliance with program attendance may have bolstered capital balance sheets, but it did not result in privatization of a financial sector that remained largely in state hands.

Structural indebtedness is part of the semicivilized condition. It cannot be solved with training programs or with specific policy shifts. The issues go back much further. Inextricable debt and concessions were central to the building of the Egyptian state, in the pattern of reforms, debt, and concessions followed by the Ottomans and Mehmed Ali alike, and characteristic of the Middle East and North Africa as a whole—what James Gelvin has called "defensive developmentalism" (Gelvin 2015). When we hold too strongly to the assumption that finance moves from the West to the East in a unidirectional imperialist channel, we miss a great deal—including the many faces of finance.

Thick Finance

Khedive Ismail did not bring finance to Egypt when he took on so much debt to fund the Suez Canal and the Khedivial Opera House. Finance was already there. Finance was already directly linked to the internal politics of the Ottoman Empire, and money and debt had always been political

(Kafadar 1986). When the Ottoman Empire is called an "Empire of Debt" (Yaycıoğlu 2022), this does not mean that the empire was indebted to the West, although the structure of finance would flip that way in the second half of the nineteenth century. Rather, it means that political, kin, communal, and commercial relationships were interwoven through a medium of debt (and credit). This is no Egyptian anomaly, nor is it an indicator of corruption and economic failure. In many parts of the world, relations of credit and debt were the medium through which ongoing ties of interdependence across space and time were articulated (Elyachar 2023; Bishara 2017).

Sophisticated global debt markets and regularized channels of finance existed in the East long before nineteenth-century capitalism in the West. As far back as the sixteenth century, the Ottoman Empire had an extensive and sophisticated financial system. Ottoman financiers made short-term loans not only to private businesses but also to the state. Members of the Greek Orthodox and Jewish communities were prominent in this realm. Kings of Poland and France turned to these Ottoman bankers for loans, which were issued as bonds in which many prominent Ottomans invested (Pamuk 2000, 80). Imperial politics in the Ottoman Empire were commonly articulated in the language of finance (Kafadar 1995).

Around the empire, merchants and money changers articulated complex commercial deals, moving channels of commerce across their domains. Along the Mediterranean Ottoman coast, commerce was conducted and accounts were balanced with letters of credit coming from French, Italian, and English commercial merchants (Clay 2000, 118). A credit nexus facing inward was part of this financial infrastructure, mediating relations of power in the most direct of ways. Finance was the "lifeblood of bureaucracy," of the state managed by the grand vizier. Finance was also the engine of growth in state capacity (86). Finance mediated power struggles between the Porte, the seat of the imperial bureaucracy, and the palace and its own distinct sources of wealth (Eldem 1999).

In the Ottoman Empire, and across the Indian Ocean, finance was relational (Elyachar 2023). Fully financialized relationships of exchange and trade over long distances were mediated with instruments of credit and debt. To go into debt was to enter into a relationship (Bishara 2017). Finance was a channel for interactions across space and time. In twentieth-century economic anthropology, this kind of monetized debt was contrasted with a fictive "gift economy," one that functioned without markets, without finance. Finance was often understood to characterize a "higher stage" of capitalism and market life. Such an understanding of finance could stand only through the studied ignorance of empires of debt and finance in the Indian Ocean and today's Middle East.

The Ottoman-centered financial order is at least as "global" or "universal" as any story of finance coming from accounts of capitalist Western Europe. The Ottoman case sounds much like the views of economists like Perry Mehrling and his "money view" account of how financial markets work: "Financial relationships are not about mediating something else on the 'real' side of the economy; they are the constitutive relationships of the whole system" (Mehrling 2017, n.p.). Finance was constitutive of politics as well, as we saw with the Saint-Simonians who influenced Mehmet Ali in the 1830s and who contributed to the early phases of planning the Suez Canal (Elshakry 2007).

In 1848, revolutions broke out across Europe. Revolutions failed and were suppressed.[10] In France, the 1789 revolution had been the first time the working class and peasants had entered the political stage: it was brutally suppressed by the liberal bourgeoisie. Bonapartism used revolutionary language and imagery to successfully sideline the liberal bourgeoisie on the political stage, carry out a coup d'état, and install a counterrevolution and a dictatorship. Financial innovations were at the core of Bonapartist industrialization. Their centerpiece was the banking firm Crédit Mobilier, founded by Émile Péreire, an ex-follower of Saint-Simon. Marx analyzed the firm in a series of articles in the mid-1850s, about five years into the Second Empire.

In the view of Saint-Simon, banks could be the "nervous system" of a rationally organized social body. Finance would be the brain and the nerves of industrial society. Saint-Simon and his disciples saw credit as a means of mobilizing and channeling funds—that were otherwise pooling up in unproductive ways—into productive spheres. Crédit Mobilier would tap the unused savings of the middle and working classes, consolidate those little pools, and put that money to productive use. Banks, by gathering up small sums of money from individuals, could put that money to work by funding massive infrastructure projects that would advance the economic activity and the health of the nation. Such techniques were mobilized in Egypt with the building of the Suez Canal and the transformation of finance into unpayable debt. This became a mark of the semicivilized condition.

We can learn a great deal about finance in general by paying attention to such arrangements of finance. Finance is not always an agent of destruction of social ties. Intertwining politics, kinship, and community with finance is not in itself a mode of corruption. We saw this with the case of Mr. Amir. Relational finance merely violates an ideal type of finance that grew from study of one empirical model in Western Europe. Borrowing the phrase "thick description" from Clifford Geertz, we can think instead of "thick finance," which is always embedded in society and is the very substance of social relations, "a web of time-dated promises to pay that stretches from now into the future, and from here around the globe" (Mehrling 2017, 1). Thick finance moving from lands of the semicivilized was no less global than financial arrangements emanating from London. But as with so many aspects of the semicivilized condition, relational finance disappeared from view.

The Waiting Room of History

The Ottoman Empire lay in an anomalous relation to the rising capitalist powers of the West in other ways as well. What was the Ottoman Empire in relation to Europe? The question returned once again in the mid-nineteenth century. Was it Europe's eternal enemy as the "infidel Turk" had been for the Crusaders? Or given the fact that the Ottoman Empire was geographically part of Europe, had incorporated the legacy of Roman law, and had signed multiple treaties with sovereigns of the civilized West, was the Ottoman Empire actually European? Scholars of international relations in the nineteenth century would attempt to bridge these seemingly disparate views: the Ottoman Empire was both European and non-European; it was part of the European system of states but not part of European society (Kayaoğlu 2010; Özsu 2016a).

Thomas Naff (1977, 107) put the logic concisely: "Even though a significant portion of the Empire was based *in* Europe, it cannot be said to have been *of* Europe." The Ottoman Empire had been a member of international order much earlier than Japan or China, given the long-standing nature of the capitulations as treaties in private international law (Kayaoğlu 2010, 108). But the Ottomans were not part of international society "because they shared only a few of Europe's interests, principles, and norms" (109). The Treaty of Paris of 1856 officially included the Ottoman Empire in the Concert of Europe and European International Public Law, specifically in Article 7 (Kayaoğlu 2010, 109–10). But the tension continued.

This debate was transformed into a question of "civilization" by James Lorimer in his classic work, *The Institutes of the Law of Nations: A Treatise of the Jural Relations of Separate Political Communities* (1883), in which he shifted the concept of civilization and civilizational difference by designating the Ottoman Empire "semicivilized." Lorimer (1883) divided the world into three spheres—"civilized humanity," "barbarous humanity," and "savage humanity"—with three corresponding "stages of recognition" toward becoming a member of the "family of nations." This was a new spin on the eighteenth-century stadial theories in which the barbarian could progress if only he would accept the gifts of commerce and a settled life. Lorimer's division of the world into three types of humanity offered the possibility of civilizational progress, however deferred. "Savage humanity" comprised the "non-progressive races" that might remain forever outside of the "family of nations" (101–2). But the "semicivilized" had the potential to progress. Once again, the link of the semicivilized to foundational theories of the barbarian in Western political thought is striking.

Putting this anthropology of gradated development that underlay most understandings of "universal history" into practice, the Mandate system—put into place at the end of World War I to manage areas of the dissolved Ottoman Empire deemed not ready for independence—consolidated the fate of the semicivilized (figure 2.1). At the foundation of the Mandates' ideology was the semicivilized's supposed ability to progress to civilization, thus becoming worthy of full independence, both political and territorial. At the end of World War I, the southern Slavic nations that had belonged to the former Austro-Hungarian Empire formed the State of Slovenes, Croats, and Serbs. That state, in turn, joined with the Kingdom of Serbia to become the Kingdom of Serbs, Croats, and Slovenes in 1918. Recognition of that state may be seen as part of the wave of the rushed recognition of successor states to the Austro-Hungarian Empire, which was meant to prevent the spread of Bolshevism farther west into Europe (Elyachar 2021). The legal basis for the formation of such states was the "right to self-determination," which was pushed mostly by the American delegation at the Paris Peace Conference and by President Woodrow Wilson.

Under the Treaty of Rapallo of 1920 between the Kingdom of Italy and the Kingdom of Serbs, Croats, and Slovenes, the Slovenes and Croats living between the Julian Alps and much of the Adriatic coast came under Italian rule rather than being granted independence. The Balkans remained fixed in the Western imagination as the realm of the semicivilized (cf. Jezernik 2004; Todorova 1997). The semicivilized status of the Balkans was certainly a legacy of the Ottoman Empire that had ruled over those lands. But more than the continuity of Western relations with and attitudes toward the Ottomans was involved. The Balkans' semicivilized fate consolidated the epistemological and political challenges posed by the Ottoman Empire to an international order formed with Western Europe at its center (Jezernik

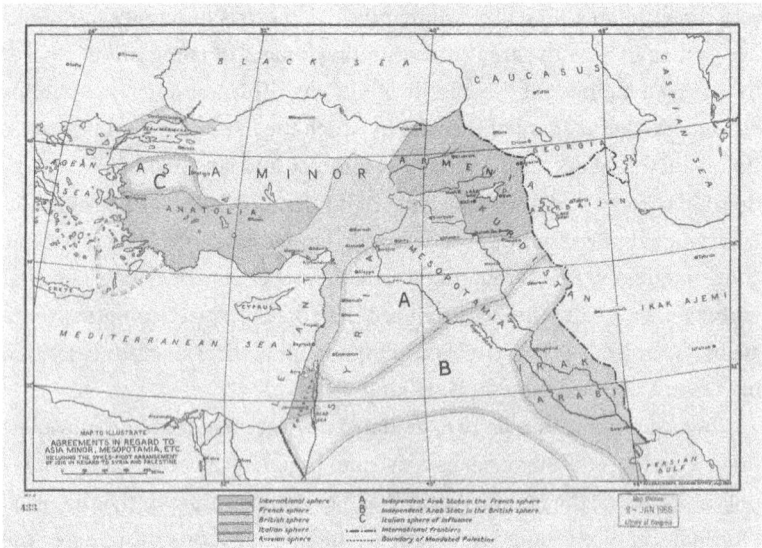

2.1   Map to Illustrate Agreements in Regard to Asia Minor, Mesopotamia, etc.: Including the Sykes-Picot Arrangement of 1916 in Regard to Syria and Palestine. London: Foreign Office, 1964. This map shows the French, British, Italian, and Russian "spheres of influence" in the former Ottoman Empire as well as Mandatory Palestine. Library of Congress, Geography and Map Division, 2014587996.

2004). The Ottoman Empire was dealt a very different fate at the conference in Lausanne than was its ally, the Austro-Hungarian Empire.

The Arab territories of the former Ottoman Empire were governed under British and French Mandates tasked with the endless work of rendering the semicivilized *ready* to be bestowed sovereign status.[11] Egypt would not escape this fate, as was made clear to Egyptians who aspired to "full independence" and territorial sovereignty according to the Wilsonian promises of self-determination at the Paris Peace Conference and the League of Nations. During World War I, Egypt's continued ambiguous status as simultaneously Ottoman and a British protectorate almost dragged the Ottomans into the war months before its entry in October 1914 (Genell 2019). During the war, Egypt became a laboratory for "British thinking about the location of formal sovereignty in relationship to imperial control" and, thus, a "model for thinking about British imperial control in the Middle East after the war" (Genell 2019, 78). It became a learning lab for thinking through how to organize the Mandates that would administer the semi-civilized without claiming colonial rule or bestowing upon them the rights to territorial sovereignty.

Two days after the armistice, a group of Egyptians met with British General Wingate, the high commissioner of Egypt, to request permission to send an Egyptian delegation, led by Sa'd Zaghloul, to Paris and the negotiations at Versailles. This delegation, or *wafd* (in Arabic), told Wingate that they would present Egypt's aspiration for full independence at Versailles. The British government refused to consider Zaghloul's "programme of complete autonomy." London was focused on keeping Egyptian questions out of the Paris Peace Conference, particularly any discussion of Egypt's legal status. London insisted that Egypt was "an imperial and not an international question" (Genell 2019, 88).

Zaghloul and the *wafd*, however, emphasized Egypt's status as an "autonomous province," as guaranteed in international law by treaty. Ottoman sovereignty, Zaghloul and the *wafd* maintained, could be transferred to the Egyptians. They "refuted Great Britain's title to Egypt by recapitulating the history of the 'Egyptian question' in international relations from Mehmet Ali through the protectorate" (Genell 2019, 88). Zaghloul's memo to Georges Clemenceau on "Egyptian National Claims" lays out the argument for sovereignty and a road out of the never-ending trap of the semicivilized. Egypt, Zaghloul argued, had never really been part of the Ottoman Empire. Egypt's relation to the Ottoman Empire had involved only the "payment of an annual tribute, some limitation on the military establishment, and the observation of any treaties signed by the Sublime Porte" (89). Here Zaghloul presented Egypt in terms of the territorial nation-state that it aspired to be, erasing traces of the multilayered nature of sovereignty and its belonging to the empire through exactly such mechanisms. Indeed, he argued, Egypt's autonomy had been recognized in international law: the Convention of London in 1840 had constituted a "Charter of Egypt" in which the rights of Egypt were recognized both by Turkey and by the Great Powers.

A delegation from the Hijaz had been admitted to the Paris conference. Why would Egypt not be admitted? Egypt was "richer, more civilized" than provinces whose delegations were being received—delegations from Hijaz, Armenia, Syria, and Lebanon. It had clear "civilizational superiority" over Hijaz and other Ottoman provinces that were being allowed into the negotiations, and with whom possible sovereign status was being discussed (if later denied). When General Edmund Allenby replaced Wingate as high commissioner of Egypt, the *wafd* sent him a letter as well, making the case that "Egypt had a stronger claim to independence than any other part of the Ottoman Empire on the basis of its internationally guaranteed legal status, its civilization, and the fact that Egypt had supported Britain during the war."

These arguments did not gain the *wafd* entry to the Paris Peace Conference in 1919. The British government refused to accept the delegation and arrested Zaghloul, which led to the Egyptian Revolution of 1919, Britain's recognition of Egyptian independence in 1922, and the new constitution in 1923. Egypt's declaration of independence in 1922 put a formal end to the British protectorate but left in British control four key matters that rendered moot the notion of territorial sovereignty. The British government retained de facto rule over the Sudan, under the preexisting Anglo-Egyptian Condominium Agreement; control of Egypt's external defense; and sovereignty over all those who had been rendered extraterritorial in the capitulations: British citizens, "foreign interests," and "minorities." Britain also claimed for itself the right to guarantee the "security of the communications of the British Empire in Egypt" (Genell 2019, 92).[12]

Even with these limitations on its independence and sovereignty, Egypt fared better than other Arab regions of the former Ottoman Empire. At the San Remo Conference of April 1920, wartime allies France and Britain divided between themselves the Mandates for Syria, Mesopotamia, and Palestine. Greater Lebanon was created in September 1920, carved out of greater Syria by the French as part of its Mandate. In December 1922, the League of Nations issued the terms of Britain's Mandate for Palestine, which made the Mandatory power "responsible for putting into effect" the Balfour Declaration, with its commitment to "the establishment in Palestine of a national home for the Jewish people" (Arsan 2021). The creation of the Mandates was explicitly justified using the logic of the semicivilized.[13] The semicivilized would remain without sovereignty over their land, and without a functional financial infrastructure to undergird an effective national economy. A century later, the straitjacket of the semicivilized remains. It can be seen in the familiar trifecta of revolt, counterrevolution, and conquest of urban space we have already seen in Cairo, in part through the long-standing mechanism of finance.

The Long Year of Finance and Contraction

In August 2022, downtown hotels and apartments in the former elite neighborhoods of Cairo filled up with visitors from the Gulf States escaping the much hotter climes of home. Talk of debt and devaluation was everywhere that summer, at least for Egyptians who were facing worsening conditions of life most every day.

I no longer knew many anthropologists or scholars from the United States or Europe who spent time in Cairo. Until the Egyptian Revolution of 2011, Egypt had been seen by westerners as the "one stable country in the Middle East" where students could do research and experts learn their language skills and from which reporters and corporate staff could live and move around the region as needed. That assumption was long gone by 2022. Along with the missing Western visitors and now-absent home offices of corporations, NGOs, development agencies, and schools went the foreign exchange that they had brought to the Egyptian economy. Power of an authoritarian military leader did not extend to control over a currency losing its value on global financial markets.

With the Egyptian pound devalued over and over, no one knew if there would ever be a way out of the economic disaster. Things got only worse in the next two years, when the Egyptian government continued to face regular foreign exchange and balance-of-payments crises. As the United States and the EU pulled back, others moved in to pick up the slack. Qatar, the United Arab Emirates (UAE), and Saudi Arabia provided billions to the Central Bank of Egypt in the decade after the January 25 Revolution so that Egypt would not go back into a massive debt crisis on global markets. Criticisms of economic policy and concerns about the foreign exchange situation were still published in the Arabic- and English-language press. Such discussions read as objective. It was economic logic. That kind of language had been used by Eugene Black, the American director of the World Bank whom President Nasser had torn to shreds in his popular radio talks of the 1950s.

Discussions of budget constraints were more neutral: the framing of "economic crisis" foreclosed directly political aspects of the structural situation. Certainly, as MP Mohamed Badrawy from the House Planning and Budget Committee put it in an interview with a critical Egyptian publication in 2022, the budget draft continued a policy of overreliance on debt (Kassab, al-Naggar, and Mamdouh 2022). The structural debt crisis had been going on for so long that it was no longer clear it made sense to call it a "crisis." A crisis implies a situation that is temporary, a moment off the normal distribution curve. Framing something as a "debt crisis" can foreclose deeper discussions about what is underway (Roitman 2013).

That said, grumbling was on the rise. So was uncertainty. When would the next devaluation come? How would inflation of foodstuffs and all the necessities of daily life cut into family well-being? Would devaluation occur before or after Egypt would sign a memorandum of agreement with the IMF? What would happen to prices? The value of the Egyptian pound, and thus the price of so much of everything, was wrapped up in these abstract debates, given the extent to which Egypt was import-reliant. Massive inflation is a matter most intimate, on which economic theory has often failed or remained silent.

The coronavirus pandemic had shut down tourism and depleted foreign reserves. Then, just as tourism was opening up again, the Ukraine war broke out. The loss of Russian and Ukrainian tourism was another devastating hit to Egypt's foreign exchange reserves. Long-standing ties to the former Soviet Union had created regular flows of tourism, and decline in that tourism from current-day Russia and Ukraine contributed to the worrisome fall in hard currency. One problem folded into another. Local investors in Egypt's bond market fled to the more secure havens of US treasury bills (Kassab, al-Naggar, and Mamdouh 2022).[14]

The global wave of inflation in the wake of the pandemic had made things worse: Egypt's dependence on imports meant that foreign currency reserves were again declining. Imports had to be paid in "hard currency" rather than in Egyptian pounds. All this exacerbated the structural crisis in Egypt's foreign currency holdings. The numbers were shocking to read. In the first two quarters of 2022, Egypt owed $22 billion in debt servicing (that is, in interest payments) alone. Debt servicing was poised to consume 50 percent of the 2022–23 government budget expenditures (Kassab, al-Naggar, and Mamdouh 2022).

No one seemed to know exactly what the right numbers were. How much did Egypt owe to the West, or to the Gulf States? What were gifts and what were fictive loans that would never be repaid? Negotiations over debts were no longer conducted with the Foreign Office of Great Britain, as they might have been in the late nineteenth century. Egyptian debt was not debated in Parliament among great political economists, like in the mid-nineteenth century. That said, international agencies were still evaluating the state's capacity for rational behavior befitting the civilized. Now, Saudi Arabia, the UAE, and Oman were involved in these discussions.

The loans, aid, and conditionality programs continued without end, until they did not. Increasingly by 2022, and under the tutelage of top financial firms from Saudi Arabia, the UAE, and Qatar, the Egyptian state's lands, territory, and wealth were being financialized and subject to professional norms of financial conduct. No longer were they simply siphoned off as "private wealth" to the president and his sons' friends, as had happened under Hosni

Mubarak. Rather, the state's wealth was being quietly sold off on financial markets in ways that did not attract attention. Egypt's debt problems in the 1860s had been linked to the khedive's efforts to perform Egypt's sovereignty as separate from its ties to the Ottoman Empire and in the communicative space in which Bonapartist politics and financial policies were formed. No longer was the aspirational goal to be European. Egypt's finances and debt obligations were moving toward the Gulf. The three circles of Egypt were indeed shifting.

In 2022, the UAE, Saudi Arabia, Kuwait, and Qatar deposited $13 billion (US) of foreign reserves into the Egyptian Central Bank, leaving Egypt with a total of $37 billion foreign currency reserves (Ezz and Medhat 2022). Deposits of foreign currency from the Gulf States had become a way to maintain macroeconomic stability and thus to forestall political upheaval. By November 2022, 85 percent of Egypt's foreign reserves were made up of deposits from just three Gulf states.[15] Of its crucial long-term deposits of $15 billion, about one-third were from the UAE ($5.7 billion), another third from Saudi Arabia ($5.3 billion), and a bit less from Kuwait ($4 billion). Short-term deposits amounted to $13 billion and could disappear quickly.[16] The UAE, with which Egypt was most closely allied, had acquired what some called a "patronage presence" in Egypt (Kassab, al-Naggar, and Mamdouh 2022). Egypt, some said in a bitter voice, had become a "private army" for the rulers of the UAE.

The Gulf Corporation Council (GCC) states were sounding more and more like the IMF. Like "traditional lenders" of the West, they were losing "their appetite for coming to the rescue in the old way of providing aid or introducing reserves," said one government official to Al Jazeera in September 2022. These states wanted one thing alone: "to buy strategic assets" (Kassab, al-Naggar, and Mamdouh 2022). Most important of those strategic assets was—and still is—the Suez Canal, which sometimes seemed to be at risk of moving back out of Egyptian control. Reports came out in the press that Egypt was selling off prime areas of land around the Suez Canal to states in the Gulf. It became a widely debated scandal.

Debts of Infrastructure

Banks, financial assets, infrastructure, and other firms had been swept up into the "public sector" of the Egyptian state under Abdel Nasser in the 1960s. This had put a decisive end to centuries of Western domination over Egypt's political economy. Global flows of finance and local inefficiencies had then forced changes in the property structure of those public-sector assets, which were often changed into joint stock companies, public-private firms, and sometimes, privatized firms.

By the 2020s, key symbols of state sovereignty, like the infamous building of the Interior Ministry, the Mogamma, and entire tracts of land around the Suez Canal, were leveraged, turned into financial assets, and swept into the coffers of The Sovereign Fund of Egypt (TSFE). There, they were further leveraged to provide new sources of funding and profits for Egyptian military companies and their corporate partners in the United States, the United Kingdom, and the Gulf, in the form of public-private partnerships.

In the words of one Egyptian official in July 2022, sixty-six years after Nasser's speech boldly nationalizing the Suez Canal, "Our focus now is to work on attracting Gulf investments" (Kassab, al-Naggar, and Mamdouh 2022). Saudi Arabia and the UAE had tired of saving Egypt from its recurring foreign exchange crises. Qatar had strained relations with Egypt after the coup that overthrew the Muslim Brotherhood–led government of President Morsi. But it appeared back on the scene in 2022 with a proposal that came full circle to the entangled stories of finance, infrastructure, and the semicivilized in Egypt. The Qatar Investment Authority, the state's sovereign wealth fund that oversaw an estimated $445 billion in assets, was on track to acquire 20 percent of Egypt's telecom infrastructure, Vodafone Egypt, from Telecom Egypt (Magdy 2022).

Telecom Egypt, earlier known in English as Egyptian Telecom, had been established in 1854 with the first telegraph line connecting Cairo and Alexandria. The line had been built by British Eastern Telegraph Company (or Eastern Telegraph), which in turn was purchased by the Egyptian government in 1881 under Khedive Tawfiq, creating the Telephone and Telegraph Authority (Rachty 1999).[17] Eastern Telegraph sent the first direct telegraph message from Falmouth, UK, to India via Egypt on June 11, 1870. Its accomplishments were astounding at the time. In the words of the 1894 trade paper *The Electrician*, "the system of submarine telegraphs which is generally known under the name of the 'Eastern' may truthfully be said to be one of the greatest monuments of British enterprise and perseverance that the world has ever seen" (Moss 2022).

Eastern Telegraph grew from efforts to speed up communication across the British Empire, which was more urgently felt in London after the 1857 Sepoy Rebellion in India that had put British rule at risk and had proceeded for weeks before anyone in London knew about it. Whether on land or by sea, cables had to pass through the Ottoman Empire. As such, all matters pertaining to the work of Eastern Telegraph—including its financing, the treacherous work of laying cables, and the hiring and firing of employees—fell under the sway of the Ottoman capitulations. In Egypt, this meant that the work of Eastern Telegraph fell under the purview of the Egyptian Mixed Courts, which adjudicated many questions pertaining to the infrastructure, as the company was exempt from oversight from, or taxation by, the Egyptian government. In a fiction that extraterritoriality continued to render legally true, it all went on as if those telegraph lines and underwater cables were not in Egypt at all.[18]

In 1957, the Eastern Telegraph Company's and the Telephone and Telegraph Authority's remaining assets were transferred to the Egyptian Ministry of Communications and renamed the Egyptian National Telecommunications Organization. In 1980, that organization became an "autonomous public utility" of the kind that proliferated with public-sector reforms; in 1998, it became a joint stock company over which the government retained full ownership (Rachty 1999). By the January 2011 Revolution and subsequent events, telegraph lines and the companies that owned them became a strategic platform of contestation between the state and activists. And in 2022, the strategic communicative infrastructure of Telecom Egypt was sold off to Qatar.

This was not the only economic infrastructure sold off. Gulf investors combined strategic reliance on Egypt's stability with astute professional financial analysis at the highest level of skill and wealth, together with top investment firms in the United States and Europe. For the sovereign wealth funds, the Egyptian pound's low value was an incentive to purchase and gain value through the exchange process. The lower the Egyptian pound fell, the greater investors' net value gain was. Market valuation of the assets was increasingly attractive.

Valuation proceeded through professional financial teams. By 2022, the UAE was purchasing so much Suez land that high levels of the Egyptian government were concerned (Kassab, al-Naggar, and Mamdouh 2022). Egypt turned increasingly to Qatar to balance out some of the power of its patrons. Other companies affiliated with the Suez Canal were also up for acquisition, with Qatar, the UAE, and Saudi Arabia competing for the opportunities.[19] Meanwhile, the UAE had become a major security and military power in the region, ranging from the Red Sea, where it had bases in Berbera and Somaliland, to Bosaso, Somalia, to coastal ports in Yemen. Abu Dhabi Ports had taken over the management of Egypt's Ain Sokhna Port and, in 2022, acquired 70 percent of the Egyptian IACC Holdings' assets, "including majority stakes in two companies operating in the Red Sea: Transmar and Transcargo International" (Kassab, al-Naggar, and Mamdouh 2022).

Pipelines were also being fought over. Given the Ukraine war and attacks on pipelines from Russia to Germany and the bombing of the Nordstream pipeline in 2022, Egyptian pipelines were increasingly attractive to Qatar. Negotiations began to extend pipelines to transport Qatari gas through Saudi Arabia to Egypt (Kassab, al-Naggar, and Mamdouh 2022). Thus continued a long story of infrastructure, finance, sovereignty, and infrastructure channeling through Egypt and its territory.

Sovereignty beyond Territory

By the mid-nineteenth century when the Suez Canal was being built, the semicivilized was already an established category in international law (see Özsu 2016a). As the semicivilized had signed treaties in private international law with countries of the Christian West through the capitulations, the semicivilized were considered were part of the "international order." But they had too many "civilizational differences" to be part of "international society" (Özsu 2016a) or to be considered "civilized." Instead, relations between the "capitalist West" and the Ottoman Empire were mediated through commercial and financial infrastructures and in private international law, through the key concept of extraterritoriality.

In its modern incarnation, *extraterritoriality* refers to exemption from local rule of law for staff and families of diplomatic missions and consuls, or for military personnel on bases in foreign lands. In the Ottoman Empire and other empires where the promotion of commerce predated the establishment of territorial states, extraterritoriality was closely linked to the notion of "the personality of law," dating back to the Roman Empire. In such a system, sojourners moving through the lands of other sovereigns carried with them a *laissez-passer* from the sovereign of their place of birth or abode.

Extraterritorial arrangements consolidated in the Ottoman capitulations began as a courtesy to weaker Western polities. But with the rise of territorial nation-states, the Ottoman Empire came to be at a disadvantage. By the mid-nineteenth century, these extraterritorial arrangements with Western sovereigns, and the porous nature of "boundaries" in the empire, left the semicivilized without sovereignty over *territory* in international law.

We must understand this distinction to understand the nightmare of the semicivilized that we still live with today and see in places like Egypt, Syria, and Palestine. At Versailles, the Egyptians were denied the opportunity to make their case for independence on the international stage, even as their debts were accorded full privileges on international financial markets. Discourse of the semicivilized and barbarian lingered in the denial of claims to peoplehood, sovereignty, and independence. That discourse was racialized by scientific missions sponsored by the United States before and after World War I.

Such scientific commissions from the United States in the period bolstered "scientific" claims to the reality of the "semicivilized" and thus provided the scientific justification for denying Arabs territorial sovereignty in their own lands. These studies included public opinion surveys, archaeological research, and skull measurements to assess racial characteristics and civilizational capacity. Woodrow Wilson requested formation of the King-Crane Commission to the Levant during the Paris Peace Conference in 1919 to "canvass the opinions of its inhabitants." While destined to fail on its own terms, the petitions the commission gathered "constitute a rich archive of this historical moment's indigenous thought" (Arsan 2021). Most people surveyed called for an "independent greater Syrian state" that would never come to pass. Those charged with carrying out the commission had a prior stance on the very "capacity of non-European peoples to become modern—and therefore up to the task of being sovereign over their own affairs" (Arsan 2021).

During World War I, Wilson had authorized the creation of a War Data Investigations Bureau, later just called The Inquiry, which began in the New York Public Library and soon moved to the offices of the American Geographical Society (Khalil 2016). The Inquiry undertook a series of reports on the civilizational capacity of what was called, in a May 1918 report, the *Mohammedan World*. The report was authored by Leon Dominian, a "recent Armenian émigré from Anatolia," and a "staffer at the AGS [American Geographical Society]" albeit with reputed "Greek bias" (Khalil 2016, 18). In another report, Dominian argued that "independence for the majority Arab Muslim areas would be a 'menace to unhampered intercourse between Europe and the regions of Southern Asia and the Far East'" (19).

Another such report was penned for the Inquiry by Princeton archaeologist Howard Crosby Butler, who relied on research he and his team conducted in greater Syria on the physiology of the Arab peoples to conclude that independent sovereign status for Syria was not advisable (Khalil 2016, 20–21). In *Just and Practical Boundaries for Subdivisions of the Turkish Empire*, the Western Asian division of the Inquiry drew on some of these "scientific findings" to lay out racialized boundaries of civilizational difference in the former empire and "to advocate for the postwar establishment of protectorates" (21). In Anatolia, according to classics professor William Westermann's *Just and Practical Boundaries for Subdivisions of the Turkish Empire*, a race of "Turkish" people predominated over other peoples, but in other parts of the "Turkish Empire," no large enough "Nations" existed in "the sense of peoples of one blood, fairly pure from racial intermixture, who are massed in someone given area" (Khalil 2016, 21).

Also joining Butler's mission to Syria was a young anthropologist, Henry Minor Huxley, who had just graduated from Harvard University in 1899, with an undergraduate concentration in anthropology (Browman and Williams 2013).[20] Huxley was brought on to study what was called the physical anthropology of the people of Syria and Palestine, through techniques of anthropometry—the systematic measurement and study of the morphology of humans. Huxley had a brief training in anthropometry and use of a caliper—an instrument for measuring human morphology in use since the 1600s—on living subjects by none other than Franz Boas, one of the most important anthropologists of the twentieth century who would be at the center of debates about race in the decades to come.

Members of the mission carried out their research to mark out different "peoples" and "nations" by skull size. Only the "desert Arabs," they concluded, were a "people practically untouched by infiltration of foreign blood" and thus could be treated "in an entirely different manner from the rest of the Empire," where unfortunate mixing of peoples prevailed (Khalil 2016, 21). In this way, a racialized notion of civilizational difference was linked to fateful discussions of territory and readiness for sovereignty. The Mandates would move the semicivilized along on the civilizational scale, like commerce was supposed to have done for those more overtly labeled "barbarian" in eighteenth-century civilizational schema. Such missions were part of global processes racializing subjects of dissolved empires deemed semicivilized in ways that have consequences through our own times.

Too important to be left alone, too strong to be ignored, too "civilized" to be treated as primitive, "semicivilized" Egypt was left with an ambiguous legal status and a legacy of debts that continue to this day. Thanks in part to Mehmet Ali's successes in securing relative independence for Egypt from the Ottoman Empire in international law, Egypt was spared indignities of the Mandates. Despite its long and celebrated history as the "cradle of civilization," Egypt was unable to gain entry to the Versailles conference and did not escape the curse of the semicivilized and the burdens it imposed. Those denigrated as "primitive" in the civilizational logics of the nineteenth and twentieth centuries went through bloody wars of national liberation and anticolonial struggles. Those designated "semicivilized" experienced different bloody aftermaths.

We still live with nightmares of the semicivilized. This is most dramatically apparent in cities and countries whose urban fabric and infrastructures have been destroyed since the beginning of the twenty-first century. Millions have been killed and whole ecosystems have been destroyed since the US invasion of Iraq in 2001 and the ensuing two decades of its war on terror and cities and life itself. Other urban centers of the former Ottoman Empire were also attacked in the wars of succession to Yugoslavia. Such attacks on post-Ottoman urban centers in Bosnia were analyzed as a case of urbicide. They continued through to the wholesale destruction of educational, religious, cultural, health, and commercial infrastructure of Palestinians in Gaza. Debts of the semicivilized accumulate in accelerating and multiplying fashion. More than pure financial debt is at play: semicivilized infrastructures are multifaceted. They also entailed sorting and sifting out people by their embodied sovereign status. I move next to this process of sorting things and people.

SORTING THINGS OUT

I first encountered the Mixed Courts of Egypt at a secondhand book market in Cairo: the famous outdoor al-Azbakeya market. I would often go book shopping there with friends in the 1990s, browsing through volumes in Arabic, English, French, and Latin. Egypt was flooded with foreigners. It was home territory for Western journalists, academics, and corporate employees working all around the Arab world. Booksellers knew their market and what interested foreigners. The prices for works of Egyptian literature were high, as were the works of the most famous Arab historians. Books about debt and finance sold for next to nothing.

One day as we approached a stall, the owner started pulling out books he assumed my friends and I would want. But other books drew my eye— books off to the side about debt. Among those books were leather-bound masters' theses from Cairo University's faculties of law and commerce on various aspects of Egypt's debt. Their titles reflected a broad sense of outrage about indebtedness to foreigners in the late nineteenth and early twentieth centuries. I found books about the history of banking in Egypt written in Arabic and French; books in French about particular banks and their history; and books about the Alexandria stock market. I also came across a full set of volumes of the jurisprudence of the Mixed Courts of Egypt and a set of court cases from the years 1870–1910. There was no market for any of these, and the prices were cheap.

I had written papers and a thesis on debt and finance in college, had worked at the Federal Reserve Bank researching debt crises, and had written a master's thesis on the Public Debt Administration of the Ottoman Empire. This topic touched on my family history as well. I had a note from the original (British and French owned) Ottoman Imperial Bank among my grandfather's papers. And in his exit documents from Palestine, my great-grandfather had listed his profession as *sarraf* (banker or broker, in the Ottoman Empire). I was fascinated. Why were so many young Egyptians writing about debt and finance, about the unjust burdens of debt imposed on the nation, and about the outrageous offense caused by the Egyptian Mixed Courts to Egyptian national pride?

Published as *Gazettes of the Proceedings of Mixed Courts*, edited by Phillipe Gelat Bey, these bound volumes of proceedings and jurisprudence of the Mixed Courts were written mainly in French, the language of commerce in the region, and the lingua franca of the Mixed Courts; but they incorporated the languages of the jurists of the Mixed Courts, as well: most often English and Italian—never Arabic.[1] The books are an archive of an Egyptian institution and its workings in three cities of Egypt—Cairo, Mansoura, and Alexandria. But they are also an archive of extraterritorial commerce across a ghostly inter-imperial world facing new kinds of pressures and reforms. In these pages can be found the vast infrastructure of sorting out bodies according to norms of extraterritorial commerce and distributed sovereign rule.

The cases from the volumes reflect the scope of this infrastructure of sorting people out and the immense amount of labor it required. Here is a different archiving of lives in Cairo, Alexandria, and Mansoura. I read of streets and neighborhoods I knew well in accounts of an import-export firm established; a business dissolved; a dispute between two Egyptians, one with extraterritorial privileges of protection from a Western power, which landed them in the Mixed Courts. These cases tell fragments of lives lived on these streets yet enmeshed in a geography of global commerce shaped by the Ottoman capitulations and their legacies.

The *Gazettes* discuss Mixed Court cases in detail. Routine cases often have only three lines. The information recorded is simple: names and addresses of the two parties; name of the enterprise being dissolved, going bankrupt, or facing legal action; and designation of one side as "indigène," "native," or "Egyptian" and the other side as extraterritorial or foreign. Many cases record granting—and sometimes taking away—extraterritorial status of local people claiming rights of protection and embodied sovereignty linked to European sovereigns—and thus exemption from Egyptian rule of law. In these *Gazettes*, we have an archive of the semicivilized as viewed from one locality in Egypt. Each case tells a story of people with multiple sovereignties engaged in commerce in its dual meanings of market exchange and communication. Each case deals with far-ranging matters of economy, commerce, and infrastructure.

Some of the cases seem small in scale. There are cases of bankruptcy or the dissolution of import-export firms. There are cases about inheritance disputes and fights to gain access to a promised pension. There are also disputes about the need to pay or not pay customs taxes (anyone extraterritorial or deemed "foreign" did not have to pay such taxes). There are discussions of the legality of moving enslaved Africans across Egyptian territory in the mid-nineteenth century, including through Ottoman-Egyptian ruled Sudan (annexed to Egypt in 1821 by Mehmed Ali and consolidated under the rule of his grandson Khedive Ismail until the Mahdist Revolt of 1881), and about projects to build transoceanic telegraph cables like those being laid by the Eastern Telegraph Company across the British imperial world in the 1920s. All such matters, large and small, fell under the rubric of the capitulations prior to 1876, and under the purview of the Mixed Courts thereafter (or at least until 1949). In some of the cases, Rue el Khurunfich appears—a street to which I have a personal connection.

As I mentioned in the opening of this book, my grandfather owned a small burgundy suitcase that he carried with him from Palestine to the United States when he emigrated in 1930. Inside were a stack of neatly tied brown office folders and stacks of letters wound up in twine. Poking out from one of those files was a yellowed page with Arabic calligraphy at the top (figure 3.1). The vivid red of the name in French, the black calligraphy writing of the name in Arabic above it, and the contrast with the block black print of typewritten words in French right below had caught my eye.

The very fact of this document being typed was interesting: I had been looking through papers written by hand in a mix of languages ranging from Arabic to French to Hebrew to English. When did commercial houses in Cairo begin to have typewriters? When might such a small firm have used a typewriter to correspond with counterparts—this time in Galata, Constantinople (now Istanbul), where my forebear Nathan Coronel was based? The first telephone was installed in Egypt in 1881 and quickly transformed the nature of gendered conversation, channeling communication, speed, and delay among the *effendi* and *afrangi* classes of Cairo (Barak 2013, 206–7). The typewriter was invented in 1875, began to be used, and was quickly deemed essential to commerce by 1885.[2] Perhaps it reached Galata in Constantinople

3.1 Order letter from Boursaly Frères and Co., Cairo, sent to Nathan Coronel, Galata, Constantinople, July 4, 1910. Collection of the author.

and Rue el Khurunfich in Cairo by 1890. So this document's date had to be after that. The mix of writing styles and genres confused me.

The location of the firm and writer was printed in French: *Le Caire*. The day and month were easily legible, *le 4 Juillet*, as was the printed stationery year "191–." But something blotted came after that where the final number should be. It took me a few more minutes to realize that this blot was an

Arabic zero, a dot, written on the French side of the page. The letter was written in 1910, in Cairo under the rule of Khedive Ismail, four years before the outbreak of World War I. The letter is from someone writing from "Boursaly Frères et Cie., Rue el Khoronfich [*sic*], Caire," addressed to Nathan Coronel at his post office box in Galata, Constantinople. It turned out to be an order slip for confectionery ingredients, with prices and a discussion of pricing and expediting shipment, and order forms, and permissions.

> *Boursaly Frères and Co.*
> *Rue el Khoronfich [sic], Cairo.*
> *To: Nathan Coronel*
> *P.B. 268*
> *Galata, Constantinople [Istanbul]*
>
> *Sir,*
>
> *We received a letter from your enterprise in Jerusalem stating that you require confectionery ingredients. Please send us a list of the articles you require, and we will do our best to expedite your order. It would be helpful if you could note your current market price for our records. In turn, we would like to order an amount of the product known in Arabic as "Bondoque" and in English as "hazel nut" from the province of Anatolia. If you could prepare us a shipment of this article as well as another shipment of the article "melon seeds" we would be grateful.*
>
> *Regarding pending shipments, we were pleased to read in the newspaper that tea may now be shipped without the permits that have caused us such delay. We hope to be able to ship the tea and soap soon, but please note it will not be from the same lot, which was liquidated and sold off since we were unable to get those permits. Please note that in the meantime the price of soap has gone up to 14–15 piastres a kilo and the price of tea to 400 a kilo. Please let us know if you are interested and if so we will then send out the shipment.*
>
> *(formal closing)*

The writer of this letter worked with a small import/export firm, Boursaly Frères, located on Rue el Khurunfish (or Khoronfich, as written in the letter). This famous street is in El Gamaliya, off Port Said Street and parallel to Muski Street, close to Haret el Yehoud (the Jewish Quarter). Rue el Khurunfish was already famous in Fatimid Cairo, where the cover, or *kiswa*, for the Ka'ba in Mecca was produced. (The Fatimids established and ruled from Cairo from approximately 970 to 1171 CE).

By the mid-nineteenth century, Rue el Khurunfish was a meeting place for public personalities and was home to many Egyptians, mostly Jewish, engaged in commerce around the region. Egyptian President Gamal Abdel Nasser's father rented a home there when the family first moved to Cairo, and Nasser himself lived on the street in 1933. I knew that name from an oral history with my grandfather, who mentioned that his engagement party to my grandmother had been held at his cousin's house on Rue el Khurunfish.

Nathan Coronel was my grandfather's second cousin by marriage. His *maison* moved items essential for the running of coffeehouses around Palestine, Cairo, and Constantinople. These items—sugar, tea, and hazelnuts (for sweets)—were raw materials in the production of conviviality and communication that were a necessary part of commerce. Coffeehouses supplied by Maison Coronel's import/export firm were nodes in a vast communicative infrastructure of commerce. I assume this deal eventually went through. I found no other papers about the matter in my grandfather's suitcase. But (to indulge in a counterfactual), what if things had gone wrong? What if Boursaly Frères had been sued or dissolved before the deal was completed? Where would the matter have been adjudicated? Would it have been in the Mixed Courts?

As a civil case, it would have fallen within the extensive commercial code of Egypt and the Ottoman Empire shaped by the capitulations, agreements for the conduct of extraterritorial commerce between the Ottoman Empire and sovereign nations of Western Christendom. As such, this kind of matter would have been referred to the consular courts, which were held in a European nation's consular (extraterritorial) domain, where the local rule of law had no sway. In short, lurking behind the trivial details of this letter sent from Rue el Khurunfich to Galata, Constantinople, about sugar, tea, and hazelnuts was a vast infrastructure of global commerce and international private law.

This letter traveled with the goods it described to Jerusalem via Constantinople by Ottoman post, which stretched across the vast reaches of the empire in a crucial communicative infrastructure (Koh 2021). This order did not come from the national economy of a territorial state. Nor was it from "the colonies," despite Egypt being in Africa and this being the era of high colonialism. This order does not track with Egypt's political economy of labor-building industry or with its long history in the political economy of the movement of enslaved Africans through and from Sudan (Sikainga

1996, Powell 2003). This was not extraction of sugar from a plantation colony, theft of raw materials, or state-to-state export. Rather, these goods for sweetshops or coffeehouses moved along communicative channels of commerce stretching across imperial domains. The letter invites us to consider commerce and sovereignty differently.

Capitulating Commerce

The capitulations were part of the essential infrastructure of the world in which Nathan Coronel, a resident of the Ottoman Empire since birth, lived and by means of which he was exempt from Ottoman jurisdiction—even though his offices and homes were in two important Ottoman cities: Jerusalem and Constantinople (Istanbul). They shaped a world in which "men of capital" built enterprises, debated economic theories, and organized consumption practices in Palestine as they did in Egypt (Seikaly 2015). Without understanding basics of the capitulations, we cannot make sense of this letter moving from Rue el Khurunfich in Cairo to Galata, western Constantinople, through which most of this global extraterritorial commerce flowed along channels of financialized relationships. Life on Rue el Khurunfish and around Cairo was shaped by Egypt's variable inclusion in the Ottoman Empire and as part of a geography of the Levant, shaped by the range and reach of the Ottoman capitulations.

As we have discussed, the capitulations were a kind of treaty granting extraterritorial privileges to merchants, their assistants, their families, and their protégés traveling around, or living in, Ottoman domains across the vast stretches of the empire. When the Ottomans conquered Constantinople in 1453, they incorporated jurisprudence of the Byzantine Empire, capitulations included, into their legal infrastructure. Granting factors (or agents) of the trading corporations—or nations, as they were called—the right and obligation of self-regulation was nothing remarkable. As mentioned previously, such agreements were standard in the Ottoman Empire as well as in other regions of the former Roman Empire, the Hapsburg Empire, and the Venetian Empire.

Capitulations between the Ottomans and the Venetians incorporated terminology from earlier agreements between the Byzantines and the Venetians. The capitulations were pragmatic and synthetic. Byzantine treaties with the Varangians (in today's Russia) were also regularly renewed (such as those in 907, 911, and 944 CE) and were nothing exceptional under common practices of personal law (Thayer 1923, 208). Such agreements were standard practice with the Hanseatic League as well, whose factors "were judged by their own law wherever engaged in commerce abroad."[3]

In the Ottoman Empire, these capitulations were granted to the nations of factors representing these new companies with new forms of legal personhood and sovereign rights (Schmitthoff 1939). The concept of "legal personality" arose to denote a consequential division between natural persons and legal persons that we live with to this day. This innovation opened up space to discuss "the juridical nature of corporate bodies and their relationship to their individual members" and the concept of "legal person," as opposed to natural person, was applied to groups such as monastic communities and universities (*persona quoad iuris intellectum*) (Brundage 1995, as cited in Anghie 2012, 100). The monopoly corporations and joint stock companies established by Queen Elizabeth I of England at the end of the sixteenth century were part of this growing tradition of corporations as "legal persons" and as "corporate sovereigns" (Keene 2004; Wilson 2008).

Over time, the capitulations changed in nature as they were extended to the English, the Dutch, and other "Christian powers" and then to locals with protected status. The capitulations shifted to the status of treaties (if "unequal treaties") between two sovereigns and, as such, shifted from the terrain of "private" to "public" international law. As treaties, once signed, these capitulations would be considered binding forever. By the middle of the nineteenth century, thirteen Christian nations of Europe and two of the New World nations possessed extraterritorial privileges in Turkey (Thayer 1923, 211). In this context, acquiring the status of "foreigner," being linked to those carrying passports of other sovereign states, through shared cultural capital gave one crucial material privilege. Capitulations provided freedom from local jurisdiction to some locals, called *beratlis*, but not to others. Cultural and religious differences in the empire became a gateway to exterritorial privilege, enshrined in international law, and shaped the flows of global commerce that made up the emerging world of commercial society in the eighteenth century.

No one could reasonably claim that the Ottoman Empire needed the West to bring it commerce. Commerce was a well-practiced art in the realms of the Ottoman Empire. Carrying things over long distances through the "well-protected domains" of the Ottoman Empire, to use the Ottoman Turkish expression, was a source of prestige and state legitimacy, and it was a means of provisioning the cities and generating tax revenue within the empire (Erkal 2020). From countless chronicles, books, and articles, we know that commerce (*tigara*) was highly valued in the Ottoman

Empire long before the first travelers from Western Europe arrived bearing goods and representing queen and country. The reasons were many. Commerce involved the movement hither and thither of people conveying things and moneys over land and across seas. Commerce and the long-distance travel it entailed were a source of tax revenue and of bounty.

Trade brought taxes, work, and profits for local craftsmen and consumers in urban centers, and it displayed the ruler's power and legitimacy through the safety of roads and routes and the ample places to pray, sleep, drink, and eat. Infrastructures of commerce along roads and routes and in the urban centers were funded as waqf, which (much like the word's literal translation) stopped the hand of the state from appropriating these properties and real estate. Waqf protected assets across the generations and provided income for family trustees, just like trusts of the wealthy in our own times.[4]

This infrastructure of commerce—what Laleh Khalili has called the "sinews of commerce" (2020)—was built in material form along roads and routes and in the great cities and towns of the empire. It was a public good (to use the term loosely); use by one did not reduce its possibilities for use by another; its use was intended for all. Buildings such as the *wakala*, the *khan*, or the caravansary gave merchants and other sojourners a safe place to stay and store their goods. They encouraged internal trade, cross-imperial trade, and trade across the Mediterranean.

Building and maintaining a *wakala* or *khan*[5] brought in artisans, their craft guilds (also a source of revenue for the state), and guards. The *waqfiyya* of the Mamluk ruler Baybars II, for example, "provided good livings for four hundred sufis and one hundred soldiers and children of mamluks" (Williams 1984, 40, citing Al-Maqrīzī [1270] 1854, 2:417).[6] Sufis from across the Islamic world were housed there, in Cairo, and engaged in trade as well as prayer. The *rab* was one such building—a "dormitory" with a distinctive architectural form. It housed sojourners from other regions of the empire and from across the Islamic world who were traveling to sell wares, purchase goods, and conduct all kinds of commerce associated with the neighboring *wakala*, or caravansary. It was "a kind of furnished hotel where up to ten or fifteen apartments can be rented, each lodging up to ten people" (Raymond 2000, 57, citing Clerget 1934, 1:316–17).[7]

This ecosystem of hospitality and of cultivated mobilities was not in itself Islamic, Arab, or Middle Eastern. This infrastructure spans a vast stretch of time and a geographic range wider than the Roman Empire, with its long history of property law pertaining to hospitality.[8] The great fourteenth-century Arab scholar Ibn Khaldun left us both a description and an analysis of this infrastructure of commerce and the guiding logics of its political economy in Egypt, where merchants built many madrasas, *zawiyas*, and *ribats*, and endowed them with waqfs that yielded income. A share of the income thus generated was given to their descendants, who functioned either as supervisors of the endowment or as its beneficiaries, "as well as from a general wish to do good and receive recompense for their good intentions and good deeds" (Williams 1984).

The entry of Western Christian nations such as the English into networks and ecosystems of the Levant trade changed the nature of this world of commerce and eventually exercised enormous power over these channels of commerce.[9] The Ottoman capitulations would be transformed from a beneficence granted at the discretion of the sultan to a burden the Ottomans constantly tried to shrug off. With their legacy of attributing sovereign status to bodies that moved through space rather than to anything affixed to static, bounded territory, sorting things out had become more complex. Which person, which body, was linked to which sovereign? The Mixed Courts of Egypt inherited the labor of sorting all this out in 1876.

Sieving and Sorting

The Egyptian Mixed Courts were a response to perceived shortcomings of the infrastructure of global commerce running through the Ottoman Empire, including Egypt.[10] The courts were established to normalize and regularize the capitulations in a semiautonomous Egypt with sovereignty distributed among the British, the Ottomans, and the Egyptians (Brown 1993; Genell 2013). Under terms of the capitulations, any dispute between Egyptians and foreigners—or between two residents from Western nations who had gained protected status—would be resolved in consular courts, where Western powers were much stronger and Egypt had little influence. In this landscape, the Mixed Courts were an "ingenious solution" that aimed to "protect the country's financial interests, without alienating foreign bondholders who could cause the country's fiscal collapse" (Brown 1993, 34).

First established for a trial five-year period, the Mixed Courts lasted seventy-three years. They were proposed in 1876 by Nubar Pasha, "an ambitious and creative politician who served the Egyptian government in a variety of capacities (including three terms as prime minister) under both the Khedive Ismail and the British occupation" (Brown 1993, 34). It was a moment of vast transformations in Egypt, formalizing Egypt's status outside of the institutions of the Ottoman Empire (even if neither a colony of the

British or the French nor a sovereign territorial state). The Mixed Courts heard cases of "mixed" sovereignty, between those deemed "foreign," or subject to extraterritorial rule, and those deemed "local" or *indigène*.

The jurisprudence of the Egyptian Mixed Courts was part of international law. It was issued by an international group of judges. Proceedings were conducted in four judicial languages: French, Arabic, English, and Italian; but most of the records are written in French. While the British conceded the courts' language to the French as compensation for their own dominant role in Egypt (Genell 2016), the British handled key aspects of the courts' administration and managed their finances, even as formal sovereignty remained with the khedive, in an arrangement of dividual sovereignty that we have seen throughout this book. Three court systems came into existence: the native or *indigène* courts, the consular courts, and the Mixed Courts.

The Mixed Courts handled cases as large and consequential as the laying of underwater cables by the British Eastern Telegraph Company near the Suez Canal and as small as the dissolution of a two-person partnership of the kind reflected in the letter from Rue el Khurunfish. These courts aimed, in the framing of their Egyptian founders, to protect Egypt's resources and interests against the constant incursions of Western powers who had endless claims against the Egyptian government under the terms of the capitulations. Looked at from a different perspective, the Mixed Courts pandered to concerns of investors, engineers, and financial architects of Western colonialism of the nineteenth century about the safety of their capital. Yet, it is more generative to look at the Mixed Courts from the actually existing reality and the regularity (rather than exceptionality) of dividual and embodied sovereignty as a mode of governance around the world.

The Mixed Courts emerged from the extraterritorial system of capitulations—of which the Ottoman Empire was a linchpin. They were part of an ensemble with other initiatives undertaken by Khedive Ismail to perform the reality of a sovereign state: remaking Cairo, building the Khedivial Opera House, commissioning *Aida*, and opening the Suez Canal. The Mixed Courts were part of this moment of disentangling Egypt from the Ottoman Empire in a complex field of power including the British and French Empires (see Genell 2013). This entailed reframing the capitulations as *Egyptian* (if international) law inside Egyptian territory.

The "Mixed" in the name Mixed Court referred to mixed cases; a case could be between one Egyptian national (in a modern sense of the word) subject to local rule of law, and one Egyptian with extraterritorial status, subject to the sovereign and law of another country. Rather than applying a category of racialization, this sorting practice works out which body of law pertains to which body. The Mixed Courts carried forward into the modern era a system of sovereignty based not on territorial integrity but on place of origin (be it fictitious or not) and, importantly, as carried through space by the human body. Locals who were cultural brokers for Westerners could become legal subjects of a foreign power and thus be exempt from the legal system of their own country. In the process, cultural practice and bodily comportment became markers of privilege in terms of both political and property rights.

What cases, and which people, belonged where? Who was native or *indigène* and who was foreign or extraterritorial?[11] This was a practical dilemma for those engaged in this labor of sorting things out. The divisions they came up with and the practices they reflected and reproduced pose challenges to categories like colonizer/colonized, subaltern, and indigenous/settler. These were not simple questions. But they were also not new: processes of sorting people out were inherent to embodied sovereignty. The Mixed Courts offer a clear, and easily examined, case study of multiple attempts to redo and revise the extraterritorial arrangements of the capitulations. They were a kind of "neocapitulatory" regime regulating the vast and accelerating speed and reach of commerce that would also allow a degree of local sovereignty over economic space.

The usual frameworks of colonial studies or imperialism emanating from the developed capitalist West do not allow us to grasp these dynamics of dividual sovereignty and personal law. According to a theory of personal law, we carry the body of the sovereign in our own person as we move through space. It helps to use historian Lauren Benton's (2002) term *sojourner* to describe people who traveled, in days before airplanes, long distances, quite often, and who stayed in foreign lands for long times.

Sojourners in the Ottoman Empire might live there for years. Factors of the Levant Company usually did. Communities of merchants living in the "factory," in their capacity as factors of the corporate sovereign, could be called and treated as a "millet" or "nation." The factory in which they lived, the commerce they conducted, and their activities were under the jurisdiction of their home sovereign. Those individuals protected under capitulations were not subject to the jurisdiction of the local sovereign. In the decades and century to come, a growing number of locals gained access to membership of this "nation" as well. First were the translators, or drago-men, who were present at any interaction with the Ottoman bureaucracy or courts. Matters expanded from there.

From the point of view of theories of sovereign territorial nation-states (if not always the practice), the anomaly is even greater. Over time, large numbers of locals gained access to the status of sojourner and were exempted from the law of the land in which they and their forebears were born. In today's terms, the capitulations granted extraterritoriality to some locals but not to others. It should be obvious that a system granting "immunities from jurisdiction" not only to foreigners sojourning in the Ottoman Empire but also to indigenous communities—such as Syrian Catholics or Egyptian Catholics, "protected" by foreign powers under the capitulations—could become irritating to local populations.

The Mixed Courts absorbed cases that might otherwise have gone to consular courts. In a system of embodied sovereignty, a man sojourning within Ottoman domains was subject to the sovereign law attached to his body. Prior to the establishment of the Mixed Courts, if a Frenchman got into a dispute over business or pleasure with an Egyptian in Cairo, the two parties would appear in the French consular court to settle the matter.[12] From the Ottoman perspective, this system was problematic for many reasons, and things got really messy by the 1860s. That decade saw a huge increase in the number of resident foreigners in Cairo, including resident workers on the Suez Canal and other infrastructure projects. The Mixed Courts were created to ameliorate the chaotic situation this created.

Western signatories of the capitulations were not eager to let go of either the capitulations or the consular courts. The US Congress took up the topic in 1920 in the context of discussions about the Treaty of Versailles. "The cri-terional feature of the capitulations," the author of a report to the members of Congress explained, "is the principle of exterritoriality, i.e., the government of settlers in a foreign land by their own laws and magistrates." The origin of capitulations, he continued, was remote, going back to 526 BC and arrange-ments for the Greek traders based in Egypt (Ravndal 1921, 5–7). Commerce in this tradition, the author noted, continued in ancient Greece, which per-mitted foreigners to reside in its city-states (6). On the island of Rhodes, in particular, "a more human view of international relations appears to have flourished. Guided by the idea of creating the fullest possible freedom of trade, the lawmakers of that country developed a code of maritime and mer-cantile legislation which became a model throughout the Mediterranean and as annexed to Roman law (Lex Rhodia) was handed down to future ages" (7).

Consular institutions were useful "in the protection of the interests of commerce" (Ravndal 1921, 84). Their object, the report said, was "1. The protection of commerce and navigation. 2. The personal security of those engaged therein. 3. The conservation of the privileges obtained abroad. 4. The maintenance of good faith in commercial transactions (including proper standards of value, weight, and measurement). 5. The administration of justice, promptly and impartially, in civil and commercial matters by national judges" (86). Such "prompt and impartial administration of justice," under this system of capitulations and consular courts, swept in all local Ottoman subjects who were one party to a dispute.

Much as the US Congress wanted to keep this situation in place at the end of World War I, consular courts lost their authority soon enough. The capitulations were finally abrogated by the Treaty of Lausanne in 1923. The consular courts were dissolved—except for diplomatic consuls and their staff, who retained extraterritorial privileges. But in Egypt something like the consular courts lived on longer, thanks to the Mixed Courts. Even though the category of the extraterritorial who had had access to those consular courts was dissolved, the divide between the extraterritorial and the local did not go away. Legacies of the extraterritorial are easy to see and track in regions of the former Ottoman Empire that were placed under the control of British and French Mandates and perhaps most dramatically also in Egypt (cf. Hanley 2013; Culang 2019, and Genell 2019).

By the nineteenth century, the consular courts, and workings of the capitulations inside Egypt, with its distinct emerging political structure, caused immense challenges for the project of rationalizing the legal system. Figuring out who was local was a full-time job in the Mixed Courts of Egypt from 1876 to 1949, in the police stations of Alexandria in the late nineteenth century (Hanley 2017), and in the offices of taxation in the Venetian Empire (Rothman 2012). "Local" referred to all those without extraterritorial privileges and protection from a Western sovereign. It could be an English language translation of the Arabic *mahaliyya* (Hanley 2016) or another way of saying of "native," as in "native courts." "Local" might also be a translation of the French word *indigène*, which was the dominant term used in other parts of North Africa colonized by France.

Behind the larger-scale dramas and lengthy cases of jurisdiction over infrastructures of canals and telegraphs, of enslavement, and of commercial deals bringing in state-to-state negotiations and public debt repayment plans, the archives of the Mixed Courts of Egypt record the endless labor of sorting people out, fixing—if but for one encounter, one exchange—a nationality or a citizenship, as such things became more in demand and more readily produced. The process marked out bodies as *attached* to different sovereigns.

One by one, case by case, hearing by hearing, session by session, court by court, application by application, the sorting and sieving of people living in one locality, one region, one country continued. Over seventy years of changing geopolitics and legal categories of political belonging, claims to the status of local or foreign, extraterritorial or *indigène*, were enacted, accepted, or rejected in cases brought before the Mixed Court. Shifts in status appeared in moments of exit and entry, the payment of taxes, creating a firm or going into bankruptcy, or settling an estate of a loved one who had lived a lifetime of overlapping sovereignties and multiple citizenships in an ecosystem of extraterritorial commerce and distributed sovereignty.

As taxes marked the relation of subject to the imperial state, tax exemption was the "most important marker of legal status in the Ottoman Empire" (Hanley 2013, 42). As such, the concept of the local is linked to embodied sovereign status and taxation: Who is linked to which sovereign? *Local* means being a "local subject," or *ra'iya*—someone who is subject to paying tax or tribute to the state and subject to the local rule of law. By contrast, *askeri* elite were those who received a part of those taxes. Within those two categories existed multiple and sometimes overlapping political memberships. This kind of situation is common with dividual sovereignty and is "more common than experience of [unitary] citizenship" (Hanley 2013, 97).

This logic carries through to nineteenth-century Egypt, where the local subject becomes a "comprehensive, collective category that . . . was used primarily by foreign powers uninterested in the distinction between different kinds of nonforeigners or in police work or access to local subjects." Just as outsiders were described generically as "Europeans," anyone without foreign protection could be described as "native" (Hanley 2017, 262). My great-uncle's reply to the question of "nationality" with "local" on a document from Mandatory Palestine has a great deal to do with life in Cairo too (see figure I.2).

While "local" was a common term in late nineteenth- and early twentieth-century Egypt, it was far from the only category used in the archives to designate local populations. Before the Mixed Courts in Egypt, an essential division tracked was between those who were "under the control of the authorities" (*dakhil al-hukuma*), or local, and those outside of their control" (*kharij al-hukuma*) (Hanley 2013, 97–98). Some government bureaucracies tracked five subcategories of local: *ibn al-balad* for city dweller; *fallahi*; *ibn 'arab*; *barbari*; and *ra'iya* (Hanley 2017, 262).

Categories were demarcated differently during the earlier French Occupation of Egypt. In the 1800 *Description de l'Egypte*, French orientalists marked out "national groups," of which Egypt's population was said to include eight: "Egyptians, Turks, Arabs, Moors (specifically, Maghrabis), Greeks, Syrians, Jews, and Europeans" (Hanley 2017, 45). By 1840, the Egyptian census divided the population in a simpler way, between those under local authority (*dakhil al-hukuma*) and those beyond government authority (*kharij al-hukuma*) (Hanley 2013, 97–98). Then, in an 1882 census, the Egyptian population was categorized by "national type" once again.

These categories of "national type" were problematic on many levels. In a system of overlapping sovereignties, identity was assumed situationally to interact with different kinds of administrators. Such national labels entailed no access to rights and were irrelevant for travel as well—as with my great-uncle's travel document in Palestine. In the "complex legal landscape of turn of the century Egypt," the closest thing to what a twentieth-century observer might think of as nationality still meant, more or less, which sovereign "exercised jurisdiction over the bodies of the territory's subjects" (Hanley 2017, 44).

Until the end of the nineteenth century in Egypt, "national categories such as 'Ottoman' or 'Egyptian' were of little use to local authorities" (Hanley 2017, 261). Categories that were "usable and meaningful locally" appeared in police records: "Name, profession, and residence" (259). Again, we saw such categories in the exit documents from Palestine in both Ottoman and Mandate bureaucratic forms (figures I.1 and I.2): this was a much broader ontology of categories and ways of moving through the world and of regulating policy.

Locals did not "assert subjecthood" in legal terms that would make sense to foreign consuls (Hanley 2017, 259) charged with ruling on any dispute between a local and someone holding extraterritorial status. In a system of embodied sovereignty under the capitulations, anyone with extraterritorial status—even if just one party to a dispute—would appear before a consular court. When a consular court needed a local as a witness in a case, it "code switched" to local categories, identifying individuals in ways that would allow the individual to be located and called forth.

The issues being worked out here involved multiple levels of imperial citizenship and belonging. Could an Arab from elsewhere in the Ottoman Empire who had lived in Cairo for decades with protected status provided by France successfully claim French citizenship? Was he an "Egyptian"? Some such cases were transferred from the native courts to the Mixed Courts

(Hanley 2017, 360). Answers came case by case, bit by bit, family by family, in narratives of trivia and tragedy, wealth and impoverishment. Multiple sovereignty became a matter of "culture," "cosmopolitanism," or "nostalgia" rather than of legal status.

Sorting out Ottomans from regions of Serbia or Bosnia-Herzegovina that had been Ottoman domains before World War I continued in Egypt as well. Recall from the introduction how, for Western Europe, the Balkans had become the imaginary home of the "barbarian" by the Middle Ages. In the jurisprudence of the Mixed Courts, such former Ottomans faced multiple challenges. Before 1924, such Ottomans would have been designated as "local," in the sense of being "subject to Ottoman jurisdiction." Others might have become subjects under the capitulations of other states and thus have fallen under the status of "foreigner." The status of "Slavs" in the Austro-Hungarian Empire created another twist. In one case considered by the Egyptian Mixed Courts, a local resident of Cairo identified as Slav "had been employed by the Egyptian government in June 1907. In November 1914 he had become protected by Russia, and after the war his place of origin, Dalmatia, became Yugoslav. He too claimed the benefits of the 1923 law for the retirement of foreigners in the government service. It was held that he was a local subject. None of his changes in nationality or protection derogated from his status at birth, which the court assessed had become an international issue" (Hoyle 1987, 361–62). Such national categories would come increasingly into play in cases from a wide range of locations that today would be considered parts of completely different and incommensurate regions: the Middle East, the Balkans, Central Europe, Western Europe, and Russia.

Legacies of the Mixed Courts

The capitulations had generated a de facto category of foreigner: one who was not subject to local rule of law. Foreigner was a bucket category. It was demonstrated through an accumulation of small events documenting status and sovereign affiliation in any encounter with the police, the tax authority, the army (to prove exemption from conscription), or the search of one's home. "The foreigner was he who was not local. The local, in turn, became an empty signifier, holding the place of the nonforeign" (Hanley 2017, 258). The work of linking signifier to signified—of linking body to category—grew more complicated over the course of the nineteenth century, and even more so after the end of World War I.

After dissolution of the Ottoman Empire and the end of the capitulations with the Treaties of Lausanne and Sèvres, the process of sorting people out in Egypt became exponentially more complicated. Were former Ottomans in Egypt local or foreign? What about people from former Ottoman regions now ruled as part of the French or British Mandates? Former Ottomans from Palestine, Syria, Lebanon, and more had no state to grant them citizenship. What would their sovereign affiliation be?

The Ottoman Empire might be studied now as part of Middle Eastern studies, but one-third of the empire was in Europe for much of its history. Complex international politics at the vortex of the dissolution of the Ottoman Empire were at play involving Ottomans from regions of Europe. Were Bulgarians the same or different from other ex-Ottomans (Hoyle 1987, 360)? Similar issues unfolded for residents of Cairo whose parents had come from Ottoman Greece, or who were native-born Cairenes who had gained status as "Greek" thanks to their ties to the Greek Orthodox Church. The case of one Damianos, who was trying to get access to his pension by bringing a case to the Mixed Courts, was written about by former Judge Hoyle of the Mixed Courts as follows: "In the *Damianos* case, the plaintiff had enrolled as a policeman in the Egyptian police in January 1910. He was an Ottoman subject from Crete, and as an Ottoman he was not entitled to a pension. By the Treaty of Athens in 1913, Damianos was given the right to opt for Greek nationality, and he did so. He continued to serve in the police until 1924, and on retirement claimed a pension on the basis of a 1923 law setting out the terms of retirement for foreigners in the government service" (Hoyle 1987, 361).

Legacies of the Austro-Hungarian Empire appear in these deliberations as well, as does the Kingdom of Italy, which after 1866 included Venice, the center of the Venetian Empire that was once the Ottoman Empire's ally in regulation of the Mediterranean and then its opponent in a war for its control. Deliberations on one man's, and one family's, future course rested on terms of the Treaty of Vienna signed in 1866. In 1925,

the grandson of a Jew born in the Papal States who was himself registered in Egypt as an Austrian protégé was held to be Italian. The court made it clear that if the executive authorities of the state could not agree on a person's nationality it was up to the Mixed Courts to do so. The previous month the case of Pini v. Pini, MCA, 28 Apr. 1925, GTM XV, p. 161 decided that the descendant of a Venetian sailor, resident in Egypt, was Italian. The operative fact was Venice's inclusion into the Kingdom of Italy in 1866 after rule by Napoleon, then Austria and then a status as the Cisalpine Republic, rule by Italy and again by Austria. When Venice was recognized as part of Italy by the Treaty of Vienna in 1866 the right to Italian nationality became a primary right and could be exercised by a descendant. (Hoyle 1987, 362n15)

For the privileged, the solution to the nationality problem was resettlement (Hanley 2017, 293). Over time, most of those who could leverage their multiple sovereignties into foreign papers and citizenship did so. Those who could substantiate European protection as a modern form of citizenship did so and moved to places where their privileges of *laissez-passer* (increasingly understood in its modern meaning as a right restricted to diplomats and those with diplomatic papers) could be turned into passports of a sovereign territorial state. Those who could became privileged citizens of the emerging global order.[13] Those whose prior claims to extraterritorial status failed, or those who simply fell through the cracks over years of inattention, were rendered local—subject to the expanding jurisdiction of a territorial state.

No case appearing before the Mixed Courts in these years after the Treaties of Versailles and Lausanne is completely local or personal. No case is devoid of international law and overlapping jurisdictions. One example is a case from 1926, *Risgallah v. Zahar*, which discussed the question of where this civil case should be heard. Did cases involving Syrians—former Ottomans—belong in the Mixed Courts as foreigners? Or in the native courts as *indigènes*? In this particular case, it was ruled that they were not within the jurisdiction of Mixed Courts as foreigners, since Egypt had not recognized the Treaty of Lausanne, "so no status dependent on that treaty could be automatically recognized." (Hoyle 1987, 358fn9). Furthermore, the ruling went on, the "Mixed Courts would not extend its jurisdiction over former Ottomans because the Ottoman Empire had not submitted to the Capitulations and therefore could not benefit from them" (359).

Such issues and cases and shifts in the nature of the sieves through which people were sorted out, rearranged, and quite often moved to another place and another territory, whether by decree or by choice, did not rest there. Also in 1926, *Zachari Meckdachi and Bros. v. Egyptian Customs Administration* decided "that Syrians were foreigners for the purposes of jurisdiction" (Hoyle 1987, 359). This fateful decision happened, too, through rulings of commerce, shipping, and the moving of goods through ports. Customs authorities had seized Meckdachi's goods. He appealed to the Mixed Courts for relief, claiming that the Egyptian Customs Administration had no authority. The

Customs Administration, of course, disagreed. Since the firm was Syrian, and registered in Beirut, under Lebanese law (under the French Mandate), this matter was befitting for the "native Courts" (359).[14]

In a 1926 article on the Mixed Courts of Egypt in the *American Journal of International Law*, Jasper Brinton, a justice of the Court of Appeals of the Mixed Courts, opined that "next to the Church, the Mixed Courts are the most successful international institution in history" (Brinton 1926, 670). The Mixed Courts and its legal bar were "among those institutions which do the highest honor to humanity," according to Leon Duguit, dean of the Law School of the University of Bordeaux and the Law School of the University of Egypt (670). Not everyone agreed. Numerous Egyptians denounced the Mixed Courts as a "means of foreign domination" from which Egypt only escaped by degree after the 1920s (Brown 1993, 33). On June 29, 1936, the Egyptian newspaper *Al-Musawwar* called the Mixed Courts "a crime against humanity" (Brown 1993, 33).

Brinton was an American jurist appointed to the Mixed Courts; his auto-ethnographic account of the courts is illuminating to read. While the Mixed Courts began with a "modest output of judicial labor and a highly unstable tenure of existence," they had by the 1920s become "an institution which has stood like a rock at the foundation of the prosperity of Modern Egypt, an institution which, with a personnel of sixty-five judges, recruited in no small part from among the leading jurists of Europe, and fifteen hundred employees, renders annually some thirty thousand written opinions, maintains a great land-registry system, is responsible for an annual net revenue to the government of a million pounds), and exercises legislative functions of a unique and most important character" (Brinton 1926, 320).

The Mixed Courts were not abolished until 1949. Many had claimed credit for their establishment in 1876. And many claimed credit for their abolishment, including the Egyptian government. A stamp celebrating their end was issued on October 14, 1949 (three years before the Free Officers coup), in Arabic and French (figure 3.2). On the left-hand side are the scales of justice and the price of the stamp, 10 mills. On the right is the name of the country, in French ("Egypte") and Arabic (not the Arab Republic of Egypt, as it would soon become), and a legend, also in French ("Fin du systeme judiciare mixte") and Arabic ("End of the Mixed Court System").

These stamps and medals celebrating the end of the Mixed Courts are now sold on another platform of global commerce: eBay. I found some items discussed at the "Gentleman's Military Interest Club," an online forum where an item being sold on eBay labeled "Egypt Khedivate Judge's Badge" was

3.2 Commemorative postcard and stamps marking the abolition of the Egyptian Mixed Courts, October 14, 1949. Collection of the author.

under discussion in 2018. A user asks for information about a "1949 medal from an auction taking place on 18 May, 2018, on Sixbid.com/Stephen Album Rare Coins (lot 1776) [that] shows King Farouk I on the obverse and the inscription of the commemoration of the end of the Mixed Courts and judicial symbols."[15] Petty commerce on eBay in memorabilia of the celebration of the end of the Mixed Courts seemed a poignant end to global infrastructures of the semicivilized.

This was not the only endpoint to the legal infrastructures of the semicivilized. Sorting out the local from the extraterritorial also culminated in the waves of nationalizations in the financial sector that I outlined in chapter 1, when President Nasser expropriated the wealth of remaining Egyptian extraterritorials to build a national economy, and with the stamping of some Egyptian passports with a one-way *laissez-passer*, with the words, "never to return" (Tignor 2010, 269). It is no simple matter to sort out who is extraterritorial and who is local. Practices of sorting people out, assigning nationality and sovereign belonging—linking body to sovereign in distributed fashion—reverberate to this day.

What exactly makes one obviously an *afrangi* or a *khawaga*—as extraterritorials or their offspring might be called—became more difficult to enunciate in words. It became harder to define what made a person local, or *sha'bi* (one of the urban masses) even, crucially, as this status identity was obvious to all. These categories remained essential to how people moved, interacted, built, shopped, worked, and lived in common in the neighborhoods and on the city streets of Cairo. I approach all this in relation to that notion of being "in common" next.

COMMONS GOODS

"Defend our country." "Be part of our land." "Defend our resources." "Reclaim our water." Calls such as those rang through Cairo, in Egypt, and resounded around the world in 2010 and 2011 and after the great financial crisis of 2008, when mass protests erupted in cities across the United States, Europe, and North Africa. The slogan of Occupy Wall Street, "We are the 99 percent," expressed this new political moment in which an old issue of progressive politics, "the commons," once again came back to the fore.[1] Lauding a new politics of "the commons," Western political theorists imported images of mass revolt from across these spaces, from Cairo especially, into calls for resistance against the ravages of neoliberal dispossession around the world. In the words of political theorist Étienne Balibar (2019), the issue of the commons was "knocking on the door."

As many Arab scholars and participants in the January 25 Revolution of 2011 have shown, the Egyptian uprising was about many things, some of which were grounded in politics of the country and region, and some of which were part of a global revolt against unfair outcomes of the 2008 financial crisis and policy responses that shifted immense amounts of wealth from the public sphere to the world's wealthiest. Around the Mediterranean and North Africa, governments had sold off state-owned resources for a pittance in the name of economic efficiency. Revolts large and small were underway across the towns and stopping points of the old Levantine world of commerce within the former Venetian and Ottoman Empires. Greece, for example, was being told in 2010, and again in 2015, to sell off islands that were part of its national territory to qualify for loans with which to pay off interest on previous EU loans.

I watched events unfold in Cairo from Split, Croatia, in the summer of 2011. There, discontent with the country's pending ascension to the European Union simmered and members of the government were condemned as "traitors to the homeland." Every day, crowds flocked on foot and in ten-year-old diesel cars to their end of the Adriatic to enjoy their seacoast as a public good while they could. In Egypt, where the Mediterranean hit the shores of Alexandria, the city was still mourning the martyred children who had died in such high numbers during the January 25 Revolution. Some of my friends who lost their children, friends, and nephews never quite recovered. But all around the shores of the Mediterranean in those years, and all around the world, the commons continued "knocking on the door," to repeat Balibar's framing.

The commons knocked to mark the failures, hopes, and an auspicious moment of history: a moment of kairos. The ancient Greek concept of kairos sounds like the English name for Cairo. Perhaps for this reason, perhaps for others, images of Egyptian masses assembled in Cairo's Tahrir Square at the height of the mass revolts in 2011 that forced President Mubarak out of power and became known as the January 25 Revolution proliferated in a new literature on the commons. Tahrir Square became the poster child of this new commons, or "common," as it was dubbed by Michael Hardt and Antonio Negri (Butler 2011; Hardt and Negri 2011; Negri 2000). In the process, essential lessons from commons of the semicivilized disappeared from view.

Literature on the new commons was largely grounded in Western political theory by theorists from the West. It proceeded along a parallel track that did not intersect or cite a substantial literature by scholars from the Middle East on the unfolding, meaning, and significance of the January 25 Revolution in Egypt. The politics and experience of "time out of time" directly invoked by the notion of kairos was brilliantly analyzed by Hanan Sabea in the midst of unfolding events of revolution and counterrevolution (Sabea 2013).[2] Multiple activists and public intellectuals documented what was going on and what had happened in writings that have now been reissued in collected volumes (Attalah 2019; Abd el-Fattah 2022) and preserved in the archives of the websites *Mada Masr* and *Jadaliyya*. Young scholars were not only active in organizing, writing, and publishing as events unfolded; they established new communications infrastructures such as *Mada Masr* and *Jadaliyya* in order to communicate in closer to real time with a global audience (Elyachar 2012b). Scholars, activists, and "techies" remade digital space and communicative channels to better mesh with global communication platforms, making it possible to tweet in Arabic for the first time (Sakr 2023). All this was rendered invisible in publications invoking Tahrir as a central image of the commons and the global uprisings of the period.

Lionizing Tahrir as the poster child of the global commons misses key dynamics of the revolution/counterrevolution in Egypt, erasing local dynamics and local scholarship. But that is not all. It also leaves intact the deep attachments of theories of the commons to the very civilizational logics that relegated the semicivilized to the status of less-than-human, thus rendering invisible the persistent flourishing of the other commons of the semicivilized. Here, I want to bring together with ethnography from Cairo alternative genealogies in the history of political thought related to the commons. Doing this will allow us to enter into a discussion of the commons by looking at how people—some people, some bodies, some commoners—move, cross streets, drink tea, gossip, pass cigarettes back and forth, and how "the spiritual *sense* of the being-in-common is embedded in the material *sensorium* of everyday experience" (Rancière 2010, 89). Such simple, everyday practices on the street create and reproduce what I call "social infrastructures of communicative channels" that run through nerves, muscle, ground, and wire, across multiple nodes of distributed agency and the grounds they provide for the survival, flourishing, and reconstitution, against all odds, of the urban commoners.

These communicative channels are a valuable and ethnographically tractable resource of the urban masses in the Global South. Commoners, those of the "commons," share a set of embodied resources that are linked to material privilege and resources. In Cairo or in other cities of the former Ottoman Empire, such resources might be water fountains of waqf property or small fields lying behind homes carved out of former *miri* state-owned land. Communicative channels of the urban masses move through neighborhoods, shops, and streets, and appear in sayings, modes of address, and gestural resources of daily life as well. In Cairo, the praxis of "personal law" that marked movement across realms of empire—in which the travelers in foreign lands carried with them ties to the sovereign of their home—helped lay down these communicative channels.

Recall how this mode of sovereignty is embodied rather than linked to territory. It is ethnographically tractable in modes of collective movement and distributed agency across space over time. In a system of personal law, travelers or sojourners (Benton 2002) carried with them their sovereign affiliations, even as infrastructures of extraterritoriality promoted flows of commerce through inter-imperial worlds. Channels of mobility and finance moved through this global infrastructure of the semicivilized and, in a city like Cairo, became a collective resource, or a commons of the "locals," or commoners, of Cairo. Re-created as living vital infrastructures (Tadiar 2022) in the present, these pathways and channels of the commons carry along embodied history in movement down the street.

We all carry history on our backs. But in some towns and cities of the semicivilized that have not been destroyed, this is more obviously apparent. The living encyclopedia of Cairo is reproduced and cultivated through the interlocking networks or communicative channels of its people and neighborhoods. Such social infrastructures of communicative channels weave together extended families, communities, and workplaces across multiple generations living on the streets and in the homes of the city's popular neighborhoods. These social infrastructures were then integrated into platforms of revolt in the 2010s in Egypt and countries across the region, with Cairo's Tahrir Square only the most prominent and visible hub.

A vast literature on the "new commons" would be published in the decade following 2011. But troubling entanglements of the concept of the commons going back to Western moral philosophy, civilizational logics, and colonialism remained largely unexamined. In anthropology, the commons is usually seen as a pure good (just like neoliberalism is usually taken to be a pure bad). But the story is more complex. The commons has been lionized in contexts that might horrify anthropologists and critical political theorists. Take the seventeenth-century argument of international lawyer Hugo Grotius that channels of commerce across the ocean should be a commons, but only for competing sovereign powers of Western Europe in their bloody pursuit of commerce and profits across the Atlantic (Grotius [1609] 2004).[3] Or take the theory's entanglements with Christian legacies of the Garden of Eden, colonialism, and the corporation that go as far back as thirteenth-century writings of Thomas Aquinas, for whom the world was God's property and had been given to the human species for collective stewardship (Aquinas 1975, as cited in Hont and Ignatieff 1983, 27). When Adam and Eve were expelled from the Garden of Eden, they were condemned to toil by the sweat of their brow—a curse and obligation that was passed on to their children. It became their duty and obligation to toil in the soil of the earth and to live through labor.

Aquinas considered collective stewardship of the Garden of Eden to be the first "competence" of humans as trustees of the world's resources; as such, the Christian tradition considers this responsibility to be the original commons. Yet, as Aquinas went on to say, this collective relationship to the world's resources existed in tension with a second competence of human beings: private property (Hont and Ignatieff 1983, 26–27). Only with "arrangements of private possession" would each person take more trouble to "care for something that is his sole responsibility than what is held in common by many." The moral dilemma stemming from God's donation of the world in exclusive dominion to Adam and his heirs, and its subsequent "individuation," "made possible a responsible and productive management of God's estate." Such a conception of the commons was central to the evolution of natural jurisprudence and moral philosophy (42). From the start, the notion of the commons was entangled with the kind of exclusionary civilizational logic that rendered the commons the shared legacy and wealth of Christians, or the civilized, alone.

Given this entanglement with civilizational logic, it is not surprising that the commons would go on to play an important role in Western European colonial praxis and constitute a cornerstone of "indirect rule." Henry Sumner Maine, the legal scholar who was early in his career an employee of the British East India Company, defended the commons in his analysis of reasons for mass revolts in India against British rule in 1857 (Mantena 2010). British imperialism, Maine argued, should abandon its misguided attachment to liberal individualist ideology, which undermined the Indian commons/corporation. Despite the civilizing efforts of English liberal imperialists, "inscrutable sentiments" still shaped far too much of Indians' behavior (Mantena 2010). Individualized relations of the "contract" (as opposed to relations of "status") were not for them. Rather, colonized natives needed to stay rooted in the commons, here figured as the communal family with its strong links to communal property. Such communal units were a "corporate entity," which maintained its viability via shared ownership of land over time. Like corporations such as the East India Corporation, the Indian communal family persisted over the generations, outlived its individual members, and was indispensable for indirect colonial rule (Maine 1986; Kuper 2009).[4]

Commons never disappeared. But they were not at the center of political discourse in the twentieth century, which was shaped by "the grand dichotomy" of the public and the private (Bobbio 1996). Usually thought of as shared resources that are collectively managed by groups outside the strictures of state law or the free market, the commons was neglected in the grand story of this great clash in political theory. Yet, in the early twenty-first century, attention to the role of the commons in politics came back in. The global movement for which Tahrir Square was taken up as poster child would articulate the voice of a new political subject—the common, to use Hardt and Negri's terminology—that would transcend the divisions of class-based politics and the private/public divide.

We need better conceptual language to talk about what is going on. Once we let go of lingering assumptions of territorial sovereignty or even territory as the grounds for social and political theory, other ways of think-ing can emerge. To make this kind of conceptual shift in thinking about sovereignty and the commons, it helps to remember that the commons are not always shared goods or natural resources. Nor are the commons, as "re-lations among humans," for the sons of Adam and Eve alone. The commons can extend beyond the "communal family," linked to shared communal property, as an anchor of colonial governance. The commons emerge from other kinds of "grounds" as well—semiotic, embodied, local, and shifting. We can develop a richer vocabulary to think about struggles for public things and vital infrastructures by the poor urban majorities of the world and to imagine peoplehood outside the bounds of nation-state territorial sovereignty. The semicivilized, and the extraterritorial, can help us do so.

Being Local in Common

As part of a global infrastructure of commerce resting on personal law and embodied sovereignty, the extraterritorial relied on the labor of "sorting out" who was extraterritorial and who was local. This process of sieving the extraterritorial from the local occurred around the Ottoman Empire and in other imperial spaces shaped by norms of embodied sovereignty. Status as "local" in Ottoman and post-Ottoman political orders is distinct from the category of the colonized. To call Egypt postcolonial and leave things there would miss so much—including localness (*mahalliya*) as a set of strategic legal practices. In postimperial worlds of the semicivilized, much that is spoken of in social theory as "culture" is a marker of political status: sover-eignty is embodied, theories of personal law shape mobility practices, and sovereign affiliation is carried through space in dividual imperial domains. Much that Western theory has come to call "culture" or "cultural practice" is an index of privilege, or a pathway to its attainment. To be local is a political status in a regime of extraterritoriality. In Egypt, to be local is to be a commoner, one of the locals tied to the "living encyclopedia" of Cairo.

I adopt the category of the *commoner* from the legal language of the late Roman Empire. The Ottoman Empire extended over the former Roman Empire's eastern domains, via the Byzantine Empire, which was defeated by the Ottomans in 1453 with the conquest of Constantinople (today's Istanbul). The Ottoman Empire absorbed into its jurisprudence the logics of rule and legal systems of the empires and the lands it incorporated. Two of those principles were extraterritoriality and personal law, in which extraterritorials (*beratlis*, sojourners, factors) carried through space their effective ties with their sovereign from their place of birth, no matter how long they might reside as sojourners in domains of empire. Commoners, by contrast, were part of the local urban fabric and were subject to the local rule of law. The quality of being local, or a commoner, did not disappear with the abolition of the last vestiges of the Ottoman capitulations. To be one of the urban commoners was not merely a matter of law under the infrastructures of the semicivilized. Being local was also an ongoing, embodied practice of being local, together and in common.

Being local has multiple attributes: being from a certain city and neighborhood; living daily life in ways indigenous to Cairo; moving and interacting on the street in ways that clearly convey to others of the same status group that one is indeed local, a commoner, part of the popular urban masses. Locals have a shared intergenerational experience of place and time, on streets and in neighborhoods, experienced in common. Multiple categories, norms, honorifics, and concepts in Egyptian Arabic are linked to this notion of the local. In Egyptian Arabic, to be "local" refers to indigenous categories such as *sha'bi* (popular), *ibn al-balad* (literally, a son of the town), or *mahalli* (of the local place). Local status is communicated in public space in ways that extend beyond written or spoken language. Those who live together over generations in particular neighborhoods of urban spaces, as we learned from Sayyid 'Uways (1989), have multiple grounds for instantaneous communication.

But how, specifically, were *locals* identified and tracked by state administrations? Before establishment of the Mixed Courts in 1876, one essential division tracked in Egypt was between those who were "under the control of the authorities" (*dakhil al-hukuma*), or local, and those who were outside of authorities' control (*kharij al-hukuma*). As we have seen, later in the nineteenth century, this essential divide still obtained, but government bureaucracies tracked five subcategories of local: *ibn al-balad* for city dweller;

fallahi; ibn 'arab; barbari; ra'iya (Hanley 2017, 262). At the same time, the condition of being *local* preceded and exceeded these nineteenth-century categories of the local.

Being local also points to a much broader discursive universe in the Islamic/Arab world relating polity to place and land to identity. *Local* in Arabic implies deep affective attachment to place, home, or geography. Concepts of home and homeland, of *watan,* and of affective investment in place in the Arab/Islamic world need to be understood on their own terms (Antrim 2012), including points of intersection with and divergence from dominant Western concepts of nationality, patriotism, or nation. There are many grounds to the local.

The local is constituted in a structured pair with the extraterritorial. Take, for example, the Egyptian Arabic concept of *afrangi,* which refers to an Egyptian whose cultural practice or extraterritorial status links them to European Christians, or Franks. Another such concept is that of the *khawaga.* In Egypt, someone who could benefit from the privilege vested through the capitulations was often called a *khawaga,* a Persian/Ottoman Turkish term that could refer to a Jew or non-Coptic Christian whose family may have been local for centuries. Over time, the term came to mean any non-Muslim resident foreigner or a local who had acquired the legal rights of a foreigner. (In my own family papers from Palestine in the nineteenth century, my grandfather or his brothers and male cousins were sometimes addressed as "khawaga Elyachar.")

In Egypt of the late twentieth century, the local was also linked to the changing meaning of the native (*ahli*) and the national (*watani*). Two mass revolts, in 1882 and in 1919, "bookend the rise of an explicit Egyptian nationalism that began to propagate rights claims for Egyptians that mimicked the terms of foreign subjecthood. A collective generic sense of a local counterpart to foreign national communities began to emerge under the signs of *ahli* (native) and *watani* (national), terms that gradually acquired political force" (Hanley 2017, 258). In the nineteenth century, "Egyptian" (*misri*) identity became increasingly meaningful in a nationalist political register, even as it remained limited on a legal register (258). However, the unity of the *misri* identity "was ephemeral and rhetorical" and, as Will Hanley notes, "Actionable, appreciable rights were (and are) secured under other headings" (258).

Indices of the local also take on aesthetic expressions that are important in times of mass revolt. Semiotic resources of the "local" in Cairo are recorded in countless novels, films, poems, and chants in Egypt over the decades—nay, centuries—written, chanted, and sung in Egyptian Arabic ('*ammiya*) and recorded in the vast archive and historical storehouse of what is called, in a misleading term in English, "popular culture" (Ambrust 1996). Those collective resources are captured in phrases of Egyptian Arabic, in which the *ibn al-balad*, the *gad'a*, and the *futuwwah* are exemplars of manhood and morally upright behavior and in regular and changing use (Ismail 2006, 145; El-Messiri 1978; Elyachar 2005, 137–38, 158–59, 233fn1). The *futuwwah* were historically the defenders of the community and community value; if, over time, the word's usage had shifted to emphasize one of its meanings as thug (as during the 2011 Revolution), it could still mean a defender of collective resources and community.

The politics of the embodied practices associated with such categories of the local were again elucidated during the political upheaval of the 1970s in Egypt, when protesters on the streets of Cairo sang the song of Sheikh Imam and Fou'ad Nagm, "Houma min wa ihna min?" (Who are they and who are we?). This song clearly expresses key divisions in Egyptian society of the 1970s in terms of embodied and locomotory practice. "We" in the song are those who eat *ful* (the beans that are the staple of the poor) and travel by public-sector bus. "They" can eat meat whenever they want, drive around in expensive cars, and travel by airplane to foreign countries. Through the early 1970s, it was still possible for Sheikh Imam (1918–95), the great Egyptian popular composer and singer, to help mobilize mass protests in Cairo through reference to these embodied divides. Divisions between those who ride in private luxury cars and those who ride public-sector buses remain relevant to this day.

The divisions emerged again in 2011 in the mass revolts surrounding the January 25 Revolution. And elements of popular culture appeared in tweets, documents, and YouTube clips that helped bring Egyptians to the streets. Invoked over and over during the revolution, the *ibn al-balad*, the *futuwwah*, and the *gada'* were a communicative channel through which people were called to the street to defend their collective and national resources. These exemplars of moral behavior also point back to the market, in a word like *fahlawa*, the kind of street smarts characteristic of the *ibn al-balad*, possessed, as we have seen in chapter 2, by Mr. Amir.

A master of *fahlawa* would know with whom he is dealing and how to act in any situation, in the market as in politics. With Mr. Amir, we saw how street smarts from the market made their way into the public sector in Egypt with nationalization of the banking sector by President Nasser in the 1960s (Elyachar 2012a). The semiotic resources of the commons were absorbed into the public sector in Egypt, as well, and flourished in its sprawling, and ironically unregulated, bounds (Tignor 1998). Tacit knowledge coming from street smarts—or ways of knowing that rely on intuition, gesture, and semiosis—was both crucial for market success and a source of community value to the urban commons. This was most visible in the vast terrain of "*baladi* capitalism": the workshops in urban centers that were often completely left out of formal economic statistics (Adly 2020, 177–207; Elyachar 2005).

Egyptian craftsmen I worked with in the 1990s would talk about exchanges with colleagues and customers in a language that emphasized the preservation of long-term value in their community as opposed to short-term gain. These were claims of an alternative schema value among the "local," a reclaiming the meaning of economic worth. The term they used was *bil-gad'ana*, exchanging in the way of a brave young man who preserves community value, to give a very loose translation (Elyachar 2005). A common translation of this word in English can be "brave." But brave does not capture the references at play. The *gada'* is a young man of the popular classes. He is local, one of the commons.

What if the commons are a shared resource associated with this status of the local in a political field shaped by extraterritoriality and embodied sovereignty? Then, rather than as shared natural resources, we can begin to see the commons as a "vital infrastructure" of the urban masses (Tadiar 2022).[5] Sometimes platformed for revolt, sometimes enclosed for profit, and always with a surrounds (Simone 2022) that defies capture, these urban commons are a resource that exceeds the dominant frameworks of political economy or colonialism, and whose grounds remain to be understood.

Common Grounds and Communicative Channels

Language is one classic "shared ground" of communication. But there are other shared grounds. All kinds of semiotic events can be analyzed in relation to the grounds of communication and the channels through which that communication takes place. Shared grounds can involve status regulated by state law, including the passport(s) we hold or are denied access to; or the side of the border we were born on. But often shared grounds involve status that is not, or no longer, regulated by the state—for example, the way in which the status of being extraterritorial or local was once a juridical status in international private law.

Indices of status often make relatively public the rights and responsibilities that a person holds. In the context of embodied sovereignty, these indices can communicate crucial questions such as what rule of law a person is subject to. In empire, as a form of state, the link between indexical signs and status is often explicitly regulated (Burbank and Cooper 2011). Clothing, color, and type of cloth were the subject of both traditional and regulated practice in the Middle East as well as in India (Tarlo 1996). In the Ottoman Empire, forms of dress and use of color were overtly meaningful and regulated signs of communal and individual status (Quataert 2000). Sumptuary codes were common in the Mughal and British Empires of the Indian subcontinent. The British in India worked hard to understand and insert themselves into a semiotic politics of rank in imperial law (Cohn 1996).

Language was part of this process as well. By the nineteenth century, the semiotics of rank and power had become wrapped up in an anticolonial politics. The adoption of Western dress or the refusal to wear a fez in the Ottoman Empire was political (Campos 2010; Sharkey 2017). Attempts to speak French, shed native clothes for the garb of the European, or adopt the ways of walking and moving that such dress entailed could be marked both as a form of political betrayal in late nineteenth-century Egyptian nationalist anticolonial movements, or as a form of anti-British discursive tactic. In Cairo of the same period, using French in daily speech or wearing Western pants became politicized both as a statement of real or aspiring status and as a form of betrayal against the movement of "Egypt for the Egyptians."

Sometimes it is at least as important to look at the channel through which a sign moves as at the sign event itself (Kockelman 2010). The channels through which people move can be indexes of status distinction. Never neutral, the channel appears as a semiotic ground that allows another person to instantaneously move from perception of an index of a type of transport (a microbus versus a private luxury car, for example) to an identity. A channel is "that which translates material across space and time from one node to another." But the channel is also a locus of transmission and translation: it "takes in some kind of input (say, a sign) and puts out some kind of output (say, an interpretant)" (Kockelman 2010, 410). In regimes of distributed, embodied sovereignty of the semicivilized, as well exemplified in Cairo, channels of movement through urban space index status and power.

Nowhere was this clearer than in times of mass revolt in Cairo, where communicative channels were mobilized in multiple ways. But we do not need dramatic events to see the importance of locomotory practices as a grounds of the commons. The politics of channels appears in mundane ways all the time. In Cairo, like in many urban spaces, one can generally infer a great deal about the status of a person from the channels they use, such as the type of vehicle in which they habitually move through space: public-sector bus, microbus, car with driver, helicopter. Or from how the channel as an index is aestheticized and politicized in poems, chants, graffiti, and songs. These channels are a transgenerational, collective resource: a commons.

One day in 1995 I was sitting in a minibus on the way from northern Cairo to downtown when I saw two minibus drivers weaving in and out of traffic among a crowd of cars, minibuses, trucks, and buses. A rider owed the driver the fare of one Egyptian pound (about thirty US cents at the time). He tried to pay with an Egyptian twenty-pound note, calling to the driver to ask for change. The driver shook his head no. No one else in the minibus had, or was willing to cede, precious small bills for a twenty. So the driver called out to the driver of another minibus moving alongside, "Got change for a twenty?" That driver sent the request behind him to the rows of his passengers. Someone in the second minibus had a surfeit of small bills and passed up to the driver a folded, sweaty bunch. That driver handed the bills across the moving traffic to the driver of the first minibus, who in turn handed the second driver the crisp twenty-pound note, which he then handed back to his helpful passenger. In the first minibus, the passenger was finally able to pay his fare.

Another day that same year, I saw a thin-bodied man in a sweat-streaked but crisply ironed shirt run down a crowded street as a public-sector bus slowed down to its stop. The bus was stuffed to the steps of its always-open doors. One man pulled ahead of the crowd hoping to board the bus, soared into the air, and then alit in a spot that was not there a second ago, but which fifteen men shifted a bare millimeter apiece, eyes elsewhere, to create. This breathtaking movement was a capacity of the local alone, the local as one of the urban masses who has had no choice but to develop this capacity since an early age.

And then on another day, two small pickup trucks moved side by side down an eight-lane street of downtown Cairo. Traffic flowed at a steady pace. A man in the back of one of the trucks took a crumpled pack of cigarettes out of his pocket. He pulled out a cigarette, patted his pocket for a lighter, and found none. He gestured to a man in the other pickup moving along the street one lane away. Without a word, the second man tossed over his lighter as the traffic continued to flow at a steady pace. The first man lit up his cigarette and tossed the lighter back. Throughout, the drivers of both pickup trucks adjusted their speed to one another, even though the smokers in the back never signaled them to slow down. The smokers, like the drivers, it bears mentioning, gave no sign of knowing each other.

This scene fascinated me for years. I kept thinking about it—and many similar moments of collective virtuosity. I wondered: How do people recognize each other as members of a shared community? How, in an instant, moving down busy urban streets, do people know to whom to turn for support, succor, or a bit of change on a bus? I could not find helpful conceptual frameworks from within the bounds of political economy, anthropology, or postcolonial studies. This is where concept work from "underlying processes that underlay and shape such events" (Wolf 1999, 21) became necessary.

It is surely a leap to think of the silent interactions of people on the street in terms of a commons. And yet, practices of urban mobility in postimperial spaces can teach us a great deal about the embodied commons of the urban masses. These commons are a transgenerational collective resource such as that which Pierre Bourdieu wrote of in terms of habitus and field. This language can help consider how collective locomotory practices on the urban street are historically grounded.

History exists, Pierre Bourdieu (1993, 273) said, "in the embodied state as habitus and in the objectified state as fields." Bourdieu formed many of his theoretical insights through fieldwork in North Africa, also tenuously part of the Ottoman Empire and subject to French colonial conquest with a much longer period of control. If we think back to the politics of mobility and embodied sovereignty that I described as an essential part of governance in regions of the Ottoman Empire and its postimperial regions, Bourdieu's focus on embodiment and habitus as political field makes lots of sense.

Once we extend bodily habitus to include locomotory practices on the street, we can begin to move beyond the static, individualized formulations of habitus for which Bourdieu has been criticized (Mahmood 2005). Habitus in Bourdieu's writing is usually the site of encounter between social ideology and strategizing individuals. But practice cannot be embodied in individual selves. A meaningful anthropology of bodily practice cannot frame the body as an "executant of the goals we frame" (Taylor 1993, 50). The self and agency are embodied from the start. That embodied self, moreover, is dialogic (Taylor 1991).

Dialogic action is more than coordinated action. As paradigmatic examples of the dialogical, philosopher Charles Taylor refers to sawing a log with a two-handled saw or dancing as a couple; what he calls "cadence" and "rhythmizing" are prominent. Dialogic action is produced by and produces a different kind of agency than does individual action. According to Taylor (1993, 52), "An action is dialogical . . . when it is effected by an integrated, nonindividual agent." If we do not analyze bodily practices as simultaneously embodied and dialogic, then it is easy to fall back into an account of the "disengaged first-person-singular self" (48–49). The disengaged first-person-singular self can transmute, when critiqued, into the body as the site of a first-person-singular bodily agent. In other words, there is no individual agent of bodily practice any more than there is a first-person-singular interiorized self. But while the notion of an internal preexisting self who forms representations about the external world has been put to rest, an individualism of the body remains.

Such bodily individualism cannot account for the kind of distributed embodied practices I wrote about above. What are other resources for thinking about an embodied commons? Another anthropological tradition has looked at bodies and meaning in terms of what people do *to* their bodies, and what people do *with* their bodies. How, anthropologists like Mary Douglas asked, does the body serve as a vehicle of communication, mediating the relation of embodied self to social structure (Douglas 1996, 1999, 2002)? What are the permanent and object-like things people do to their bodies to indicate to others the social status that they inhabit and the social relations in which they are implicated (Turner 1980)? Anthropology has also looked at the things that people do with their bodies to create and evince social relations. Such is the approach of Marcel Mauss's classic "Techniques of the Body" (Mauss [1935] 1973), in which he analyzes the actions people engage in with their bodies and the way those actions are socially constructed, locally functional, and efficacious. And yet, in all this, the body is but a vehicle for expression of the self.

For sure, even if the locomotory practices on the street that I presented above tend to lie in the background of perception, they do make a great deal relatively public and unambiguous—to some. Such practices can reveal both the kind of person we are and the sort of social relations we inhabit with others. Locomotory bodily practices both evince and reproduce the social status of the persons engaging in that practice (tossing a lighter from one truck to another) and evince and reproduce social relations (between people tossing lighters or passing money). Now, to go back to my questions at the start of this chapter: How do these bodily practices (made utterly clear to everyone, and difficult to describe in language) show who is a local or a commoner? What can these analytic tools tell us about what collectives of people do with their bodies? Perhaps the answer lies in gesture.

Gesture and the Semiotic Community

Recall that tossed lighter. Remember how the patting of a hand on an empty pocket was followed by the toss of a lighter from another moving pickup truck. That interaction involved more than the two men—or four men, if we count the drivers who adjusted their speed to each other. No language was uttered. This communication was embodied and social. There were no expressed ideas or thoughts. This was gesture: the patting of an empty pocket in one pickup truck and the tossing of a lighter across the traffic by a man in another truck.

Gesture, according to George Herbert Mead, lies in "the completion or resultant of the act it initiates." The meaning of gesture becomes apparent in "the response of the second organism to it" (Mead [1934] 1967, 145). But gesture is not a matter between two individuals. Rather, it is a "triadic relation on which the existence of meaning is based." Mead also describes gesture with reference to the "peculiar character" of a great city like New York (or Cairo). The distinctive feel of each city's urban space, Mead says, rests on gesture at least as much as on its distinctive built space (145).

My goal here is not to add to theory of gesture. Rather I want to build on this theory of gesture to approach a different understanding of the commons. And this is where the notion of *semiotic community*—a concept coined by Paul Kockelman is helpful (Kockelman 2005, 261–62; Elyachar 2011).[6] A semiotic community might be a group of people in a country or a city who interact by means of semiosis or, in other words, by interpreting without conscious thought, and by reacting to signals that are meaningful to those within the community and simple noise to those without. A "semiotic community" shares a "semiotic commons" of signs and gestures (Kockelman 2005, 262), with potential for self-reflection and self-awareness. The semiotic commons can provide grounds for a community to act *for itself*, with political agency.

This gives us another way to consider different relations of body to grounds and to collective action—without assumptions of territory and territorialism. It also gives us a way to consider the embodied commons that stood up and revolted across shared regions of the Mediterranean, North Africa, and the Middle East after 2008. The embodied commons in Cairo and across the region stretched across the "data body" and physical body of all those who stood up in times of mass revolt (Sakr 2023). These regions were all part of the broader political fields of the circles of Cairo that I have been discussing—those of the Levant as a region shaped by extraterritorial commerce and of the Ottoman Empire in which extraterritoriality was a guiding principle rather than a matter of territory.

This commons extends to buildings, streets, shops, mosques, and public works of pious property in urban architecture in ways that social historians of Cairo have amply documented and that sociologist Sayyid 'Uways (1989) drew on in his studies of intertwining of the collective identity of the urban popular masses with urban space in Cairo. In his work, and in countless sayings, slogans, categories of daily speech—and aestheticized in songs, films, novels, and poetry—indigenous categories of the commoners are incorporated into a political field. The *futuwwa*, the *shabab*, the *gada'*, all defend the community and the commons (Elyachar 2005; Ambrust 2020; Ghannam 2013). Social infrastructures of the commoners enfold these infrastructures of collective life and self-defense. Such embodied commons are part of the "history that we carry on our backs" ('Uways 1989). The commons are embodied, intergenerational, and emplaced; their communicative channels convey the wishes, pleas, aspirations, and agency of the commoners, the locals. As made clear in graffiti, in writings on public-sector buses, or on small scraps of paper folded into cracks of the shrine to Saiyda Zeinab, a beloved protector of the common people of Cairo ('Uways 1989), channels of the communicative commons are real and have material effects.

Mead's distinction between gesture and significant symbol gives us a new (if old) way to think about bodily practice in Cairo and to rethink the commons. Recall, first, Mead's discussion of gesture: the way that gesture calls forth a response in the respondent is inherently social, but the first and second organisms involved need not share the same ideas or understandings about the actions taking place. With a significant symbol, the situation is different. Then the link between the two organisms is not only as a stimulus eliciting a response. A significant symbol implies both a mutual adjustment of response and, crucially, the interpretation of that response. When, within a particular social group, a gesture comes to "stand for a particular act or response, namely, the act or response which it calls forth explicitly in the individual to whom it is addressed, and implicitly in the individual who makes it," then the act or response for which the gesture stands becomes its meaning as a significant symbol (Mead [1934] 1967, 47).[7]

The distinction between gesture and significant practice matters to me neither for technical reasons nor for conceptual purity. Instead, it enables us to make sense of the local as a significant status and identity. It can help us understand how the semiotic grounds of identity and status become a channel for political protest. It gives us a way to think about how a set of practices around which identity is manifested and reproduced form the "local" as a collective of the commoners who share an embodied semiotic commons that can, in particular circumstances, become a political subject, "in and for itself." Mead wrote of gesture as being in strict opposition to a significant symbol, which implied that identity linked to gesture could not be a basis for collective action. Taylor thought differently. He wrote as if dialogic action could move swiftly and easily into political action. Writing about the 1989 Tiananmen Square protests in China, for example, Taylor (1993) referred to those political protests as an example of dialogic action.

Things are more fluid: gesture can shift to symbolic object when activated in politics or wrapped into platforms of revolt. This matters in revolt and political mobilizations. In Egypt, over time, these shared gestural resources of the semiotic commons of the popular masses of Cairo, or the urban commoners, created social infrastructures of communicative channels that rendered life more livable. This is the materiality of bodies in motion, producing signals and relations, approaching the limit of the invisible or what Jacques Rancière calls the "distribution of the perceptible" (Rancière 2010). This totality of signs, signifiers, indexes, affect, and motion can together be considered a commons. It is a precious resource and collective form of wealth from which other collective infrastructures of life and survival in the city emerge.

Uprising and Draining the Urban Commons

In the 1990s, the grounds of the semiotic commons were destroyed along with key neighborhoods in Cairo in order to build up new towers and structures that would generate more profits for their owners. Even then, one could see the constriction of the urban spaces of the local, and one can consider how the contexts in which gesture is recognized and responded to were constricted as well. This, already then, could have been seen as a form of "disinvestment—albeit unplanned—in an important if unrecognized form of urban infrastructure" (Elyachar 2011, 94). At the time, it seemed as if the spacio-temporal fabric of the embodied commons could only temporarily be disrupted. This, anyway, is what I thought in the years before 2011 and the January 25 Revolution. Sometimes this disruption appeared during Ramadan, with its global reworking of the grounds of collective movement. As I put it then: "During Ramadan, the temporal coordinates and constitution of bodily spacetime (Munn 1986) are drastically altered, which changes important aspects of the infrastructure of urban life" (Elyachar 2011,

93). In the years after 2011, the radical reorganization of bodily space-time was everywhere to be felt.

Local urban *sha'bi* culture was rooted in Cairo's long-established central neighborhoods. As these centers emptied out beginning in the 1990s, through earthquakes, neglect of infrastructure, gentrification, and forced evictions (Ghannam 2002), the embodied practices through which communication among a semiotic community was generated and replenished over the centuries began to come unhinged as well. *Sha'bi* Cairenes who were once concentrated in central neighborhoods were increasingly spread across the far-reaching city. Many others moved out of the central old neighborhoods when they returned after years spent working in the Gulf. New patterns of consumption and bodily practice adopted in the Gulf began to inscribe their traces on Cairo as these returned workers grew in number. And in the decade of urban planning as counterinsurgency following the military coup of 2013, destruction of the material infrastructure of historic neighborhoods of Cairo and the forced dispersion of residents continued this draining of the commons from within.

In 2011, when millions of Egyptians took to the streets during the January 25 Revolution to overthrow President Hosni Mubarak and to demand bread, freedom, and social justice, they succeeded in forcing Mubarak to resign—with the support of the armed forces. Yet debates immediately began about whether this was really a revolution and whether it had succeeded or failed. Those debates are not my focus here. Rather, I am interested in the communicative infrastructures that emerged from the semiotic commons and that became the platform of revolt.

Revolts are collective, willed, and condensed events. They are the outcome of many different kinds of social action and political intent. This is different from the kind of hacking into infrastructure that is a normal part of daily life in the Global South.[8] During mass revolts, communicative channels are either repurposed by groups, or they are actively broken down. Roads, phones, subways, and wires become channels through which people are persuaded to act and bodies are motivated to move. Communicative channels are also rendered visible in revolt when people are blocked from moving—when streets are blocked off or squares suffused with people—or when signals cannot be transmitted across computer or mobile phone networks. Gestural commons are platforms for revolt.

Despite the waves of privatization of public sector services that have been imposed on Egypt over the decades, the Egyptian state kept tight control over two strategic sectors of the economy: banking and telecommunications.

The state instituted a private-sector telecommunications industry only in the mid-2000s, when it granted mobile phone licenses to two private-sector firms to begin operations. Mobile phone use quickly skyrocketed. Signed contracts included a stipulation that telecom and internet services could be shut down at the authorities' discretion in case of national emergency. That stipulation was invoked during the January 25 Revolution, but the attempt to keep people from communicating, coordinating, and mobilizing through these social infrastructures of communicative channels repeatedly failed.

Egyptians quickly patched together alternative platforms for communication. These included older platforms such as landlines. Even fifty years after the 1952 Free Officers coup promised the redistribution of wealth to Egypt's poor and the remaking of the Egyptian economy, only the wealthy, well connected, or foreigners had access to infrastructure such as landlines. (Lack of landlines on the African continent, including in Egypt, made it prime terrain for the rapid and deep mobile phone penetration.) Some of those landlines were concentrated in downtown Cairo, where the greatest number of pitched battles of the revolution were fought. Landlines in apartments of activists and their sympathizers became strategic channels, sites around which people visited, gossiped, and planned.

Communicative infrastructures in Egypt were not created by Facebook: that point may be obvious now, but such a claim was seriously argued at the time by Western observers of the January 25 Revolution. That said, communicative infrastructures were crucial to the revolution. Efforts to turn off the internet and mobile phones inadvertently made visible the relational and multilayered nature of the infrastructures of communicative channels. Young activists and coders created new ways to communicate and used new technologies, which they integrated into existing communications ecologies.

An image from the revolution shows a group of young men in Tahrir Square at night, crouched over a group of mobile phones, among a tangle of extension cords wired into stores opened up by owners around Tahrir Square, under spotlights patched by activists into the state's electric grid (figure 4.1). The men are charging their mobile phones. This captures the way in which poor people in Cairo and elsewhere patch their way into infrastructure of the state on a daily basis (Simone 2004) and claim that infrastructure as a commons for themselves. This kind of slow, long-term, apparently apolitical encroachment of the poor onto land and into infrastructure (Bayat 2013) assumes overt political meaning in times of revolt.

Even as they created new modalities of communication and capacities for texting in Arabic, activists also brought out retired technologies like boat

4.1   Young men charging mobile phones during the January 25 Revolution, Tahrir Square, Cairo, 2011. Source: Christine Hauser, "New Service Lets Voices from Egypt Be Heard," *New York Times*, February 1, 2011.

phones and satellite communications. They created pirate and alternative infrastructures, patching together whatever worked to keep in contact with one another and with the outside world, demonstrating how "communities with unreliable access and connectivity to the Internet could become communities of power performing as a network, creating and demanding new forms of access and gesture" (Sakr 2023, 10).

Young people tapped into peer geek networks around the world. With mobile phones turned off, the infrastructure behind them came into view. This included communicative channels created and reproduced over time through practices of visiting, gossiping, socializing, and strategizing. This multilayered infrastructure of communicative channels jumped out from the background and became part of the action itself. This reminds us just how much infrastructure is a terrain and an object of political contestation. That much has been clear throughout this book, since the opening pages describing contests over roads and canals and other channels moving across the domains of empire. But here we see how embodied and "vital infrastructures" are also "the means for facilitating circulation and movement" essential to urban life (Tadiar 2022, 161).

Competing models of the market, socio-technologies of market life, technological innovations, engineering dilemmas, and historical layering of infrastructures in Egypt were welded together as a communicative infrastructure and a vast communicative commons. Platforms themselves became a key terrain of political contestation. Thousands of activists and hackers around the globe got involved in the January 25 Revolution via their concern about platforms and an open internet. The embodied commons of Cairo supported the possibility of dignified life for the undervalued urban masses. By this point, the embodied commons of the Egyptian masses had become a global affair.

Mass revolts create new channels for conveying meaning, for dreaming of futures and for reclaiming the past. They stand up, as a standard to be reached, and as a flag post to be taken and maybe lost. But what happens to a flagpole when the grounds on which it is staked are broken up or start to crumble? In revolutionary times, these communicative channels became a platform for revolt. In the years that followed, however, their fate became unclear. Had the grounds for the commons been smashed, bulldozed, and drained away from under the territory of a city of salt? Or would they reconstitute once again, under new conditions? This had been an open question even in the 1990s. After the decades of mass revolt, revolution, counterrevolution, and the upending of the political landscape of Egypt and the region of the Middle East and North Africa, no one really could say.

PHATIC LABOR AND
CHANNELS OF COMMERCE

By the summer of 2022, most of the old coffeehouses in downtown Cairo were gone. Essam and I sat one day at a small, rickety, round table belonging to a coffeehouse that remained open on a narrow cobblestone alley. Small groups of young people sat in clusters around similar tables set up along the street, staring at their phones or chatting. I ordered coffee: light roast, medium sugar. Essam got tea with mint. Both came in Styrofoam cups with lids. This was a lingering relic of the COVID-19 health ministry regulations enforced downtown and at other centers of the tourist trade. A few tourists walked by. We didn't stay long.

In 2011, the January 25 Revolution had been fought on some of these streets. When I met up with my friends a year later, I had been struck by its traces in their shaking hands and jumpy movements, and, more dramatically, missing eyes (the regime's security police had deliberately shot at the eyes of protesters); and further, in the regular eruption of tears for loved ones martyred on streets of Alexandria and Cairo. That winter of 2012, no one associated with the Mubarak regime, or *fulul*, had shown their face in public, certainly not in the cafes. My friends told me this as we went out and around the streets of downtown, stopping now and then for coffee or tea.

Only slowly did those *fulul* come crawling out from their hiding places at home. At first they sat in the corners of coffeehouses. Then, as the weeks went by, they moved their flimsy plastic coffeehouse chairs closer to the center, testing the waters, as it were. By the time of the military coup in July 2013, they were firmly back at the center of coffeehouse floors and public life. The coffeehouses that were still open were watched by cameras pointing down from high streetlights, posted all around downtown.

Many voices—of friends, relatives, acquaintances—had been silenced forever, shot dead during the Revolution by Mubarak thugs or run over by tanks sent by SCAF (the Supreme Council of the Armed Forces). Some acquaintances were in jail, could possibly be back in jail, or might end up there soon. Some were locked inside their homes, depressed by the course of events, unable to go outside other than to go to work and back again, much as they had gone to Tahrir and back again each day during the revolution. Some of my friends were busy with the piled-up tasks of junior faculty everywhere: classes to be taught, grades to be filed, tenure materials to be assembled, bills to be paid, children to be raised, and parents' health crises to be attended to. For a year, all this had been fit into days otherwise occupied with organizing strikes at the university, volunteering at clinics for victims of SCAF violence in Tahrir, and testifying at hearings. Others were silenced by the collapse of hope that seemed so clear a year ago. They returned to the day-to-day job of getting institutions functioning again. For some, politics had become a full-time occupation. For those in the United States and Europe, the revolution had to somehow become the means of academic reproduction: papers, conference presentations, and books. For those writing from Egypt, it often seemed impossible to finish a paper taken up, over and over, in moments wrested from other pressing tasks of the day. When each day brings a radically different reality, narrative continuity becomes hard.

Ten years later, in 2022, my friends still hadn't recovered from the physical toll of the revolution: the tear gas, the bullets, the broken limbs, the toll of urban fighting on those no longer young. The shaking hands were gone, but lots of signs remained. Some friends had passed on from one random illness or another. Others remained but, although still relatively young, were no longer able to continue. Those who could leave continued to do so. But life looked something like normal. Cars moved down the street and got stuck in traffic; people walked down the street on half-restored sidewalks; people went into stores and bought things, at least at those stores that hadn't gone out of business.

Many coffeehouses in downtown Cairo—core institutions of cultural, political, and intellectual life for centuries—were done and gone.[1] Essam and I went to visit some of them one summer day in 2022. I took a picture of him outside of the empty Nadi al-thaqafa, whose name was still visible in faded script on the window outside on the quiet small alleyway. Even the illustrious coffeehouse Ali Baba on the periphery of Tahrir Square, near the largely shuttered downtown campus of the American University in Cairo, where the great Egyptian novelist Naguib Mahfouz used to sit, was shut down and stood empty, its ghostly presence bearing witness to what had been.

After our tea and coffee in that cobblestone alley, Essam and I headed on foot back to Tahrir Square, passing acquaintances along the way. Essam exchanged greetings, handshakes, hugs, inquiries about material shared and not returned, words of concern, and chitchat about nothing much with each in turn. Every encounter these days bore the potential of further disaster too hard to hear: illness, death, and hardships of all kinds. So sorry for being out of touch, we all might say: I've withdrawn from the world, closed in on myself ('Afil ala nafsi). Everyone was in a state of qabd, contraction.

Soon, we arrived at Mounira, near the famous neighborhood of Sayyida Zeinab. Near El-Mounira Palace, a few fawanees (Ramadan lanterns) hung from the trees that still shaded and gave oxygen to these wide streets, which had been built for the French Army to move through in its short-lived conquest of Cairo. Here, the café tables spilling out onto the streets were all full, and there were flat-screen TVs hanging from the trees like kites trapped midflight. A Liverpool match was on; the Egyptian star Mo Salah was playing. Tea here was served as it should be, in glasses.

Once upon a time in Cairo, things had come to a stop on the street whenever President Nasser spoke on the radio. Today, the image of President Sisi was everywhere, on posters and in framed pictures on walls, and constantly on television screens, with his smiles and handshakes and beneficence. The struggle to survive ground on; none of his utterances stopped time or movement on the street. But the streets shut down for Mo Salah, star of Liverpool and captain of the Egyptian national team (figure 5.1).

We sat on Essam's balcony on this warm summer night, and cheers from the coffeehouses floated up to us. Traffic flowed or was stuck on the major streets of Qasr el-Aini and along all the major roads leading south from Tahrir Square to Garden City, or down Helwan Street and farther south to the new cities to which the population of Cairo that had the option to move had moved. The air was strangely fresh that evening, but I couldn't stop feeling that the ground was sinking underneath our feet. Through it all, day and night, the coffeehouses (or some of them) remained.

The coffeehouse is more than a building or a neutral shop. It is a familiar place where friends and acquaintances sit and chat, where a peaceful break to the day can be enjoyed, and where ethnographers debrief on what just

5.1 People gather at a Cairo coffeehouse to watch a Liverpool match; Egyptian soccer star Mo Salah's image is painted on the wall behind them, May 27, 2018. Source: *Telegraph* (UK).

happened in the field and take notes. When Essam and I worked together in the 1990s, the coffeehouse was where we would regroup, figure out our next moves, talk over what had happened, and watch life unfolding around us. This fit with the longstanding role of the coffeehouse as a node of commerce and communication across the region.

Coffee and coffeehouses have appeared multiple times in this book. Coffee was at the center of the letters of the Boursaly Frères in Cairo in 1920 (see figure 3.1), placing orders for hazelnuts, for sweets and tea to drink, requests that traveled from Cairo and Istanbul (or Contantinople) to Jaffa, Palestine. Coffeehouses were a waystation of communicative channels of commerce around the region and across the Ottoman Empire. And in late twentieth-century Cairo, Mr. Amir, the public sector banker described in chapter 2, deployed coffee to oil the channels of sociality flowing across his desk in the bank. Coffee and cups of hot tea were carried on a small metal tray by a young man with fleet step and elegant movements whose job consisted of exactly this.

To talk of coffee and coffeehouses anywhere, as Paul Manning (2012, 35) has put it, is to talk of talk. The coffeehouse has been associated with the rise of a public sphere in Ottoman history and historiography no less than in Europe. News of coffee came to Cairo at the beginning of the sixteenth century. As one anonymous person recorded, and as recounted by historian Cemal Kafadar (2002, 53), "The news reached us in Egypt that a drink, called *qahwa*, had spread in Yemen and was being used by Sufi shaykhs and others to help them stay awake during their devotional exercises"; early use of coffee took place in "sufi confraternities, homes, and small street stalls."

From sufi confraternities, coffee moved into commercial spheres. Merchants of coffee beans took the "entrepreneurial step" of opening a "new institution for its consumption," the coffeehouse (Kafadar 2002, 54). As would occur later in Europe, the coffeehouse became a "novel social space where distinctions of rank were ignored, social, intellectual and political information was exchanged, and various forms of entertainment took place" (Çaykent and Tarbuck 2017, 206). Political authorities feared the coffeehouse's potency as a space of conversation across rank more than they feared the beverages it served. Literature on coffee in the empire and in the West includes a whole genre of regulating, banning, and advocating for the coffeehouse. Attacks on the coffeehouse and its dangers may have faded away, but the potency of such a node where all status ranks could converge remained. The coffeehouse was a place where the duality of commerce and communication and its potential to unsettle—which I have discussed throughout this book—came into view. This was quite evident during my long-term dissertation fieldwork in Cairo back in the 1990s.

The Grand Central Coffeehouse

I conducted part of that fieldwork in a neighborhood constructed a decade earlier to house industrial and service workshops relocated from other areas of northern Cairo. When residents first arrived, the new neighborhood was still missing many things. Streetlights were few, streets were unpaved, and many workshops were without the water they needed to open for business. Workshop masters quickly organized themselves into an association to voice their concerns directly and vigorously to the government. They went on strike to force the municipality to finish the essential infrastructure for their new neighborhood and workspaces: lighting, electricity, and paved roads. Workshop masters did not strike for a coffeehouse. Yet the coffeehouse was also part of that essential infrastructure.

In workshop neighborhoods of Cairo, as in many cities and towns of the former Ottoman Empire, the coffeehouse is a place of hospitality and exchange of information along channels of commerce and communication. Providing the goods and means for a coffeehouse to survive and thrive entailed commerce and exchange across empire, from Yemen to Cairo and on to Jerusalem, to Istanbul, with tea and sugar and coffee and hazelnuts for sweets moved along well-established commercial channels. Each of these inputs to communicative production is brought together in a coffeehouse that is firmly rooted on a particular street of a particular neighborhood where customers are known, and strangers appear mediated by well-known others. I first entered coffeehouses of Cairo in the late twentieth century as a student, then as an ethnographer, and most often with friends. In popular neighborhoods where I conducted fieldwork as a graduate student, the coffeehouse was a place where deals were made, information exchanged, workers located, and opportunities pursued. The coffeehouse was a beehive of sociality, where men from workshops chatted and gossiped over instruments of conviviality: coffee, tea, and water pipes (*shisha*). Workshop masters would come to the coffeehouse to settle disputes, arrange deals, and learn about new customers or supplies from new sources, and to see if workers with skills they needed were available for hire. Workers shared information about possible jobs and gossiped about their current employers. The coffeehouse has been called an "informal institution" of the Egyptian labor market (Assaad 1993). More broadly, it is a place where channels of communication in the public economic space of workshop communities come together and become visible, like train tracks come together in Grand Central Station in New York City.

Women were never to be seen in coffeehouses in this kind of neighborhood, and yet, without their labor, nothing would have worked. I first realized how essential women were to keeping the coffeehouse going when I got to know ʿUm Muhammed, who lived above the one well-established coffeehouse in town.[2] ʿUm's furniture was simple but colorful, and the walls of her apartment were dotted with pictures of family members, framed posters of Alpine scenery, and framed surah from the Quran. Among the photos was one of ʿUm Muhammed with her husband, Abu Muhammed, at their marriage; one of the two of them with their two young children together with ʿUm's mother; and one of Muhammed, ʿUm and Abu's son, when he was young.

In one corner, a television and VCR were tucked away behind piles of videocassettes, which Abu Muhammed brought to the coffeehouse once a week for the enjoyment of children and adolescents who worked until late at night. Children came and went to and from the coffeehouse; one might carry a flat of twenty-four eggs up the stairs to the apartment while another carried down plates of sweets for the coffeehouse or hot food that Muhammed, who by then had finished his schooling, sold from the pushcart out in front of the coffeehouse.

Abu Muhammed's family had been sweets-makers for many generations in their original home in a neighborhood of central Cairo. From the
proceeds of the sweets she made, 'Um Muhammed took out money to cover
the costs of running the household, and she gave the rest to her son, Muhammed, to put toward his future marriage expenses.

Unlike many of her neighbors, 'Um Muhammed kept pretty much to
herself. She stayed out of the back-and-forth communication and exchanges
that marked neighborly relations in this community. Other women I knew
would always go to a neighbor if they needed something, but not 'Um
Muhammed. She explained, "If I needed something like sugar I would never
go to a neighbor. That wouldn't look good! If I need something, I go and
buy it. I have little to do with my neighbors, I know them from the balcony,
but we don't go into each other's houses."

'Um Muhammed moved around much less than her neighbors. She
generally went only from her apartment to her husband's coffeehouse, to
the homes of her immediate relatives, and back again. Her limited mobility may have been due in part to a slight limp. But if so, the contours
of her social world had become shaped around those limitations to quite
productive ends. Her life was oriented around her nuclear family and her
time was spent inside the home; but 'Um Muhammed could not be called
a housewife. Nor did she spend her day reproducing labor power to be sold
on the market for a wage.

As a loving wife and mother, 'Um Muhammed's affective labor was crucial to creating the possibilities for her son to become a fully social man
who could marry and head an economic enterprise and for her husband
to enjoy his reputation as a man of honor who had the resources and the
temperament to help others in their times of need. But she did more. 'Um
Muhammed was a maintenance worker on the essential infrastructure of
communicative channels. Like anywhere, control over these communicative
infrastructures did not go uncontested. Telecommunications and fintech
firms were still in their infancy. Communicative channels had not yet been
given a direct economic value on markets. This was instead fought out on
gendered grounds. It was not a direct fight most of the time.

"I don't like women's talk" (kalam as-sittat), Usta Ahmed said to me
and Essam Fawzi one day in 1994. Usta Ahmed had been a leader of the
community in the early and tumultuous days of the move to this new
neighborhood—then still in the desert—in the 1980s. He was a carpenter
whose business consisted mainly in making full bedroom furniture sets for
young couples about to start out in married life. Since the first days in the

neighborhood, he had become a leader of the workshop owners' association that had negotiated with the municipality for infrastructure after their forced move to the neighborhood.

The phrase stayed with me. I heard it any number of times from other men who owned and operated small industrial workshops (*wirash*) and who came from *sha'bi* central neighborhoods of Cairo. Men who owned microenterprises they had opened with funding from the state, development agencies, and countless NGOs voiced the same sentiment, although many of them worked in more "women-friendly" fields, like textiles. Toward the end of 1996, I was thus surprised to learn that, in his capacity as president of a local NGO, Usta Ahmed was helping to organize meetings in his neighborhood to promote women's empowerment. A few other men in the NGO were helping as well. This would only make sense to me in years to come, when I began to see how NGOs functioned as a translation device for outsiders to access the value flowing through communicative channels of the popular neighborhood.

Most of the women I knew in this neighborhood were busy with their daily pursuits, living a life apart from the male workshop world. They spent a great deal of time on housework and on provisioning their homes with food and other necessities, like women everywhere. Their neighborhood was still quite new and lacked the density of shops, homes, and people on the street characteristic of older parts of Cairo. Here were just people, apartments, coworkers, and nuclear families. Ties to places, streets, neighborhoods and shops had been torn asunder. Patterns of shopping as well as visiting had been disrupted. At that time, the destruction of popular neighborhoods around the edges of northern Cairo, close to where the president lived and worked, seemed exceptional, an injury that shocked as well as hurt. Only years later would these spotty practices of destruction for commercial gain, or to "clean up" space for the president's eye, shift to an industrial scale.

How strange it was to go out specifically to buy bread, Hanan said to me more than once in the 1990s. All her life she had just bought it on her way somewhere else. Despite such problems, she and her friends were busy and active. They would visit one another, most often in their own block of apartments but also in other parts of the neighborhood. They visited women they knew from the mosque, friends they had made through other friends, and sometimes women they had met at the greengrocer. They also maintained ties to friends and family in other parts of Cairo, and much of their week was taken up with visiting around the city, which, with its then-population of eighteen million people, took both time and effort.

There was often no obvious purpose to those visits—no goal to accomplish, no occasion to celebrate, no fixed appointment to meet. And in those years, no one had mobile phones to arrange visits in advance. A landline was a luxury available only to elites and foreigners and people with connections, and it entailed a long application process. Those were years when even a foreigner like me, living in Zamalek part of the week, would have to go to a storefront with phones for hire by the (very expensive) minute to call family in the United States.

Usta Ahmad's worries about gossip were in many ways quite simple. Many times when chatting with Essam, he had referred to affairs and flirtations. (I faded into the background during such conversations, even though I could hear what he said.) But Usta Ahmad was worried about more than the specific bits of information he wanted to keep from his wife. He wanted control over women's communicative channels. Usta Ahmed was still confident that he could keep an eye on, if not control over, the channels through which gossip flowed.

He and other men of the neighborhood kept an eye on where their wives and sisters went during the day, with whom they spent time, and with whom they would be seen in public. Usta Ahmed was certainly worried about reputation and what is usually called honor. But he was also concerned about the power of communicative channels themselves. Just like Ottoman and British functionaries concerned about subversive coffeehouse chat, Usta Ahmed wanted to keep a firm hand on this communication. He and other men in the neighborhood tried to maintain adequate roadblocks to the free flow of information in the communicative channels linking together women in a social infrastructure of urban life. But not all infrastructures were under Usta Ahmed's control. Khadija's story made that much completely clear.

Infrastructural Entrepreneurship

Khadija was a madam and hashish dealer. I never spoke to her directly. Rather, I heard her tale through Essam. I rarely heard the best gossip shared among the workshop masters, except for when they simply forgot I was there. Essam had a gift for hearing and joining in everyone's communication, including in some tales of theft and corruption and allegations of spying. Information sometimes moved in all kinds of directions, and various actors in town strove to benefit from its value, from the security officer who sometimes called me in for a conversation, to anxious husbands and market-seeking new workshop masters. Usually I heard the gossip about women. But in the case of Khadija, the story moved through Essam from her nephew and some of the other workshop masters.

Khadija's main trade was in women's bodies; but she also sold hashish to her male clients. She invested her profits in productive workshops in a neighborhood on the outskirts of another middle-class neighborhood built in the early twentieth century. Two of my informants were workshop owners whose livelihoods and social standing in their community Khadija had made possible. Her name, like the source of her investment capital in these male workshops, remained veiled. Nothing indicated that the original investor in the men's workshops had been a madam rather than a bank or an NGO.

Khadija's professional life as madam, drug dealer, and investor was at its height in the 1970s, the period of President Sadat's *infitah*, or economic opening. The word *entrepreneur* was barely heard at that time. Sadat opened up Egypt to a tidal wave of consumer goods imported from abroad. This rapidly changed the lives of those who latched onto the large or petty trade in these goods and the associated paraphernalia of the high life. The economic opening also meant the opening of the labor market and the possibility of migration for higher-paid wage labor jobs in the Gulf States, which Egyptians did in droves. Wages at home for skilled workers in the construction and craft trades shot up as well, and cash flowed freely. Business for people like Khadija took off.

As Khadija's business grew, she needed lookout boys to watch for the police. So she brought in youths (*shabab*) from the neighborhood. One of the boys she brought in was a nephew who would become my informant in the 1990s. Khadija needed to do something with her profits. She also needed to buy the silence of those who knew too much about her and could sell her out to the police. Khadija accomplished both objectives by turning her preadolescent lookout boys into fictive kin. She did for them what any mother would do for her sons. Just like 'Um Muhammed, she created material possibilities for her "sons" to become fully social men in a way that would become nearly impossible to achieve by 2020. This meant buying them workshops and homes in which they could be masters, and it meant providing them with wives. She arranged marriages for them to her relatives and the girls in her prostitution ring.

In time, Khadija controlled fourteen workshops. When those workshops were closed down in 1991 because of urban renewal projects, some were moved to a new neighborhood and gained legal status for the first time. I met Khadija's nephew in that new neighborhood. He was, by then, a man well into his forties, of full body and with a large smile; he liked to dress in black button-down shirts. He was known as a generous man. He was not always the first to comply with the letter of the law or to follow instructions from the local NGO about community development. He preferred to watch out for poor people in and around the neighborhood who needed his help.

He also worked on communicative infrastructures in a more traditional way: when women in the neighborhood had their electricity cut off because of nonpayment, he would help them reconnect the wires to bypass the cutoff.[3] He helped maintain an alternative infrastructure of garbage collection as well, by staying loyal to a young Bedouin girl whose family had been evicted from their home and who now survived by collecting and recycling garbage. He resisted pressure from the local associations to switch over to the formalized fee-based garbage collection system organized by the municipality.

He was, in short, a man of honor; he was *gada'*, a man who looked out for others in his neighborhood and who protected those who needed help. Being *gada'* also meant that he protected the collective goods and infrastructure of his community. The resources his aunt had afforded him had created the possibility for his generosity and ability to maintain community resources. Khadija had put the women's bodies she controlled to work, captured the surpluses, and invested those surpluses in workshops interlinked by kin, fictive kin, wives, secrets traded, and money transferred. Khadija translated the most physical of links into essential infrastructure for the male productive world, which her nephew helped maintain.

The channels connecting Khadija's workshops were in plain sight, once I bothered to look. They were etched out in the pattering footfall of children employed in the workshops to carry tea (if they worked for a coffeehouse) or to convey small, low-value items from one workshop to another. Their footsteps in the unpaved roads' dirt left indexical traces of the channels connecting one apparently isolated workshop with another. As Paul Kockelman (2010, 416) put it, "past movements leave indexical traces which channel future movements in iconic ways: from footprints to riverbanks, from wheel ruts to worm holes." On the unpaved streets of this workshop community of northern Cairo, this was easy to see once I paid attention.

Using "beaten tracks" as a metaphor for channels is nothing new. Pierre Bourdieu (1990) wrote of channels in a similar way when he called practical reason a matter of "beaten tracks" and "pathways that are really maintained and used" (35). In the mid-twentieth century, Pitirim Sorokin (1959) analyzed how "channels of communication" inscribe geography with social meaning, shaping the movement of commodity and cultural values. Be it a "path in the mountains, a caravan road in the desert, a highway for wagons, horses or cars; rivers, lakes and sea routes navigated by canoe, boat, or ship; railroads and routes of airplanes; lines and networks of telegraph, telephone, radio; such are the main channels through which the value-objects move, travel, and spread . . . from place to place, man to man, group to group, in social space" (554).

In classic communications theory of the mid-twentieth century, a channel refers to the medium used to convey information or to transmit a signal of some kind to a receiver (Shannon 1948). C. E. Shannon's classic communication theory emerged in a world of physical telephone lines and epic efforts of communications companies such as the Eastern Telegraph Company to lay underwater telegraph lines between strategic nodes of the British Empire, say from Suez to India. In a context of physical proximity or of stable and well-maintained roads, ongoing contact allowed for the creation of stable communicative channels.

Later, both engineers and social theorists showed that channels could rest on social convention as much as on a specific, one-to-one physical or psychological connection (Kockelman 2010). A channel, then, can be understood as that which relates a signer to an interpreter such that signs of all kinds (and, crucially, not just language) expressed by the former may be immediately (even if not consciously) interpreted by the latter (Kockelman 2010). Understood in this way, communicative channels can be analyzed as a collective resource for all kinds of semiotic communication in addition to language itself (Elyachar 2010; Kockelman 2010).

I have previously shown how these communicative channels act as a semiotic commons for the popular urban masses, as part of what I have referred to as "embodied infrastructure." But as a relatively stable outcome of human practices, we can also think of sets of these communicative channels as infrastructure. A semiotic commons, in other words, can also function as infrastructure. This statement might seem too metaphorical were it not for the simple existence of countless projects to build all kinds of "thinking infrastructures" (Bowker et al. 2019) on top of preexisting platforms of social infrastructures.

Khadija's labor might seem to be the opposite of 'Um Muhammed's. 'Um Muhammed was the consummate family woman, whereas Khadija was a hashish dealer and madam. But they had a great deal in common. Both women produced and maintained sets of communicative channels in the male economic space of the workshop. 'Um Muhammed did so via her husband and son in the coffeehouse. Khadija did so by establishing a set of new workshops interlinked through fictive kinship and run by men who helped maintain the other commons of their community. Their contributions however went beyond the unpaid reproduction of male labor-power, or the ties of kinship, or the employment of boy-workers in innovative fashion.

These two women were infrastructural entrepreneurs. The value generated by the infrastructures that Khadija and 'Um Muhammed built and maintained, however, would be captured by others. This might not have posed a problem for either: both were concerned with transmitting value forward—to their sons and fictive kin—to ensure survival of their children, their kin, and their communities in a way that would become almost impossible to achieve just thirty years later.

Unlike the pathways referred to by Bourdieu in his writing about practical reason or the channels modeled by Shannon for information systems, the channels Khadija helped construct left no obvious marks on the ground or algorithms for engineers to reproduce. Yet, traces of these channels might have been documented in the "women's talk" of which Usta Ahmed was so leery. But until new actors appeared who were interested in injecting finance into existing channels of commerce and communication in Egypt and who took an interest in mapping out those channels, they remained an invisible infrastructure in the political economy of Cairo. Then, the importance of connectivity and channels became visible once again. This revived an old tradition of considering political economy—or "commercial society," in language of the eighteenth century—as wrapped up in flows of global commerce, rather than based on productive labor exerted on land or in an industrial factory. To understand this shift, the first step is to consider how sitting around and chatting in a coffeehouse, or at a neighbor's home, could have anything to do with political economy at all.

The Political Economy of Chat

Clues about the relation of chatting to political economy can be found in an early essay on "primitive language" from 1923, written by the Polish Austro-Hungarian anthropologist Bronisław Malinowski. Early anthropology and theories of exchange among so-called "primitives" (as opposed to "barbarians") that emerged at the end of the Great War to End All Wars shared many concerns about rational behavior and the meaning of the civilized versus the primitive. In the process, while musing about peoples he considered primitive, Malinowski had important insights about the workings of market societies and economic life (Elyachar 2020; Hann and Hart 2011).

In his essay "The Problem of Meaning in Primitive Languages," Malinowski ([1923] 1936, 464) writes that when a "number of people aimlessly gossip together," a situation is created that consists "in just this atmosphere of sociability and in the fact of the personal communion of these people." "Each utterance is an act," he continues, that serves the aim of "binding hearer to speaker by a tie of some social sentiment or other . . . language appears to us in this function not as an instrument of reflection but as a mode of action" (464). Malinowski called this act "phatic communion." With this concept, Malinowski shows how language such as gossip and chatting can be a means of establishing ties for their own sake rather than for conveying information in particular.

As in most early anthropological statements about the "primitive," these insights have more to do with the latent nature of market society or with a critique of dominant theories in the heart of the "civilized" world than with the practices of indigenous peoples. Malinowski's data for his brief discussion of phatic communion concerns his informants' engagement in face-to-face conversation in a small island community that he labeled as primitive. Crucial is what comes next. At stake in conversation, Malinowski makes clear, is not "just talk." Conversation is rarely only about the stylized transmission of information, abstracted from all sorts of entanglements.

Linguist Roman Jakobson ([1960] 1990) developed Malinowski's concept of phatic communion and made "the phatic function" one of the six functions of the speech event. In the process, he showed how channels exist wherever physical proximity and psychological contact between a speaker and addressee allow them to send and receive messages. Channels became part of his overall theory of speech events. The expressive function of the speech event focuses on the speaker; the conative focuses on the addressee; the metalinguistic focuses on code; the poetic focuses on sign; the referential focuses on the object, or referent, of a speech act; and the phatic function focuses on the channel through which speech is conveyed. Despite the wide range of these functions, linguistics has generally focused on the referential function of the speech event alone (Kockelman 2005, 260–61). But phatic communion can help us think through many theoretical dilemmas confronting critical social analysis.

Jakobson's was but an offhand comment. The phatic function was not central to his theorizing, which focused more on the referential function of the speech act (Kockelman 2005). He did not stray far from Malinowski's concept of phatic communion, which rests on an assumption of two people standing in close physical proximity and with some kind of prior psychological contact. It is easy to link this kind of model of phatic communion to the geographic base of Malinowski's theorizing in the Trobriand Islands. But how might a notion of phatic communion, or the phatic function, translate to Cairo, a megacity with more than twenty million residents as of 2023? Or to channels in cyberspace? How do these kinds of channels relate to the many ways in which passages through domains—rather than conquest of homogeneous territory—characterize the exercise of power over space? This is relevant for a world in which the struggle for control over channels and passages increasingly shapes geopolitics more than struggles to control territory do.

Members of a semiotic community maintain and reproduce their commons and communicative channels, we have seen, without explicit intention or decision. Phatic communion refers to the forging of contact and channels through language. Those moments of communion take kinetic expression in locomotory practices in urban space. In Neferti Tadiar's (2022, 161) framing, these are "vital infrastructures," composed of "distributed, coordinated, rhythmic human capacities and social routines that have to be continually generated, repeatedly performed, endlessly negotiated and modified (in a word, improvised) and occasionally, often periodically, revamped." As a concept, "embodied infrastructures" can miss the materiality of the traces such practices leave behind. But viewed at a distance from the embodied practices that create and reproduce them, communicative channels clearly have their own vitality and materiality.

Channels of these vital infrastructures are scalable. That is more evident when thinking from Cairo than from the Trobriand Islands. Communicative channels cross state borders in conditions of ongoing circular migration, whether from the Philippines to the United States, or from Egypt to the Gulf States, as in the 1970s and 1980s, when millions of Egyptian men traveled as sojourners to labor in and to build up the human and material infrastructures of these still new and underdeveloped nations. (At the time, it was impossible to imagine that the wealth and capital these laborers helped generate in the Gulf States would provide others the resources to buy up much of the strategic wealth of Egypt under the reign of President Sisi in the 2010s and 2020s.)

Communicative channels rooted in Cairo's popular neighborhoods extended into the Gulf region together with migrant laborers who lived there for years, if without the rights granted to sojourners from the Christian

West in the Ottoman Empire, before returning home. On the way, those Egyptian workers in the Gulf left "beaten tracks" and "pathways that are really maintained and used" (Bourdieu 1990, 35), which became channels for the homeward flow of money, emotion, and new kinds of consumer goods. Following Sorokin (1959, 554), these "channels of communication" inscribed geography with social meaning, shaping the movement of commodities, cultural values, and finance.

Such "pathways maintained and used" by migrants and their families to transfer money, emotion, and news materialized in forms as simple as a neighbor carrying an envelope, a friend carrying a cassette, or a fellow worshipper carrying cash. Some of those channels became formalized in institutions like the Islamic investment companies that funneled Egyptian migrants' savings home to their families during this period and grew to play a key role in the political economy of the Middle East in the 1980s, until they were crushed by the Egyptian state when they were perceived to be a threat to it. Such cross-border flows of money along the pathways of circular migrant labor to the Gulf funded new housing and entire regions of Cairo and other cities of Egypt that came to be known as "informal" or "unorganized" regions, built on land zoned for agriculture or on "empty land" that, under Ottoman rule, was de facto the "property" of the state.

Linking communicative channels to political economy is nothing new. And there is nothing particularly "Ottoman" or "Oriental" about this entangling of commerce and communication, as we have seen throughout this book. In the West, early modern definitions of commerce designated it as a way of being and selling together and as a form of liberty. This meaning was extended by Hugo Grotius in the seventeenth century to mean that the right to commerce was part of natural law. No sovereign possessed the oceans through which commerce must flow to bring one part of the world into communication with another, albeit through violent conquest. The oceans should be like a commons, or a channel for communication for all.

The channels of commerce moved conceptually from oceans to land in the early nineteenth century, when James Maitland, Earl of Lauderdale, used the concept to critique a growing "scourge of accumulation." "Capital floats," he wrote, "in all the variety of channels to which extended commerce destines it" (Maitland 1804, 212). The language of channels appears in late-nineteenth-century writings of administrators and military engineers of the Ottoman Public Debt Administration, who conducted surveys, built roads, and worried about maintaining better communicative channels by which to move troops to India, if needed, and improve flows of commerce to markets (Elyachar 2022).[4] Analytic focus on channels was largely displaced in the mid-nineteenth century with the rise of political economy and its own conceptual frameworks organized around a labor theory of value and the primacy of accumulation.

This intertangled nature of commerce and communication is even more prominent and influential in German. In a German-English dictionary of 1859, to begin with, the word *Verkehr* is translated as "intercourse, commerce, traffic, trade" (Thieme 1859, 2:495, as cited in Shell 2019, 15). It can refer to something as broad as "all the forms of relations of work, exchange, property, consciousness, as well as relationships among individuals, groups, nations, and states" (Mattelart 1996, 101, as cited in Jones 2018, 11). By the end of the nineteenth century *Verkehr* was "used by the strategists of the Kaiser's empire as a synonym for what the French called 'communication(s)' and we might call infrastructure" (Jones 2018, 11). Writing in German, Marx used the term *Verkehr* to refer to the sense of "commerce" we are familiar with by now, or employed it in the sense of "social relations" (as in *Verkehrsform* and *Verkehrshältnisse*), which become, in most discussions of Marxism, the "relations of production." Theorist Michel Serres thought that the Marxists were too concerned with production and that the problems of communication would take center stage (Serres 2003, 230). For Serres ([1980] 2007), the key figure for analyzing communication was Greek: Hermes, the god of commerce.

By the 1990s, the communicative channels' importance was taken up with a vengeance when adventurers roamed the world to try, once again, to civilize the semicivilized. This time, the adventurers carried loans and grants and NGOs' best-practices guidelines. In Egypt, and in many countries around the world, tens of millions of dollars at a time were injected into "the informal economy." This happened through a replica of arrangements of dividual sovereignty from the mid-nineteenth century, when multiple institutions and sovereigns were involved in the governance of Egypt and other parts of the Ottoman Empire. Only this time, it was the NGOs, banks, state institutions, and international development organizations that got involved with funding and lighting up these preexisting communicative channels created through what I have called phatic labor, a concept that brings together Malinowski and Marx (Elyachar 2010).

Communicative channels produced through phatic labor can transmit not only language but also all kinds of semiotic meaning and economic value. The period of "empowerment finance" (Elyachar 2002, 2005) in the 1990s made the communicative channels created through phatic labor visible as a social infrastructure on which other projects oriented around the pursuit of profit could be constructed. By the turn of the twenty-first century, these communicative channels were being studied and mobilized in new contexts. Malinowski's model of the kula, a Melanesian system of symbolic exchange, was adopted as a business model by Vodafone, and talk of the kula was recognized as important in "viral marketing" (Knight 2004). It was also drawn on as an organizing concept for alternative economic projects (Narotzky 2008). Perhaps it was just a matter of time until other aspects of Malinowski's research, such as his concept of "phatic communion," would also be mobilized for economic projects.

Communicative channels were the infrastructure of numerous projects in what came to be called the "payments space" (Maurer 2012). Across most of the African continent, colonizers had neglected communications infrastructures other than what was needed to export wealth and maintain power. Few Africans had telephones. So, all kinds of private-sector actors moved in to supply mobile phones and their associated communications and payments technologies to millions of poor people and members of their extended families overseas. By 2020, fintech was a dynamic and growing part of the economy and capital markets in Africa and around the world (Roitman 2020). The notion of "payments space" was native to this world of corporate, philanthropic, and academic actors.

Systems constructed in payments space transformed channels created by commoners who had migrated overseas and sent money home, and who had developed ingenious ways of transferring this money as well as information and affect, all of which anthropologists and development organizations studied and supported as the informal economy. Whereas microfinance focused on supporting the individual actors within that informal economy, this new systemic focus placed much greater emphasis on uncovering, developing, and mobilizing the infrastructures of communicative channels built by the "bottom of the pyramid," the world's poorest—on building upon them to create new kinds of financial and information services for profit.

Phatic labor produced outcomes that can be compared with laying cables or fiber-optic lines or building railroads. It allowed for goods and use values of various kinds to flow, even if quite different use values than those analyzed in most approaches to political economy. The outcomes of phatic labor—communicative channels—allowed for the flow of reputation, information, and emotion. They allowed for the transfer of finance and the creation of new kinds of equivalences. They became a necessary, if not a sufficient, condition for the realization of other, more classic forms of economic value. Increasingly, they were recognized as having use value, and intrinsic value, in themselves. But making those channels recognizable in the creation of economic value, and as economically valuable in themselves, did not happen on its own. The story of my informant Huda, one of many global players in this process, is instructive in this context.

Infrastructures of the Phatic Pimp

Huda came of age in quite a different moment than Khadija and Um Muhammed, who had both been children during Gamal Abdul Nasser's rule, a time of solidarity across the postcolonial Global South and of development models based on national economy and public-sector development. Huda came of age in the late 1980s, when Hosni Mubarak was president. The public sector created under Nasser was being privatized in fits and starts, and disinvestment in state-owned infrastructure had become the norm. Huda grew up in public-sector housing built by Nasser and named after him; she graduated from high school and went to work as a secretary.

Her brother was a car mechanic who had run his business on the street until he was shut down by the municipality, after which he relocated. The municipality gave him a workshop in a new neighborhood, along with an apartment, which he subsequently sold to his sister. Huda was at home among the workshop families, given that her brother was a workshop master and she was from a *baladi* family. But because of her employment as a consultant's secretary, she felt herself to be not only more educated but also better than her neighbors.

Huda was the only woman I knew in the neighborhood who held down a regular waged job. She commuted to work every day, catching a ride with one of the masters she knew through her brother or waiting on the dusty road half a mile from her apartment for the minibus to stop on its way to points south, which, not long ago, had lain on the northern reaches of Cairo. Her employer had given years of his life to leftist oppositional politics and, like others who had paid a high price for their politics with their bodies and years spent in jail, had made a new life for himself in the 1990s on the fringes of the development world. He was one of many former activists to work in the consultancies and NGOs they had created to catch the wave of NGO development funding. All this was in line with the old Egyptian "family ethos" of watching out for the future of the next generation (Wikan 1996) and of providing children with the necessities of middle-class life, which were increasingly monetized by the 1980s.

Huda sometimes worked from home so she could stay with the children while her husband was at work. She would bring home the manual typewriter from her workplace on the weekends or when her young son was sick. Part of her job was to supply her boss with local color about *baladi* women she knew for his various funding-agency reports. During the hot summer months, she sometimes left the doors and windows of her apartment open. When a troublesome male neighbor chose to understand the open windows as a signal that Huda was open to an approach, rather than as a concession to the heat, he walked in to test his interpretation. Huda kicked him out. Her brother and other male relatives immediately confronted the man to make clear to him and others that she was not, as she told me later, just from a family of "some clerk" (*muwazaf*), all alone in the world with no one to defend her and her reputation.

Toward the end of that period of my fieldwork, Huda began to search for women whom her boss could call "empowered" in his reports to development funders. Like Usta Ahmed, she took advantage of the ethnographers in her midst to seek out more names than she would have been able to uncover on her own. Who did we know in the neighborhood? Where were these women? Could we introduce her to any of our informants? The information she and Usta Ahmed gathered and the reports they helped write were then incorporated into other reports. Huda was part of a vast global process in which individual agents and agencies mapped out apparently random data about who knew whom, who helped whom, who trusted whom, and who funded whom. This activity might seem to be about social networks once again, but something else was underway.

The phatic labor of Huda's neighbors and forebears had created countless nodes of connectivity within the semiotic community of Cairo. Huda facilitated the creation of new kinds of nodes in those channels, incorporating different kinds of receivers for which signs had to be translated and interpreted. Inserting such nodes into Cairo's existing communicative channels subtly altered social infrastructures. The process of uncovering channels and translating their meaning to new kinds of actors was essential in making legible and accessible to outsiders social infrastructures of communication that had been built up over the centuries by the phatic labor of Huda's forebears.

Here it is useful to think for a moment back to Khadija and the men of honor she helped create. As Malinowski showed long ago, honor, fame, and value are created and reproduced through the flow of communicative resources in space-time (Malinowski [1922] 1999; Munn 1986). Fame, reputation, information, and value can be rerouted to different end points and undergo material and symbolic transformations in the process. Huda's phatic labor helped effect such transformations. Signals moving through channels that had been instantaneously understood by members of a semiotic community in Cairo were now entering into new chains of meaning and equivalencies. Names, reputation, and gossip acquired not only use value but also other kinds of value. In the process, channels along which signals and signs could travel were themselves being reshaped as a particular kind of sign—as a commodity (cf. Kockelman 2006).

If Khadija was a procurer of women's bodies, Huda might be thought of as a phatic pimp. Khadija prostituted women's bodies. Huda, by contrast, prostituted signs of women's bodies and outcomes of phatic labor. She was the trickster figure—Hermes, the god of commerce—who could move through all worlds. She helped generate and transmit signs of women to new actors in an emerging political economy in which communicative pathways would have strategic economic value. The channels for which she provided nodes of access were empowered by Huda's transformative labor. Through practices her peers related to as just hanging out and visiting, Huda made subtle but crucial shifts in the infrastructure of Cairo's communicative channels. She applied some of the lessons she learned through her experimental labor to her own family ethos and opened an NGO of her own in 2005, becoming wealthy enough to purchase apartments for her daughter, nieces, and nephews ten years later.

Usta Ahmed, 'Um Muhammed, Khadija, and Huda present very local, very Cairene cases of the infrastructural work of phatic labor. These infrastructures are not themselves particular to Egypt, despite their importance in restructuring Egypt over the last several decades. At the turn of the twentieth-first century, ethnographers, market specialists, NGO workers, ecotourism specialists, lawyers in intellectual property rights among indigenous peoples, and others were finding new forms of economic value in meaning, culture, and practices. This was a vast process of revealing economic value where something quite different was understood to exist before as inalienable possessions: culture, sociality, and wasting time.

Forms of meaningful action understood as "culture" or "conventions" came into a different kind of relation with power; new kinds of "relation among relations" (Kockelman 2006) were created. In the process, communicative channels came to be visible—and then accessible—to new kinds of outsiders, via new kinds of relations mediated by money, debt, empowerment, and

NGOs. The channels themselves—not just the money or value that flowed through them—acquired economic value. They were integrated into platforms for economic projects in telecom, payment systems, and more. They became part of thinking infrastructures in organizations, companies, NGOs, and community projects.

First, microfinance and telecom in Egypt built on social infrastructures, starting in the NGO sector and moving into the private sector. Disclosed and made visible to outside actors and agents in the 1990s, social infrastructures of communicative channels became a strategic interest of corporations. Channels reverted to the world of commerce from whence they had come in the sixteenth and seventeenth centuries—in the early years of warring ships of corporate sovereigns fighting it out on the oceans—which had provoked Grotius to claim those channels for commerce as a common for all European sovereigns. Now, these channels were getting incorporated into different kinds of corporate ventures.

This was a rapidly changing terrain. First was a wave of NGO microenterprise and informal economy projects to empower poor people through enterprise (Elyachar 2005). Next came a "bottom of the pyramid" approach to corporate strategic planning that attempted to access and profit from the know-how, resources, and social infrastructures of poor people (Prahalad 2010, 5; Elyachar 2012c, 112). Bottom-of-the-pyramid approaches sidestepped development and the critique of development altogether.

The seventeenth century created new infrastructures of commerce across the oceans and seas, led by the new company form and corporate sovereigns pursuing bloody commerce around the globe. The long nineteenth century, in turn, was "known as a time of large-scale material infrastructure investments in roads, rails, and wires stretching across Europe and its Empires as well as in the United States" (Bowker et al. 2019, 1); the early twenty-first century was notable for investments in thinking infrastructures. Social infrastructures created by poor people in urban centers were once relegated to "culture" or maybe "traditional social practices." Such things had nothing to do with economy. Until, once again, they did. In the first half of the 1990s, the lifeworlds of common people were financialized and rendered visible as channels and regular streams of data. By the early 2000s, such low-tech efforts were superfluous.

By 2020, everything was lit up for easy tracing and tracking. Corporations and large bureaucracies across lines of private and public sectors invested in following the channels, tracking these flows in real time, and rendering relations and connectivity explicit in emblems, data sets, and ongoing technology development (Power 2019, 118). Tracing out relations was no longer a practice of the poor, of the disenfranchised, or of the NGO micro-loan worker making out on a piece of paper who knew whom, who owed what to whom, and who was related to whom, as countless NGO workers and bank employees did in countless places around the world in the 1990s.

The largest corporations in the world were tracing and monetizing these channels. Tracing and then packaging and selling the traces of that which used to be considered the real economy—producing, distributing, and consuming stuff—thus become the "pipes and channels through which value flows and is reformatted by thinking infrastructures, with their capacities to influence thought and action" (Bowker et al. 2019, 4). Traceability infrastructures are associated with new technologies, but they are also "as old as record keeping and writing itself" (Power 2019, 121). They are also as old as the channels of gossip and relationality built into a workshop neighborhood (Elyachar 2010).

Empowerment finance had begun the story (Elyachar 2010). Tracing then moved into spheres of circulation, speeding up turnover time across space and time and flowing back into production itself, where it had in many ways all begun with logistics (Cowen 2014). These thinking infrastructures for governance and for profit were built on relationality rendered visible, in which relations and nodes of connectivity among channels have been traced out via financialization or NGOification of social relations, friendship, and mutual aid (Elyachar, 2010, 2014; Federici 2014; Bowker et al. 2019). Relations, relationality, and the stable channels they created and reproduced in social infrastructures had been financialized, platformized, and politicized (Srnicek 2016; Bowker et al. 2019).

In Cairo of 2022, the grounds for the embodied commons' survival were collapsing through direct attacks and the daily chipping away of value through inflation and generalized revaluation schemas. The social infrastructures to which those commons were linked were repeatedly revalued as platforms for profit and revolt. It was clear by now that they were essential to the most modern kinds of telecommunications, payments, fintech, and data-mining initiatives of twenty-first-century profit-seeking, where they seemed likely to last longer than they did as platforms of revolt in the January 25 Revolution of 2011. They were essential as well to the endless surveillance of life in Cairo and so many other places in the world, in emerging interfaces of profit-making, surveillance, and thinking infrastructures. But even in times of contraction of possibilities, the commons of the semicivilized would not be fully enclosed.

ACROSS THE *BARZAKH*

"The workers want resignation of the management!" called out workers occupying the offices of an oil infrastructure firm on a side street in southern Cairo as I passed by one day in 2012. Along the low brick walls of a telecom company that owned much of the city's communicative infrastructures was splashed graffiti of the Ultras, one of Egypt's football support clubs, whose members had taken to the streets to support the revolution and paid a high price with their lives. A sign warning the public to stay away merged into drawings of a fist raised high, the image of a martyred young revolutionary, and the phrase "Long live the revolution."

Strikes and takeovers were still taking place everywhere, in the universities, in factories, and on the streets. We drove through New Maʿadi, past the offices of Telecom Egypt, the sandy expanse of land from which their massive dishes sprouted, and then down Palestine Street, past the offices of GUPCO (Gulf of Suez Petroleum Company, a joint venture between British Petroleum and the Egyptian General Petroleum Company). Far less crowded here, these streets were also marked by revolution. As we approached GUPCO's entrance, chants rang out. We came to a halt on a smoothly paved street, grass and small trees growing behind brick walls in front of neat five-story family buildings. "The people want the downfall of the regime! The workers want resignation of the management!" It was the end of the workday.

Sounds of the street faded away as I entered my friend Lamia's house. Rays of the late afternoon sun turned a deep yellow as they shone through the dusty, neglected windows. A doctor, Lamia had saved many lives and served many Egyptians, rich and poor; her life was now coming to an end from a metastasized cancer. Here, aftermaths of revolution appeared differently: in the medicine she needed that had disappeared from the pharmacies, in her fear of entering the hospital, and in all the tubes of joint inflammation cream she handed to me in a small plastic bag one day from her sickbed. I laughed at her excess, as she told me about the multiple treks of her *bawab* (doorman) to pharmacies all over southern Cairo, in search of stock. All too soon, I came to appreciate her foresight: the German-Egyptian factory that produced the medicine had shut down in Cairo, perhaps for good. When I passed GUPCO on the way to downtown, the workers had gone all home.

"Resistance everywhere" was a common slogan in Egypt and around the world in the decade after the 2008 financial crisis. It could be found in graffiti, posters, hashtags, and writings. It often appeared with that image of the upraised fist, sometimes attached to the arm and torso of a young man, head thrown back. The raised fist has been an iconic symbol of resistance since the nineteenth century. It points up in the air, rather than down toward the ground, like a fist wielding tools in nineteenth-century images of the productive working man in socialist working-class movements of the time.

The raised fist was a key image of Black resistance movements in the twentieth- and early twenty-first centuries. If the raised fist of resistance points upward, mass revolt made visible much that was down below: infrastructure (Elyachar 2022).[1] Mass revolts do more than express resistance to diffuse forms of power. They do more than take the state—and then maybe lose it. They create channels for new claims to accountability, memories of the past, and pathways to the future. They upend the grounds of once-obvious realities and the sensation of the ground on which we stand. Ten years after the revolution and coup, it had become urgent to rethink the assumption of stable ground on which the resisting subject—and the exploited extracting productive worker—stood.

In the background of images of resisting subjects and productive male factory workers lay stable ground. But the ground had come unhinged—in both a semiotic sense of that which brings together a sign with its meaning and in a literal sense of the earth under our feet. In the aftermath of a decade-long revolutionary and counterrevolutionary situation of which the Middle East was an epicenter (El-Ghobashy 2021), and amid rapidly changing regional geopolitics and accelerating global climate change, no one imagined there would be a return to "normal," or normal as it had been lived before 2011. At any moment, a car, a person, a community, a country could be flipped around, unhinged, forced to regain footing.

This precarity became clear to me one day in 2017, when I was returning from northern Cairo where I had attended a friend's dissertation defense. The degree-granting institution was just one in a growing industry of Gulf-owned educational institutions that hired Egyptian academics caught in the growing ranks of the "in between" (Simone and Rao 2012, 4; see also Abaza 2020, 10), neither middle class nor poor, yet unable to get through a day, let alone a month, on their official salary. None of us at that time knew how quickly that "in between" would collapse over the coming years of spiraling inflation.

The event was held in the Saudi-owned luxury mall Citystars in Nasr City, not far from Madinat al-Hirifyeen, which had been built by the municipality of Cairo to house displaced workshops; it was where I had spent so much time in the 1990s, an area around which the state-owned desert land had since filled up with buildings both occupied and empty, in various stages of legality and recognition (Elyachar 2005). Citystars itself, owned by Citystars Properties under the proprietorship of chair and Saudi billionaire Abdulrahman Ali Al-Turki, was a different kind of real estate. It was constructed with capital accumulated from oil drilled in Saudi Arabia and then deployed in Egypt to buy up strategic companies of Egypt's former national economy and to invest in high-value real estate (Hanieh 2018). Citystars Properties was one of the Saudi real estate companies facilitating the proclaimed "opening up of Egypt's property sector to the international market" with an aspirational "boom in real estate" across the country, including the creation of the New Administrative Capital of Cairo.[2] Citystars heralded the remaking of real estate in Egypt and the revaluation of homes, land, and property its financialized entry into the market entailed. But I did not know that at the time.

After the defense, I headed downtown in a taxi. The driver's mobile phone, its GPS lit up, dangled from the mirror. "The advantage of GPS," the driver explained, "is that it shows you where the traffic is so you can go around it." But with everyone using their GPS, any benefit was canceled out. Nearing Tahrir Square, traffic opened up, and we moved faster toward Kasr el Nil bridge. Suddenly, a car spun out and swirled around to land at a 180-degree angle from where it had started. The car's driver looked stunned. No one hit him; everyone waited for him to get his bearings, readjust, and set out on the road again.

"You see this kind of thing all the time these days," laughed my driver. We traded stories from the United States and Egypt of people driving off the road, killing themselves or others, following their GPS. I saw a similar scene the next day (and then again days after that): a small black Fiat taxi spinning out 180 degrees, while the driver sat stunned. These near accidents seemed of a piece with the general situation and the complete unsettling of the ground itself that events of the past few years had entailed.

How can we think of the movement of bodies through space without the assumption of stable ground or territory on which they stand? That is a question I have been addressing throughout this book. I have shown how bodies appear, moving between two seas, along routes and across realms, in patterns that defy the assumptions of the "grounds" of territory. My material has demanded that attention be paid instead to the channels through which commerce—in its dual meanings of communication and exchange of goods for money across space—takes place and the people who create, construct, and move through, and with, them. Indeed, there are ample, and fruitful, pathways to think about the relation of bodies, mobility, and politics beyond assumptions of sovereign territorial fixity or the impasse of the male body standing upright, fist raised to the sky, with feet planted on solid and passive ground.

Unsettled—and unsettling—times invite us to move beyond the assumptions of stable ground on which the productive laborer stands. Unsettled times invite us to find a different conceptual language for rethinking collective agency and ground in the long aftermath of mass revolt, for considering different groundings of collective movement in times of endless uncertainty, and for expanding our understandings of the relation between peoplehood, territory, and sovereignty. I propose now that we turn to the idea of proprioception—conscious awareness of the body in space or of the parts of the body of one another—together with a concept from the holy Quran as interpreted by Ibn 'Arabi (1165–1240): the *barzakh*, or estuary.

Barzakh and the Space Between

For politics to appear, wrote curator Tarek Abou El Fetouh in 2015 for an art exhibition about the 2011 protests across North Africa and the Arab world, "the plural collective body has to appear and occupy spaces. Each participant in these protests offers his or her individual body, which then exists between two forms, the individual and collective, within conditions that are enigmatic." In times of revolt, "the body changes its condition into an ambiguous state that can be termed *barzakh*" (Bailey 2016). Abou El Fetouh draws on an interpretation of surah 25.53 of the holy Quran by Ibn ʿArabi (1165–1240), often considered the greatest Islamic philosopher.[3] Translation of this surah has been debated, often centering on the translation of *barzakh*, an Arabic word from the Persian that can mean barrier, obstacle, hindrance, isthmus, or the place between heaven and hell, similar to purgatory.[4]

Sometimes *barzakh* is interpreted as an estuary, a place where saltwater turns to sweet; sometimes *barzakh* refers to that which is ambiguous and un-bridgeable, even while constituting a united space between these two. Read as "isthmus," *barzakh* plays an important role in plant and animal geography. It offers "a path for the migration of plants and animals . . . a channel between the two land masses they connect." In the body, the isthmus can be a "narrow space of connection between two organ parts or structures."[5] This perspective was important in the writings of the French utopian socialist Henri de Saint-Simon. It was operationalized by the Saint-Simonian engineer Barthélemy-Prosper Enfantin, who wrote in poetic prose about carving passages through the Isthmus of Suez and is credited as one of the founders of the Suez Company. The canal would bring together East and West, male and female, in a great unity of the circulation of finance, industry, and wealth. As we have seen, it would also embroil Egypt in debt relations that it still lives with today, even as the holders of that debt shifted and expanded.

None of the Frenchmen involved cited Ibn ʿArabi, but they might well have. In the writings of Ibn ʿArabi, *barzakh* can "designate anything that simultaneously divides and brings together two things, without itself having two sides, like the 'line' that separates sunlight and shade" (Chittick 2020). *Barzakh* becomes a way to discuss "the activity or actor that differentiates between things and that, paradoxically, then provides the context of their unity" (Bashier 2004), much like Abou El Fetouh proposed about the individual protestor in times of mass revolt.[6] *Barzakh* is a productive concept for unsettling the grounds of territorial sovereignty and the relation of body to ground. In such conditions, cultivating capacities of proprioception becomes an urgent task.

Proprioception, as a concept, was coined by Charles Scott Sherrington (1857–1952), a British physiologist and medical doctor. His book, *The Integrative Action of the Nervous System*, published in 1906, is still in print; its ideas are still cited, studied, and considered relevant in the early twenty-first century (Burke 2007, 889; Fuentes 2019; Sherrington 1906). Sherrington also coined the term *synapse* in English (from the Greek *sunapsis*). Proprioception can be translated as awareness or perception of self. It refers to our knowledge, without conscious awareness, of where our body is in space and how elements of the physical body relate to one another. The term *proprioceptor* refers to a physiological element of the nerves and ligaments and muscles of the body. *Proprioception* at once thus refers to a physiological element of the nerves and ligaments and muscles of the body and to a more metaphorical sense of balance or a "sense of where you are" (McPhee 1999). Work on proprioception in physiology, neuroscience, and neuroanatomy is ongoing and rapidly evolving.[7]

Reading Sherrington with Ibn 'Arabi, we can think the synapse—also premised on an unbridgeable space between two objects (in this case, two neurons)—as *barzakh* and as a channel through which information, signals, and value flow (Elyachar 2010; Kockelman 2010). Without the space between two neurons, no communication happens, no information is transferred, and no movement is possible. Just as *barzakh* is central to Ibn 'Arabi's thinking about *wujud* or ontology, the synapse was crucial to Sherrington's reworking of being and the human. Proprioception across the *barzakh* offers a helpful framework for moving through injury, including the vast global injury wrought by the "scourge of accumulation" without end (Maitland 1804) that turned ground into empty terrain, inviting conquest and exploitation. It is particularly helpful for thinking from Cairo and across times of expansion and contraction, enmeshed in different geographies and circles.

Urban space is mutually constituted with and through millions of bodies carrying out embodied locomotory practices in contemporaneous plurality (Massey 2005, 9). Writing in the 1990s, Nigel Thrift and Doreen Massey each describe urban space in terms of "parcels of time-space" (Thrift 1996, 43) or parcels of movement that are co-constitutive *of* space rather than happening *in* space. Increasingly, after 2011, notions of a shared urban space— whether called colonial, underdeveloped, or neoliberal—came unhinged. How, then, to relearn movement in space in times of shaken grounds and profound uncertainty? Might other ways of thinking about space-time and the urban be helpful?

I have conducted a lifetime of intended and unintended research on proprioception. Only recently did I realize the deep connection of the proprioception that I cultivated in one sphere of my life to my research in another. As a teenager studying ballet with Alfredo Corvino in a crowded walk-up studio above a peep show on Manhattan's 8th Avenue and 46th Street, long before the neighborhood was gentrified, I knew how to quickly adjust my grip on the barre and the angle of my feet and hips when another dancer slipped in line right before our forty right legs kicked high in a grand battement. I knew how to instantly shift direction when suburban middle-aged men approached from across the street to solicit a teenage girl. Like every dancer who performs through pain or fever, I knew all about injury and the search for recovery.

But I began to learn systematically about proprioception only in 2011, when I found myself in a small gym in a former warehouse of the John Wayne Airport, in Orange County, California, where I would spend many hours in the years to come repairing multiple injuries from my youth. There I relearned how to stand and sit and how to raise and lower my ankles while made unstable by a wobble board or a foam pad. Cultivating instability helped me cultivate new capacities and range of motion and develop a more dynamic relation to ground in recovery. Proprioception came from physiology, I learned, only later realizing the connection to the social theory I worked with as an anthropologist.

Proprioception matters as a concept in the history of thought, in neurology and physiology, and as embodied collective practice amenable to ethnographic analysis. Thought together with *barzakh*—that which is ambiguous and unbridgeable, even while constituting a united space—proprioception can help critical inquiry move beyond lingering assumptions of stable, inert ground as a stage for the human drama. When the ground literally dissolves into sinkholes that erase political boundaries (Popperl 2018) and swallows up cities and island nations whole, proprioception and *barzakh* deserve further attention in anthropology and beyond.

The Self in Motion

Charles Scott Sherrington was born into a middle-class English family in 1857, the first year of the Sepoy Mutiny against rule by the East India Company over the former Mughal Empire, an event that led up to the direct colonization of India by Great Britain and the construction of the Suez Canal by France and Great Britain two years later (Mantena 2010). Sherrington thus was born at a time of two modes of imperial power: the territorial colonization imposed on India; and the semicolonial domination over space, channels of commerce, and armies, achieved through infrastructure building, engineering, and debt, imposed on the domains of the Ottoman Empire in general and Egypt in particular. As a medical doctor, physiologist, writer, and person deeply interested in movement, Sherrington saw his career take shape in a world where physiology had a wide and influential reach. He began with studies on the cortex of the human brain but soon shifted his focus to the spinal cord.

These two shifts—from the brain to the spinal cord, and from thinking and perception to reflex and what Sherrington came to call proprioception—shaped neurophysiology over the next one hundred years, with enduring relevance for anthropology.[8] Equally important at the time was the motor theory of perception, which can be traced back to Rudolf Hermann Lotze in 1852 and was revived in the twenty-first century (Berthoz 2000; Lotze 1852).[9] The motor theory of perception was eclipsed by analytic neurophysiology influenced by Sherrington in the twentieth century (Berthoz 2000, 11; Viviani 1987). For anthropologists, both approaches are generative to think with in times that exceed the analytic bounds of resistance.

Sherrington was a student of Frederick Matthias Alexander, developer of the still popular Alexander Technique. F. M. Alexander, as he was commonly known, was a former aspiring Shakespearean actor who developed innovative techniques in the early twentieth century to help his students become aware of and free themselves from engrained bodily habits and inefficiencies that lead to injury and unhappiness. Alexander taught John Dewey and William James, in this way impacting American philosophical pragmatism and thus anthropology. James wrote the introduction to one of Alexander's books.[10]

It was perhaps more common for physiologists, philosophers, social theorists, and clinicians to be interlocutors in the mid-nineteenth century, when stimulation, perception, and movement were considered highly integrated. In 1852, Lotze argued that "the spatial organization of visual sensations results from their integration with a muscular sense" (Berthoz 2000, 9; Lotze 1852). Théodule A. Ribot argued that personality varied with organic physical sensations and that unity of the ego was intrinsically dependent on both consciousness and physiology. In this way, something like the unconscious had its origin in the life of the body (Bixler 1945; Morgan 2010, 2; Ribot [1895] 2009; Ribot 1897). Psychiatrist and anatomist Johann Christian Reil, in turn, coined the term *cenesthesia*, often defined as "the vital sense," for the pervasive but undifferentiated complex of organic sensations by which one is aware of the body and bodily conditions and which shapes personality itself (Starobinski 1990, 24–25).[11]

The young Sigmund Freud was part of this world. He introduced the phrase "contact barriers" to describe the points where neurons touch "and suggested that interactions between neurons across contact barriers make possible memory, consciousness, and other facets of the mind" (LeDoux

2003, 38–39). In fact, when Sherrington introduced the synapse, he was building on Freud's initial idea. But by 1900, Freud had taken up positions against his original neural theory of mind (39) and the predominant theory that dreams were a result of stimulation to the senses.[12] Dreams became instead an expression of the unconscious, with the body but a vessel of the unconscious and vehicle for expression of the inner self. Interpretation of the truths of the unconscious, with its labyrinthine potential for creativity and obfuscation, became the project of psychoanalysis. Meanwhile, in sociology, Émile Durkheim approached the body as a vehicle for the expression of the social. Thus, in both psychoanalysis and sociology, the body became "a house" with no direct connection to its contents or, for that matter, to consciousness itself (Morgan 2010, 3).

Not everyone held that view. In philosophy, phenomenology and hermeneutics continued the tradition of seeing the body as much more than a vehicle for carrying around the self. In the 2010s, scientists doing popular writing in neuropsychology drew on Maurice Merleau-Ponty, citing his argument for the body as the primary site of knowing the world, as opposed to most Western traditions in which individual "consciousness" observes the world from a brain encased in a skull.

Philosophers such as Edmund Husserl, Martin Heidegger, and Merleau-Ponty all made clear that a first-person point of view on the world is never a view from nowhere. An individual's view on the world is "always defined by the situation of the perceiver's body, which concerns not simply location and posture, but action in pragmatic contexts and interaction with other people" (Gallagher and Zahavi 2005). Perception is "correlated to and accompanied by proprioceptive-kinesthetic self-sensation or self-affection" (Gallagher and Zahavi 2005; Husserl [1907] 1997). This perspective showed up in early neoliberal theory as well. F. A. Hayek made physiological "tacit knowledge" essential to his arguments against collectivist knowledge and returned to his early work on "the sensory order" toward the end of his career (Elyachar 2012a).

In politics, fascists placed a strong emphasis on the relation of bodily movement to polity and the self: *Dein Körper gehört deiner Nation* (Your body belongs to your nation) was a slogan of the Nazis as they worked on the social engineering of body movement to possess the brain. Coordination of bodily movement to polity and identity has been important in Egyptian history as well. Napoleon Bonaparte presided over the traditional Egyptian Festival of the Nile after his invasion of Egypt in 1798 and organized parades of troops of the Cairo garrison to the sounds of a French marching band accompanying "chants of the Muslims" (Cole 2007, 125) and other spectacles. In the mid-nineteenth century, as I discussed in chapter 1, Khedive Ismail undertook elaborate projects of operatic infrastructure and sensory politics in Cairo, commissioning Verdi to write the opera *Aida* to celebrate the opening of the Suez Canal in 1868. And, of course, in 2021, there was the Parade of the Mummies.

Just as these operatic movements were shared across spaces, traditions, and local knowledges, debates about the self, the social, and the unconscious were not restricted to Europe and the United States. Debates were ongoing in the Arab world, including discussion of overlaps and synergy with Islamic philosophy in general and Ibn 'Arabi in particular. Salama Musa published several books on Freud and the unconscious for a lay audience in the late 1920s (El Shakry 2017, 2). The Egyptian translator of Freud, Sami-Ali, was also a translator of and commentator on Ibn 'Arabi (El Shakry 2018, 313).[13] Ibn Khaldun (1332–1406) is called the father of sociology almost as often as Émile Durkheim, and Herbert Spencer's article "The Social Organism" was translated into Arabic in 1885 (82). Physiology was also part of the "great social laboratory" of social sciences and ethnology in nineteenth- and early twentieth-century Egypt, linked to a longer history of human geography going back to Ibn Khaldun (El Shakry 2007).

Abbate Pasha, an ophthalmologist born in Italy in the 1820s and resident in Egypt from 1845 on, was court physician to the royal family and a leader in the study of "native physiology and psychology" (El Shakry 2007, 30). Abbate Pasha drew on nineteenth-century theories of physiology to locate characteristics of Arabs as a race, including the "atavistic aptitude" of Egyptian men for mechanism and reproduction (in contrast to Western capacities for invention) and of Egyptian females to carry heavy loads on their heads, postulating that "the large and regular nature of the pelvis, the normal formation of bones, and the accentuated development of the muscles of Egyptian women all contributed to their load-balancing aptitude" (36). Abbate rendered the imputed size and shape of the pelvis as a marker of moral character and mental capacity.[14]

While the "proprio" in proprioception refers to the individual (or "one's own"), when approached as a distributed collective capacity, proprioception can help us upend lingering assumptions about how humans engage with one another and the wider world, as we saw earlier with the semiotics of gesture. Critical theorists such as Catherine Malabou (2008) have pointed to the ease with which proprioception can be absorbed into accounts of a neoliberal body maneuvering in a sea of risk and a synaptic self that is always responsible for self-improvement. Instead, we can find in proprioception ample grounds for theorizing the distributed embodied self (Elyachar 2022). Proprioception provides us with a helpful "thinking device" for considering all kinds of challenges to equilibrium offered by the current situation in Egypt and around the world. Nobody moves through the world unaided. Autonomy is an illusion (Rutherford forthcoming). Just like gesture in the semiotic commons is distributed so, too, is agency distributed and collective, at every scale.

The concept of proprioception was developed at a moment when social science thinking about self and the body was in conversation with physiology. Some lines of thought got closed off by the associations of physiology with racist pseudoscience and the ascendance of theories of the "body as a house" (Morgan 2010). It is time now to explore—in the ethnographic present and in the many archives of great cities like Cairo—how people have navigated, and continue to navigate, together, in an unsteady world. Just as kinesthesia, a concept close in meaning to proprioception, refers to cooperation among multiple sensory receptors that are collectively responsible for a sense of movement (Berthoz 2000, 5; Sweigard 1974), distributed proprioceptive capacities of the collective in motion can be explored by anthropologists and others. Throughout this book, I have drawn on ethnographic moments of embodied collective action that I sometimes characterized as "gesture," or as a gestural commons. I did not do so to romanticize a utopic past before the January 25 Revolution when everything worked better. Rather, through ethnography, I have aimed to dispel the notion that proprioception is an individual capacity, even though Sherrington's term *proprioception* incorporated the Latin *proprio*, or "one's own."

Proprioception moves across the synapses and receptors on the skin enveloping the "container" of the individual biopolitical self, external to the usual organs of perception considered in anthropology of the senses. Virtuosic locomotive practices rely on proprioceptors in the nerve endings of ligaments of the hand and foot as much as on inputs from the eye or the ear. Proprioception moves through the parasympathetic nervous system. It involves "modes of awareness of one's spatial orientation and trajectory built into outward-directed perception, modes of awareness of how one's body is disposed that are derived from awareness of our own bodies, and the complex spatial self-awareness implicated in navigating through the environment" (Bermúdez 2018, 2–3). This so far remains at the level of the individual self. But what is this self that is activated by action and motion? This question brings to the fore lingering dilemmas in practice theory, particularly a lingering individualism of the body.

Practice theory moved beyond a cerebral notion of the self to consider beings who act "in and on a world," in discussions of agency linked to the critique of liberal notions of the self (Taylor 1993, 49). If understanding is situated in practice, then understanding becomes implicit in activity. Representations are but "islands in the sea of our unformulated practical grasp on the world" (50). Understanding goes far beyond. Anthropology of bodily practice fails whenever it presents the body as an "executant of the goals we frame" (50). The self and agency are embodied, intertwined, and dialogic. But this does not go far enough. In such critiques, notions of the disengaged first-person-singular self were dislodged but only to shift to the *body* as singular bodily agent, such as occurs in Saba Mahmood's (2005) important critique of liberal notions of the self, agency, and Pierre Bourdieu's (1990) concept of habitus.

Unlike prior critiques of the Western notion of the self, or of the racist or fascist entanglements of some nineteenth-century physiology, contemporary neurophysiology works well with emergent theories of distributed agency (Enfield and Kockelman 2017). But in the main, critical theory and social sciences lumber on with "fictional pictures of the brain" (Malabou 2008). It is not just that the "the brain has a history—which is sometimes confused with that of its constitution as an object of the sciences—but that it *is* a history" (1–2). Even the individual brain, like the spinal cord, is characterized by distributed agency (Enfield and Kockelman 2017). The brain needs "many more of its cells singing together to decide what to do next" (Nicolelis 2011, 13).[15] How do we know "where your body starts and ends, what it feels like to be human, what deeper beliefs you hold, and how your children and the children of your children will one day remember who you were and what became of your legacy as a human being" (19)?[16]

In the words of Alain Berthoz (2000), "Perception *is* simulated action." And in the words of Egyptian sociologist Sayyid ʿUways (1989), that movement carries with it traces of a collective past, in "the history I carry on my back." Proprioception extends outside the "container of the skin" and is a collective capacity. Just like Abou El Fetouh (2015) wrote about mass revolt, we all live in an ambivalent state between the individual and the collective, with the kind of "relational self" that was theorized by Suad Joseph (1993) many years ago. The "lingering notion of humans as moving through the world like robots carrying around brains which . . . interpret signals from the outside world, our selves ending at the container of the skin" (Nicolelis 2011, 27) is misguided in more ways than one.

Traces of the Semicivilized

I have claimed so far that proprioception on the urban street is a distributed capacity embedded in embodied infrastructures of the urban commons. Communicative channels of these embodied infrastructures run through synapse, muscle, and proprioceptor of the body, and across multiple kinds of ground and nodes of distributed agency. Such infrastructures are accessible as a commons to the urban majority in Cairo (Simone and Rao 2012), shape the politics of sectarianism and daily life in Beirut (Nucho 2016), and proliferate around the Global South (Simone and Pieterse 2017). Channels of embodied infrastructure are ethnographically tractable in how people—the common people—move, cross streets, and pass cigarettes across moving traffic. From there, it is just a step to consider the politics of shifting grounds in ways that move beyond the common frameworks of structure and resistance (Elyachar 2014).

In times of political revolt, resources generated through movement contribute to the creation of *movements* as well (Cox 2021; Martin 2006; Roelvink 2010). Kinesthesia and collective urban movement—sometimes through dance and sometimes not—are linked to the human capacity to imagine different futures (Chin 2014; Hamera 2007; Kwan 2013; Martin 2006). As Randy Martin (2006, 800) puts it, writing on the "kinesthetics of protest," "Each protest is a gesture of arrest that unleashes its own kinesthetic. What accumulates through the actions of a social movement, whether organized through a given state entity or against it, is a capacity to reformulate how bodies can associate. This, as much as the tragic tales of struggles won and lost, is what the death in politics displays. By the time it has been announced, some other contested space has already been borne by a fresh assembly of bodies." Relatedly, Aimee Meredith Cox (2015, 2021) shows how collective movement and performance in Cincinnati rendered submerged vibrant pathways of Black urban life visible and more available for political projects.

All in all, the *proprio* of proprioception is possibly a misnomer, a lingering artifact of the liberal imperialism into which Sherrington was born, even as his research made clear how much the self was distributed and relational across interlinked synapses and proprioceptors. Proprioception is linked to politics in ways that exceed the framework of resistance on ethnographic, analytic, and historical scales. Sherrington's thinking was shaped in a moment of crisis in liberal imperialism provoked by the mass revolts in India in 1857, with an ensuing shift to theories and practices of cultural imperialism, home rule, and civilizational order (Mantena 2010). Perhaps this helps explain why his concept of proprioception was so individualist. Either way, proprioception appears more intuitively as distributed when looking from the vantage point of a semicivilized world shaped by personal law, embodied infrastructures, and extraterritoriality.

Proprioception remains important in a world without original entailments of the semicivilized such as extraterritoriality and personal law. Formal arrangements like the capitulations are largely a thing of the past. But the semicivilized condition lingers. It continued in international law even after the Treaty of Lausanne in 1923 abolished the capitulations. It continued with the establishment of the British and French Mandates over Arab regions of the former Ottoman Empire, and in jurisprudence of Mixed Courts of Egypt through 1949. Even today, the waiting room of history has lingered for the semicivilized, marked by a coloniality of debt without end, the denial of sovereign aspirations in a supposedly decolonized world, and the free exercise of violence against those marked, once again, as barbarian.

Semicivilized might no longer be the marker of a waystation between the fantastical paired concepts that earmark the bloody adventures of colonialism and anthropology alike: the primitive and the civilized. It might no longer be used to describe a polity in which territorial sovereignty is chopped up by extraterritorial treaties, like the Ottoman Empire, China, or Japan (Kayaoğlu 2010; Liu 1925; Slys 2014). But the semicivilized is anything but dead, even if the concept was written out of anthropology, colonialism studies, and postcolonial theory. That erasure should not continue. Rectifying the erasure demands both archival research and concept work.

For an anthropologist, concept work is never "an end in itself": "It is always connected to the problems one wishes to think through, as well as the question of how one could make a judgement about the problems one is engaging" (Stavrianakis and Bennett 2012). As an anthropologist, I have used the methodology of ethnography to analyze events unfolding in real time. Ethnography is an unparalleled methodology for making sense of emergent relations and structures in times of vast social and political transformation. In the process, we can also show how dismantled institutions and political arrangements wield their influence in the present. Ethnographers must "go beyond the ethnographic present" and "locate the object of our study in time," as Eric Wolf has said (1999, 8).

Different kinds of violence emerged through the incorporative processes of empire and its vast infrastructure of communicative channels. Empire in what was formerly the eastern part of the Roman Empire and later the Byzantine Empire was incorporative by nature. Even Englishmen with experience in the arts of the "merchant adventurer" could enter and assume legal status as sojourners by performing the obligatory communicative rituals of gift-exchange and epistolary letter writing.[17] Sojourners were the norm, not the exception. At the same time, Englishmen like William Harborne—Queen Elizabeth I's ambassador to the Ottoman Empire—entered the region's communicative channels of commerce like a parasite, in Michel Serres's ([1980] 2007) or Paul Kockelman's (2010) sense of the term. Serres's early formulation of the parasite as the god Hermes is even more apt here.

Hermes is the god of commerce and the god of communication. He is often called a trickster. As a divine thief and god of trade, Hermes was the only god who could cross the boundary between life and death at will (N. O. Brown 1990).[18] As one who travels effortlessly across space and has mastery of all languages, Hermes shows of the intertwining of commerce and communication that I have emphasized throughout this book (and which was set aside in nineteenth-century political economy and social theory). Hermes was a master of the Greek art of "poetic gossip" (Fulgentius 1971, 60) that is so important in the mastery of what I have called "phatic labor" (Elyachar 2010). He was the original master of the arts of communicative channels of commerce. Moving across the "routes and realms" (Antrim 2012) of the Ottoman Empire would have been no problem for him.

None of this history has disappeared; its traces live with us still, although little has made its way into thinking and writing about colonialism, let alone into the thinking and writing about the so-called "primitive" with which anthropology was so concerned in the twentieth century. Traces of the semicivilized have much to teach us about life on shaken grounds. Those traces point to other pathways of thinking about colonialism, postcolonialism, and capitalism. Traces of the semicivilized erupted in the margins of the decade of the great financial crisis—including in far-away Syria, where a completely different set of historical events (it was thought) was underway. I refer of course to the so-called Arab Spring and the Syrian wars that followed. Violence against the semicivilized proceeded at a different pace there, with all the refracted reverberations and temporalities more familiar to discussions of environmental degradation and climate terror (Nixon 2019). Such violence is most dramatic in cities and countries whose urban fabric and infrastructures have been destroyed since the beginning of the twenty-first century. Violence exercised against the semicivilized is intergenerational, in cycles of expanded accumulation, of delayed colonial violence and terror unleashed in the Armenian genocide, in structural violence against the Kurds, in the practices of genocide and urbicide carried out against the cities and towns of former Yugoslavia and their residents who wore too openly their Ottoman traces.[19] And the violence against the semicivilized has continued through to the wholesale destruction of educational, religious, cultural, health, and commercial infrastructure of Palestinians in Gaza as I finish this book.

For all these reasons, the Middle East is a good place from which to consider what happens when the ground dissolves under our feet. Since the first US invasion of Iraq in 1990, one million Iraqis have been killed, tens of millions in the region have been displaced, the earth has been devastated, and the damage has blown back around the world. The ground itself has been under constant attack. It is in this context that the line, "At least we aren't Syria, we aren't Libya, we haven't been destroyed," and the implied, "So let's be quiet and move on," was often repeated in the years after the 2013 coup. Such statements were themselves a kind of injury.

Cairo had been further woven into the political economy of Saudi Arabia and the Gulf in the years after 2013 (Hanieh 2018). Billed by the government as a new city of green, Cairo was looking more like a City of Salt, to use the title of the trilogy by the late Saudi novelist and oil economist Abdelrahman Munif, *Cities of Salt* (1989). "Cities of Salt," Munif once said, refers to "cities that offer no sustainable existence. When the waters come in, the first waves will dissolve the salt and reduce these great glass cities to dust" (Banaji 2020). Just what will remain of Cairo remains to be seen. What happens when the rivers of green, larger than New York's Central Park, dry up, when the bulldozers have nowhere left to dig, and when the millions left to survive in the remnants of Cairo's living museum must draw down modest stocks of wealth accumulated drip by drip for their children to convert its disappearing value into food for the next day. One thing we can know for sure: the injury is not about to disappear.

The Injury of Equilibrium/Contraction

Back in 2017, I started writing more about injury. Injury started early with me. But in 2017, I was not the only one dealing with and talking about injury and physical pain. My friends and I were spending less time in microbuses or minibuses and more time in cars and taxis. Among my friends and acquaintances from back in the 1990s, some had made careers and small fortunes from early entry into the NGO world; but now, under President Sisi, others faced torture in jail and bare survival after years of supporting sisters and aunts and moms and children. Those who had reregistered their NGOs under commercial business law did better, as did a couple of my acquaintances who had leveraged NGO revenue flows into registered property ownership across Cairo.

Age, prison, overwork, dust, diesel fumes, and revolution had taken a toll. Ahmed had been a master of movement, hopping from moving bus to street, gliding down the sidewalk, where there was one, creating a wake it was easy for me as a trained dancer to move along in. We used to move fast from bus to minibus, from microbus to taxi, chatting along the way about interviews and coffee, plans for dinner, entering conversations in semipublic conveyances through urban space. Now, when we met, it was to go from one specific place to another, planned out in advance. "I can't do that now," he laughed one day, remembering those trips. He was not the only one in pain. My friend Aisha, too, moved more slowly now, rarely leaving her neighborhood, preferring to sit in her apartment, on the balcony overlooking streets where battles had been fought and where, now, people walked up and down, in and out of small shops, and sat at rickety small, round tables on the cobblestones, drinking tea or coffee. Other friends were sick and coping with the grief for relatives who had passed either suddenly on the street or quietly at home.

For friends whose offices or apartment buildings were supposedly going to be moved wholesale, sometime soon, to a "new capital city," the uncertainty never ended and was palpable. Certainly a few of my friends suffered from PTSD, and for a few years after 2011 they jumped whenever there was a loud noise outside. Wobble boards were not needed by anyone to force unconscious patterns of daily movement into awareness. From the blunt hand of the military authoritarian state to the local versions of GPS mapping and tracking movement through militarized streets, different projects aimed to control and to profit in new ways from urban life.

By the time of my visit in 2022, it did not seem to matter anymore if people were being watched through cameras pointed down from up on high streetlights or through the accumulating reports of spies going up the chain of command. Core institutions of cultural, political, and intellectual life were done with and had disappeared; sometimes the names of the establishments written in script still lingered on the windows outside, like at the famous Nadi al-thaqafa, empty and quiet, or the Ali Baba. All kinds of places of gathering and sociality and communication across the stretches of pathways and streetways and waterways had been shut down, remade, reopened, in a strange mimesis of what had been there before.

This remaking took place on the water as well as on land. Houses, river-walks, beloved landmarks, and entire neighborhoods were destroyed with no room for discussion or debate. Any impediment to the flow of strategic channels for the movement of armies or the free flow of investment possibilities for financialized military firms just came down. Houseboats anchored for generations on the side of the Nile were demolished. Small boats with places for music and conviviality among young middle-class people were likewise destroyed and carted away. *Fulukas*—those traditional Nile sailboats that had for centuries plied its waters and that my friends in student days had often rented for a few hours out on the water—were all gone.

Bigger, motorized, commercial boats with brightly colored lights moved up and down the Nile near the redone carcass of Tahrir Square from which commercialized remixes of *mahragan* hits from five years ago blared down onto the silent waters. The center of Tahrir Square was retaken as well, by Cleopatra's needle, installed from Luxor. Security police planters with bits and pieces of native plants and explanatory plaques created pleasant perches for young people and families strolling in front of what used to be the Mo-gamma, ghostly in its stark silent presence, the empty offices more apparent from the side by Qasr el-Aini.

Back in 2018, the rose-colored stone buildings of Saudi-owned CityStars mall in Heliopolis had seemed an anomaly. I had read of how Saudi state-owned investment funds had bought up key companies of the Egyptian public sector (Hanieh 2018). Capitalization schemes were moving differently now. International development had taken a new turn: green energy, green hydrogen, and global meetings positioned Egypt, once again, at the center—but at the center of a different world, in a different circle, with the Gulf at the helm. The layers of Cairo as a museum of life, *mathaf al-hayat* to Sayyid 'Uways, were gone. Cairo was being remade as an "open air museum," as advertised in English to visitors from the Gulf States and, if the war would ever end, from Russia and Ukraine, and from all those Western and Eastern countries to whom Cairo could hopefully again become a place of amenities and featured sites of an Eastern tour.

The transformation of a neighborhood like Heliopolis in northern Cairo was dramatic in a different way. Heliopolis was built at the turn of the twentieth century as an "oasis in the desert" by the Belgian Baron Empain. It was planned as a "model town" for the different civilizational levels and cultural preferences of a working class needed for the maintenance of the new privately owned "public utilities,"; it had quarters for the local *musulman* sensibilities as well as for the French. Children and grandchildren and cousins and nieces and nephews of those first workers of Heliopolis had lived in that tension between the growing "informal sectors" of the area that had sprung up around the planned streets of the colonial model town.

Those informal sectors had irritated President Mubarak in the 1980s, when he passed them on his way to work; and thus they were torn down to make his life more pleasant and to ease his movement and the pleasure of his way. Thirty years later, the logics of military demolition were more brutal: informal neighborhoods were stripped down, leaving only the colonial core of Heliopolis with the worn-out buildings of Baron Empain. The vibrancy of the workshops, homes, coffeehouses, and byways of an urban Cairene world were gone. And all around, on all the squares, hung the ubiquitous pictures of President Sisi, smiling down on the masses rendered subjects.

Groups had gathered and dissolved, friends had come together and left, in these years since 2011. And there was the constant march of death. Some of my old friends from the 1990s had died. Or they had withdrawn from society altogether and were sitting at home, closed in on themselves. Then COVID-19 added the finishing touches, creeping through bodies wracked with diabetes and obesity, lung cancer and joint pain. In one week in August 2022, I learned of four deaths, not of close friends, but of close friends of close friends, people I knew. Some had died in prison; some of COVID in that first year when "no one knew what it was or what was wrong," as one friend put it to me. Some just got sick and died. And no one was doing much visiting.

We were old. But old was lived differently by some. I had lived ten of the intervening years in Orange County, California, where staying young, working out, cleansing the air, and eating the right food were the favored endeavors of those with the money to pursue the privilege as "lifestyle choices," and where "healthy aging" and "slowing down time" were popular. In Cairo, in contrast, time rushed onward with heavy weight. Years in prison for some, diesel fumes only the rich could escape, and the alcohol and cigarettes that fueled sociality and politics, were all showing their impact. Commitment to place and the refusal to leave were ultimate values (in Max Weber's sense of the term) for some, and nothing to be debated or negotiated. These weren't "lifestyle choices." It was about the stubborn clinging to the right to live in one's home, a home for which one fights, and the fight to keep the "common" as a home for all local folks, for all commoners, who have no place to go, and whose spaces of movement and mobility were shrinking around them.

If Egypt had three circles, then Cairo had more. It was a node on circuits of movement across empires and trade routes and around the regions of the Arab world. Since the 1960s and especially after the "economic opening" of Anwar Sadat in 1976, millions of Egyptian men had spent years of their lives in the Arab Gulf, building up the infrastructure of modern states, constructing and staffing schools and hospitals and factories and bureaucracies, until Iraq's invasion of Kuwait in 1991 set in motion a whole chain of events, including the first Gulf War under George H. W. Bush, which evicted Egyptians from the Gulf. Egyptian men working in the Gulf returned home and the circuits of money flowing into Egypt from informal financial channels came to a stop as well.

The city and the country had changed. New buildings and new streets and new stories had been built on top of houses for the new generations on land zoned or unzoned for urban life; doors and windows and furnishings were purchased with wages earned from elsewhere, marked with pride in an explosion of building in villages and state-owned land transformation. The tenor and rhythm of movement on the streets of Cairo shifted, as it always had, over more lifetimes than any of us would know of to tell our children and children's children.

Each injury is a lesson, as my physical therapist used to say, an opportunity to note how the previous equilibrium of the body and ways of creating stability on ground had been dysfunctional. Such is the case of our outdated models of equilibrium. It is well past time to move away from such foundational ideologies that economics inherited from nineteenth-century physics. Proprioception, and thinking from the barzakh and across the synapse, can help us do so. In times of broken ground, it is fruitless to resist. Pushing onward just leads to injury, or worse. At such times, endurance in the face of uncertainty (Abaza 2020; Simone 2013) is itself a form of resistance. Attunement to the powers of proprioception, in relation to the global majority and to the shifting and dissolving ground, is called for here as well.

Looking from Cairo across the barzakh, proprioception and long-term potentiation can be more than, as Malabou (2008) suggests, just another ideology of the relentlessly neoliberal self-improving subject. Across the synapse and the barzakh, there are multiple forms of ethnographically tractable attunement to others across the channel, running across ground under attack, suffering injury that can no longer be silenced or ignored. It is time to rethink the politics of resistance everywhere that was so popular in the long decades of neoliberal rule. The politics of proprioception and potentiation invite us instead to consider what happens—and how to respond—when the ground is upended and dissolves under our feet. And they invite us to increase our capacity for proprioception across the *barzakh*, when illusions of stability and equilibrium have disappeared in waves of hope and disappointment.

Embodied Memories, New Times

The politics of proprioception and potentiation invite us to consider what happens—and how to respond—when the ground is upended and shaken and dissolves under our feet like salt. They invite us to take the opportunity to increase our capacity to live on the earth when the illusions of its stability disappear. In opposition to the endless flexibility and individual capacity to adjust, optimize, and always improve (capacities embedded in the overlapping space of neuroscience and neoliberalism), the capacities I discuss here are distributed from the start. This implies, too, politics of remembering and defending the embodied commons.

This time of challenge to equilibrium and stability—time of perturbation (Kockelman 2010)—has the capacity to increase our powers of proprioception. It can, in fact, enable our capacity to respond, instantaneously and without conscious thought, to ongoing provocations and upendings. In the best of cases, and in a relentlessly if differently utopian mode, these challenges to equilibrium can extend our little-understood powers of proprioception. Challenges to equilibrium can increase, to draw on another term from physiology, potentiation: the activation of dormant neural pathways that remain, albeit abandoned, in the body and the semiotic community. Might we consider a shift from a politics of resistance to a politics of proprioception—an awakening of dormant channels; increasing capacities to move, keep balance, move forward in times of increasing perturbation?

Long-term potentiation activates new synaptic pathways that were there all along, but ignored. It creates "long-term modifications, capable of changing form . . . and of undoing a trace in order to remake it differently. . . . In the case of potentiated connections, synapses enlarge their area of contact, their permeability rises, and nerve conduct is more rapid" (Malabou 2008, 23–24). These insights, again from a physiology of the capacitation of our collective proprioceptive capacities, give, if nothing else, food for thought, at a time of collapsed pathways of territorialism, resistance without end, and the clear bittersweet end of a centuries-old addiction to the fantasy of endless growth. The history we still carry on our backs will help shape its path toward uncertain futures.

Years of tragic aftermath to revolution, the devastation of the region by warfare, and ecocide in a time of global climate catastrophe have challenged our balance as a species. What new capacities will we develop in the face of these challenges? Music on the streets, with "Cairo Calling," in the years after the January 25 Revolution gave some signals.[20] Music exploded, at a level "below the *sha'bi*," below the long-established ground of the commons, of a semiotic community constructed in a political economy of exterritoriality tied to the rise of the Western capitalist order. Voices of the urban masses emerged from the streets of the *hawamish*, the marginalized areas outside the urban core of the city where the *sha'bi* was formed in opposition to the exterritorial privileged others.

That phrase "below the *sha'bi*" reverberated in 2017. In these years of the aftermath, the politics of left versus right, of standing on solid ground, were gone. This was well said by Okka and Ortega in their hit song of 2017, "La' la." In Islam, the imagery of left versus right is most obviously related to an embodied piety of knowing where the right and where the left lies; of knowing where the clean is, and the dirty; and of knowing where God is as opposed to the devil. In these songs, this imagery overlaps with political cosmology of left and right in the West since the French Revolution (and the imperialist conquests North Africa to which the rise of liberalism was linked). The grounds of this politics collapsed under our feet. But something was emerging from below the commons—the undercommons (Harney and Moten 2013)—expressed in the music blowing up on the internet. It spoke, among other things, of the complete upending of the world leading up to the mass revolts against neoliberalism after 2008. The grounds of resistance had changed. Other ways of relating the body to the ground and to territory were needed, through times of expanding hopes and dreams, and through times of contraction.

In Sufi philosophy, life is lived through times of expansion (*bast*) and contraction (*qabd*). Times of great possibility and absorption in political projects promising hope and transformation can be times of individual and collective expansion. If such was the period of the years of revolution, the decade following was, in turn, a period of contraction. The expansion of "spatiotemporal possibilities" in Cairo that had been so liberating for activists and intellectuals of Black internationalism in the 1960s and for young revolutionaries in 2010 had fallen inward, contracted, and collapsed.

"Most are gone now. Those who are left are staying at home, closed in on themselves," said Essam to me one day in the summer of 2022. I could not stop thinking of this image. It was then that I started to consider this period in the language of *qabd*, or contraction, after the long years of *bast*, or expansion. The long afterlives of prison, pollution, and counterrevolution ate away at some of my friends; the relentless weight of attempting to provide for one's family as life's possibilities collapsed knocked others dead on the street. This happened to the brother of one of my friends. Like most families in Cairo, they had lost one son to the thugs of the revolution. And now the heavy weight of futures collapsed made it impossible for her brother to go on, although he was only in his fifth decade of life.

By 2023, Egypt had reached a deadlock. It missed the targets demanded by the IMF for additional loans. More than half the state budget went toward servicing interest on public debt, oddly reminiscent of the situation of student debt holders in the United States, or users of the grid or disappeared public services in Puerto Rico, living lifetimes of debt that could never end. Egypt refused conditions of the Gulf Corporation Council states to privatize military-owned companies and sectors of the economy and to have them submit to proper financial review. It seemed unwilling, or unable, to face the wrath of the Egyptian people by devaluing the Egyptian currency once again—for now.

Between March 2022 and July 2023, the Egyptian pound had already lost 50 percent of its value. The government would once again try to "coax back dollars" with high interest rates and other schemes no one thought could succeed (Magdy and El-Tablawy 2023). As the year came to an end, Egypt refused to exchange debt relief for the transfer of Palestinians weathering Israeli genocide in the Gaza Strip. Even so, Egyptian military-owned corporations started to build out an infrastructure of prison camps for Palestinians in the Egyptian Sinai Peninsula. As it became clear Israel was bent on a total war of annihilation in Gaza, such camps became less important in calculations of Egypt's futures. After all, infusions of capital from the Gulf kept coming.

How long could the resourcefulness of the Egyptian masses bear the conditions worsening beyond what had been imagined as possible, under the rubric of apparently abstract and impartial economic forces? Debt and finance had never been neutral for the semicivilized. Around the expanding bounds of Cairo, new ways of living and surviving and reaching toward hope for the next generation emerged in new neighborhoods built up once again, beyond the reaches of the financialized military state, through the embodied practices of the commoners of Cairo, collectively turning aban-donment into new forms of valued life (Tadiar 2022) along the "conduits, passageways, and openings through which life can be enacted in ways be-yond capture" (Simone 2022, 28).

Semicivilized Futures

In urban spaces around the three circles of Egypt, commons of the semi-civilized seem to have arisen as an exception to an assumed normal of the territorial nation-state, the colony, or the postcolonial state. As we have seen throughout this book, things look both different and increasingly familiar when we consider common futures from the perspective of the semicivi-lized and from the streets of Cairo.

From myths of coherent territory, and teleologies of territorial colonial-ism leading to a time of postcolonialism and freedom, or from dreams of kairos projected as a neo-Marxian theological vision of the redemptive con-jecture, something apparently unstable and yet in some ways stronger ap-pears. The semicivilized were kept in the waiting room of history after World War I, where they have been ever since. But the house to which that waiting room of history led no longer exists. That house is gone, together with all the houses and buildings and streets of Gaza. The world from which the semicivilized were excluded and dehumanized as barbarians has collapsed. Channels of mobility and finance across domains of the semicivilized cut across tightening zones of abandonment and destruction for some, endless rivers of green and delight in new neighborhoods for others, and worlds of stirring refusal against this global condition of being rendered, if fully human at all, merely semicivilized.

One day before leaving Cairo that August 2022, I found myself once again walking the streets alone. It was near sunset on the Corniche that runs along the banks of the Nile for long stretches in a Cairo that was (fig-ure 6.1). The streets were full of cars and minivans and buses and trucks. I was startled to see a group of young men—and a few young women—swoop by on roller skates. In and out of traffic they wove, torsos bent forward, legs pumping, heading into the streams of cars with joyful abandonment. Roller skating was a new fad that emerged during COVID, and despite myself, I found it unspeakably beautiful.

I stood still a bit longer, watching the skaters glide through five lanes of backed up, banged up cars driven by tired-out Cairenes breathing through their open windows the diesel-infused air of a hot August afternoon. I had

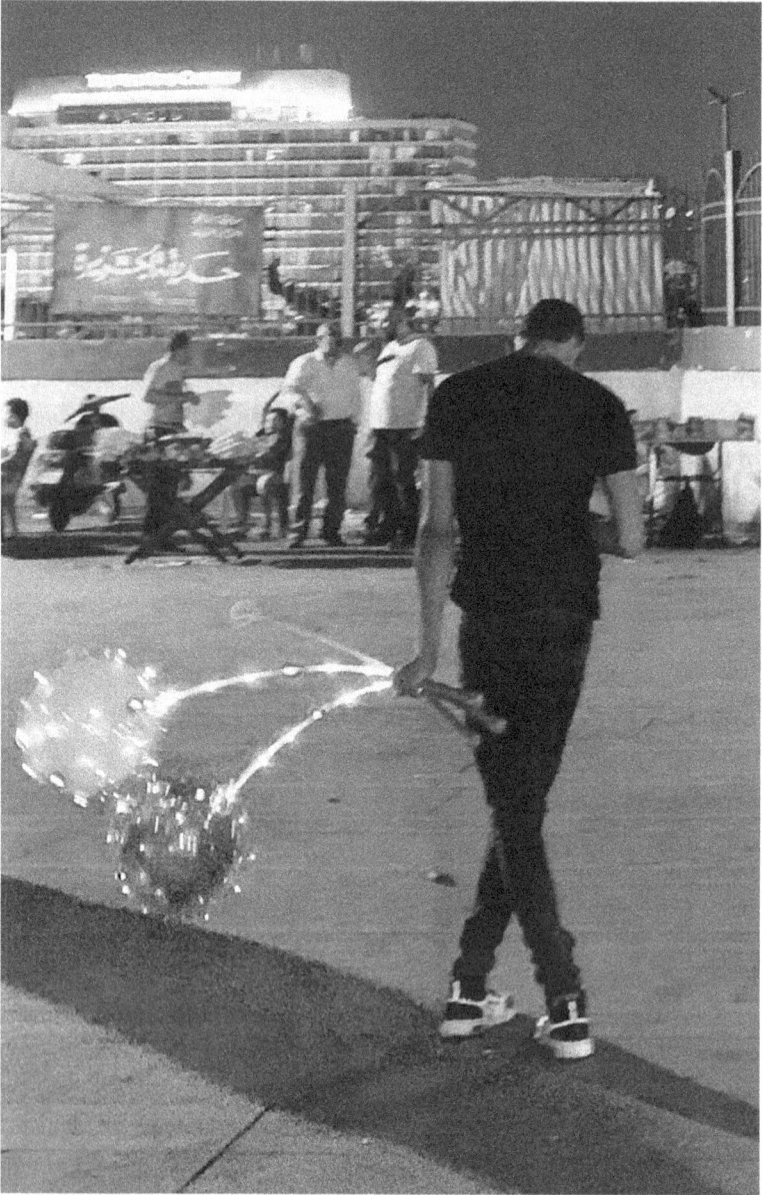

6.1 A young man holds light wands and checks his phone on a Nile River bridge, Cairo, August 2022. Photograph by the author.

found myself here after deciding to walk to my last meeting with Essam for the summer, near Garden City not far from the Nile Corniche. It was nearing sunset and the temperature had dropped to 95, which still felt unbearably hot. Other spots of beauty along the Corniche were disappearing into the voracious appetite of the financialized military.

Back in the mid-nineteenth century, Khedive Ismail had done more than open the Suez Canal, colonize the Sudan, and rebuild the capital city with operatic infrastructure. His performative sovereignty involved planting expansive gardens around palaces and lining the new, widened avenues of Cairo with trees as well. The expansive gardens and botanical museums he made in parts of Cairo were part of "botanical colonization" (Mastnak, Elyachar, and Boellstorff 2014) and aspirational sovereignty. Much like the French had done in Paris after their colonization of Algeria, Egyptian rulers built gardens and botanical museums that would attest to the civilized status of Egypt. Khedive Ismail established the fifty-two-acre Giza Zoo with plants imported from India, Africa, and South America (El Rashidi 2023). Like his grandfather, Mohamed Ali Pasha (or Mehmet Ali Pasha, his Turkish Ottoman name), Khedive Ismail planted the Nile banks with "dense vegetation and trees, including the majestic eucalyptus Cairo has become known for" (El Rashidi 2023).

Over the year to come, the last vestiges of these great gardens would be destroyed. So, too, was the ancient City of the Dead, with its famous mausoleums and homes to thousands of extended families, destroyed for yet another thrown-together highway overpass on a road to nowhere. This was called "development" by the regime. Was this a sarcastic joke or a revelation of the meaning always implicit to the word "development," which had emerged out of nineteenth-century civilizational logics? Development for the semicivilized and performative sovereignty had come to this, in a world of monetizing, financializing, and militarizing everything.

A renewed macro-economy of the semicivilized had taken shape as well. Isolated stories and snippets of experiences that first had seemed strange, unthinkable, or abnormal had become the norm. As millions of Cairenes displaced from their historic homes regrouped and found ways to survive, the embodied commons of the semicivilized reassembled elsewhere along eddies of the isthmus, across the *barzakh*, in the undercommons (Moten and Harney 2013), in the surrounds (Simone 2022).

A year after my last trip to Cairo in 2022, the right to the *proprio* of proprioception—to possess a living body—came radically into question for those relegated to the status of the semicivilized. Recall that the semicivilized was linked from the start to the ancient concept of the barbarian, to which modernity and postmodernity had added layers of dehumanization. The deadly implications of that attribution were now on full display. The right to walk without limbs being maimed by bombing, without experimental barrel bombs or white phosphorus or the weight of rubble crushing breath, for day after day in which thirst and starvation were scientifically mobilized to do their worst, was but a dream for Palestinians and others facing the violence unleashed on those dubbed semicivilized. Walking along the streets of Cairo in 2024 as the writing of this book finally came to a close, I thought of the photos and stories and faded letters written in pen of the kind I recounted at the beginning of this book, in which passages through Palestine to Beirut and Damascus had been traveled so often and so easily, along channels multiple powers had struggled to control.

Despite ongoing claims about "ungovernability," transhistorical blood feuds, or the racialized nature of "the Arab" and "the Muslim," there is, in fact, nothing exceptional about war and conflict in the Middle East. The region was left with the obscured but violent legacies of the semicivilized. The war on terror brought this concept and others such as the barbarian back to center stage, along with the violence of weaponized legal regimes to sort people out. More than one hundred years after World War I, the War to End All Wars, the semicivilized condition was anything but abolished. The right to walk on ground that had once appeared stable could no longer be assumed. The liberal language of the self, embedded in the notion of proprioception, one's own perception, is easy to critique. But the notion of a body of one's own, with the right to breathe, to walk, and to exist, had come to seem a blessed wonder. Palestinians and Cairenes have become masters of proprioception, adjusting, always, to grounds that have never stood still.

As conditions through which a life could be lived as "civilized" or as "valued" grew further constrained, the semicivilized condition of living boxed into the waiting room of history became only more relevant. The waiting never ended. But in the meantime, the house to which that waiting room was supposed to lead had been blown up by the very "civilized" actors who had constructed the house and its terms of entry in the first place. Meanwhile, along the channels and pathways of mobility around and through the ever-changing urban worlds of Cairo, vitality of the collective commons ebbed and flowed along shifting grounds of the *barzakh*, never taken, never gone, never destroyed, carried along on our collective backs.

Introduction: On the Move

1   For multiple ways in which person, community, and territory can be related in different idioms of power in today's Middle East, and the importance of connectivity, mobility, and local categories of belonging in any project to transcend assumptions of territoriality, see Antrim (2012 and 2018).

2   As Frederick Cooper put it, the concept of colonialism in postcolonialism studies is a sweeping term that is "spatially diffuse and temporally spread out over five centuries" (2005, 16). For use related to Egypt, see Huber (2012, 142).

3   Here I think of Eve Sedgwick's *Epistemology of the Closet* (2008, 1) and the difference between adding a category like "bisexual" into the middle of the "homo/heterosexual definition" in a way that bolsters the logic of gender binaries by adding a "minoritizing view," versus unsettling the entire constitutive logic of binary gender oppositions (10).

4   For some works that influenced my thinking about extraterritoriality and the semicivilized, see Genell (2016); on Bodin, Grotius, and Hobbes, see Bartelson (2011); on history of international law and the "illusion of sovereignty," see Kennedy (1997); on the "standard of civilization" in international law, see Tzouvala (2020); on dividual sovereignty in the history of political theory in a way that made clear to me that the Ottoman Empire was no "exception," see Wilson (2008); on extraterritoriality, the capitulations, and international law,

see Özsu (2016a and 2016b) and Margolies et al. (2019); on extraterritoriality and sovereignty, see Kayaoğlu (2010) and Antony Anghie's (2002) classic work on international law, colonialism, and his encounter with the Mandates. The legal infrastructure of commerce that is sometimes called the capitulations, or discussed more broadly in terms of extraterritoriality, is also key; see Slys (2014), Özsu (2016a, 2016b), Svantesson (2015), and Pal (2020).

5   Today we usually speak of *extraterritoriality*, but in the eighteenth and nineteenth century, this word was used interchangeably with *exterritoriality* (Liu 1925, 18).

6   Extraterritorial rights had been an important dynamic of early modern empire; the accumulation of rights to extraterritorial privileges of Europeans expanded without overt military intervention or legal concessions. This was a dynamic of the "accumulation of extraterritoriality" internal to the logics of the system (Pal 2020).

7   On Egyptian debt and finance from the perspective of global capitalism, see Jakes (2020).

8   This book contributes to literature building on the framework of coloniality/modernity associated with Mignolo (2007), Quijano (1992), Quijano and Ennis (2000), and Wynter (2003) by bringing into focus the place of the Ottomans, the barbarians, and the semicivilized in formative debates of "modernity" and political theory. As Maldonado-Torres (2007) notes, coloniality is different from the assumption of unitary sovereignty as a juridical-legal status by a colonizing power and "survives colonialism" (244). But coloniality is "not simply the aftermath or the residual form of any given . . . colonial relation." It is forever renewed in conditions of the present, even as it was generated in the past. It is linked to the "discovery and conquest of the Americas" in the sixteenth century and to the associated invention of the concept of the primitive (243). Coloniality is "constitutive" of modernity and the European Enlightenment as its "darker side" (44). At the same time, critics of coloniality have pointed to the need to move beyond the framework of coloniality/modernity (D. Thomas 2022), which focus on the semicivilized can help us to do.

9   The noun *civilization* was derived from much older words—*civil* and *civility*—that implied a notion of culture and manners. See *Oxford English Dictionary*, s.v. "civility"; Fisch (1992, 721); Febvre (1930); and Benveniste (1953). For a key eighteenth-century use of *civilization*, see Ferguson (1782).

10   According to Aristotle, "barbarians" were "slaves by nature" because they did not live in free cities but were ruled by god-kings living in palaces, who govern them as if they were slaves (Pocock, 2009, 11–12).

11   This is similar to what Johannes Fabian (2014) would call the denial of coevalness.

12 For a different approach to colonialism, the law, and dehumanization in Egypt, see Esmeir (2012).

13 'Uways titled one of his books "the history that I carry on my back" (literally shoulders). 'Uways uses a case-study method to gain insight into the great people of Cairo and their relation to history and collectivity as well as to "hear the sounds of silent people" (Nagasawa 2014, 74).

14 See Rohrer (2007) for a review of critiques that notes at least twelve different meanings of *embodiment*.

15 On the *hara* and a sophisticated analysis of the relation between popular and official culture in Egypt and the links of culture to politics, see Mehrez (2008).

16 Relations being reworked in the emergence of sovereignty were between king (or emperor) and land-owning magnates; between king and emperor; between the secular ruler and church authority; among kings; and among states (Hinsley 1966).

17 For a recent discussion of alternative approaches to sovereignty, see D. Thomas (2022). For a brilliant analysis of "layered sovereignty," see Nora Barakat (2023). On finance and dividual sovereignty, see Derri (2021a, 2021b). See also Audra Simpson's (2014) related analysis of the "nested sovereignty" practiced by the British Empire and its reappropriation by the Mohawk Nation as part of a politics of refusal.

18 To put that short sentence in context: "Sovereignty is a term which, in international law, indicates a well-ascertained assemblage of separate powers or privileges ... there is not, nor has there ever been, anything in international law to prevent some of those rights being lodged with one possessor and some with another. Sovereignty has always been regarded as divisible" (Keene 2004, 78).

19 Sovereignty was also divisible in British and Dutch imperial systems in the East, where the British and Dutch plugged themselves into "existing imperial hierarchies, where the principle of suzerainty was already established" (Keene 2004, 93). See also Samara Esmeir's (2012) analysis of the hybrid nature of colonial law in Egypt.

20 A new generation of Ottoman Empire and Middle East historians has shed a great deal of light on dynamics of dividual sovereignty, extraterritoriality, global finance, international law, and property regimes in the Ottoman Empire. See, for example, N. E. Barakat (2015, 2023), Derri (2021a, 2021b), Dolbee (2022), Can and Genell (2020), Can and Low (2016), Genell (2016, 2019), and Nye (2023).

21 For helpful summaries of some of that literature, see Anand, Gupta, and Appel (2018), and Larkin (2013).

22   For a related line of questioning, see Yarimar Bonilla's work on "unsettling sovereignty" (2017) and "non-sovereign futures" (2015). For a semiotic analysis of ground and grounds in the context of archeology, see Kockelman (2005, 2012).

23   Such a situation is not unique to these empires. Passports were not always used by territorial nation-states, as Torpey (2018) reminds us, and some states like Israel have no declared borders.

24   "No problem which confronted the Lausanne Conference [which followed up on aspects of ending the war and the Empire that were not settled at Versailles] contributed more to its difficulties than . . . the capitulations," wrote Lucius Thayer (1923, 207), a diplomat ("formerly engaged in work with the Near East Relief in Anatolia") whose work is cited in literature on the capitulations to this day, about the implications of the abrogation of the capitulations for the United States.

25   Cairo is an important node of a great Arabo-Islamic literary tradition that once included millions of distinct books (El Shamsy 2022, 8). Those books, like archives from the dust, faced constant dangers from the "archenemies of the written word—humidity, fire, war, insects, and censorship" (8) as well as the dangers of organized, legal, extractive theft via the free market. Here I refer to what Shamsy calls the "book drain to Europe," which intensified with Napoleon and the "Orientalists who accompanied Napoleon on his invasion of Egypt" (10) during his travels across the Mediterranean on the great ship *L'Orient*, which landed at Alexandria in 1798.

26   In the words of Malcolm X: "President Gamal Abdul Nasser was so right when he said that there are three circles: the Arab, the African and the Islamic. Only others are not as far-sighted as he is to see it." See Alhassen (2015, 16fn18, citing "Malcolm X on Islam, Africa and the US," *Egyptian Gazette*, August 17, 1964, 3). Alhassen notes that Malcolm X referred to Nasser as his "president" in this interview. The interviewer noted that Malcolm X was not only an admirer of Nasser; he was also a personal friend of many African leaders.

27   For a lucid account of this process for the non-specialist, see especially Fahmy (2009), and on the Ottoman firman of 1841 that gave Mehmet Ali "what he had been striving for ever since he landed in Egypt in 1801: an unambiguous pledge by the Ottoman sultan, backed by all major European powers, that he would continue to rule his prized province until his death, and that thereafter his descendants would inherit the governorship of Egypt and its enhanced wealth" (50).

28   On this world from the perspective of Sephardic Jewish families and their archives, see Stein (2016, 2019).

29 For some important work on settlement, property, and sovereignty in Palestine in the past and present relevant to my concerns, see R. Barakat (2018a, 2018b), Dallasheh (2015), Rabie (2021), Seikaly (2015, 2019), and Salamanca et al. (2012).

30 The Ottomans were also deeply engaged in theory and praxis of international law by the nineteenth century. See, for example, Özsu (2016b), and Can and Low (2016).

31 On Gentili and his life, see Van Der Molen ([1937] 1968), and Kingsbury (1998, 713–14). For English editions of some of his most important works, see Gentili ([1594] 1924) and Gentili ([1612] 1933) In what follows, I rely heavily on interpretations of Gentili by Wagner (2012), Kingsbury (1998), and Kingsbury and Sraumann (2010).

32 This pertains to the framework of the "English School" of international law. For a different assessment of Gentili and the law of nations and sovereignty, see Peter Schröder's chapter "Vitoria, Gentili, Bodin," 163–65, in Kingsbury and Straumann (2010).

33 This is not to idealize the law of nations. Some of the most overtly racist language about the semicivilized came from this tradition.

34 The theory of improvement is usually attributed to John Locke and his *Two Treatises on Government*, written in 1660 and published in 1689. See Locke (1960).

35 For one starting point on the Ottoman Public Debt Administration, see Eldem (2005).

36 See D. Thomas (2022) on sand, beach, and shoals as "in between spaces that disturb the certainties of territory and mapping, the colonial cartographies of sovereignty, and the divisions between Indigenous and African futures" and as "spaces, and frames, that might help us generate a 'de-colonial,' rather than postcolonial, notion of sovereignty" (250, citing Bonilla [2017] and King [2019]).

Chapter 1. Fixing Space, Moving People

1 The Egyptian constitution stipulates that the government must be located in Cairo. As such, planners of the New Administrative Capital stretched the geographical lines and borders of Cairo to insure it would be included in the expanded bounds of Cairo, rather than an independent entity. My thanks to Muhammad Addakhakhny for alerting me to this.

2 For analysis of the Egyptian military economy, see Sayigh (2019, 2022).

3 A substantial literature exists on the unfolding, meaning, and significance of the January 25, 2011, Revolution in Egypt. To touch on some relevant writings from and of the period, see Attalah (2019), Abd el-Fattah (2022),

and the entire archives of *Mada Masr* and *Jadaliyya*. On politics and "time out of time," see Sabea (2013). For some other important treatments, see also, El-Tamami (2013), Elsadda (2010), Nassar and Moodley (2020), Sakr (2023), and Seikaly and Scalanghe (2022).

4 Nora Barakat (2023) uses *state space* "to describe the landscape within a territorially conceived and hierarchical administrative and judicial apparatus and a theoretically uniform and bounded grid of property relations" (4). Here she is citing Lefebvre (2003) and Goswami (2004, 9).

5 For a lively popular account with photos, see Antoine Vanner, "The Opening of the Suez Canal, 1969: The Royal Navy Trumps the French," *Dawlish Chronicles*, February 2, 2018, https://dawlishchronicles.com/2018/02/02/opening-the-suez-canal-1869/.

6 For excellent analysis of structural debt crises in Egypt under Sisi and historically back to the nineteenth century, see Solomon (2024).

7 On this and financial innovation in Egypt in this period, see Jakes (2020). All this follows in the tradition of massive infrastructure projects since his grandfather, Mehmet Ali, undertook a canal between Alexandria and the Nile with 300,000 workers brought in through unpaid corvée labor; about one-third of these laborers died (Fahmy 2009, 30).

8 Le Père's (1809) report was published in *Description de l'Egypte*.

9 Here I touch on a large and growing literature on various aspects of the Suez Canal. To start, see Elshakry (2007), Huber (2012, 2013), Jakes (2021), Karabell (2003), Khalili (2021), and Marsot (1975, 89–93).

10 For one discussion in the broader context of the Middle East, the Balkans, and international financial control, see Tunçer (2015, 29–52).

11 This was a "neoclassical structure dreamed up by a French Egyptologist, Mariette Pasha; designed by a French architect, Marcel Dourgnon; and built by an Italian construction company, Garozzo and Zaffarani, the museum was planted in Egypt for practical reasons but was in fact meant to celebrate a heritage that Europeans had already appropriated as their own." See Rabbat (2011, 185–86).

12 As of 2018, total assets under management in sovereign wealth funds globally amounted to $7.97 trillion, with 80 funds in operation around the world. See Bahoo, Alon, and Paltrinieri (2020), who define sovereign wealth funds as "investment funds that are directly or indirectly owned, controlled and/or monitored by a government organization or arrangement (national or subnational) to stabilize macroeconomic fluctuations due to the imbalance of payments. They can have multiple objectives, such as stabilization, savings, revenue generation, and pension payments" (8).

13 For a review of literature on sovereign wealth funds, see Bahoo, Alon, and Paltrinieri (2020), and Rozanov (2005), whom Bahoo, Alon, and Paltrinieri

credit with coining the phrase. On the Egyptian fund, now called The Sovereign Fund of Egypt (TSFE), see Haroun (2021), Moneim (2020), and Sayigh (2019, 2022). Haroun (2021) is a conference presentation with English-language mistakes, but it has very helpful comparison charts about the structure of TSFE in comparison to other sovereign wealth funds globally, and about its institutional components.

14   See Sayigh's (2022) argument that real estate is now "the primary recipient of public investment and vehicle for generating revenue, driving economic growth, and attracting private investors" in Egypt (5).

15   For example, in 2014, President Sisi demanded that the Suez Canal expansion be accomplished in one year, rather than the three years that army engineers had estimated. Estimates show that this inflated the cost from $4 billion to over $8 billion (Sayigh 2022, 5).

Chapter 2. Infrastructures of the Semicivilized

1   I conducted two of three interviews with Mr. Amir (a pseudonym) together with Essam Fawzi in summer–fall 2015.

2   Nasser's Arabic was also called *bakbashi* Arabic, in contrast to the refined Arabic of the pre-1952 political elite, since Nasser was a *bakbashi* (lieutenant colonel) at the time of the coup. My thanks to Muhammad Addakhakhny for this point.

3   More recently, "technocrat," transliterated into Arabic letters, became the name of a group of exiled critics of President Sisi who critique the economic policies of the government.

4   Historian Omnia El Shakry (2007) calls this a "social-welfare mode of regulation . . . underpinned by an economic system of 'etatism'" (198).

5   During my fieldwork in Cairo in the 1990s, men in trades and who owned small productive workshops in Cairo used the word *bizniz* disparagingly to refer to clever and morally dubious action on the market aimed at gaming the system for short-term gains (Elyachar 2005).

6   For a brief history of the Faculty of Commerce at Cairo University, see the schools' website: https://cu.edu.eg/page.php?pg=contentFront /SubSectionData.php&SubSectionId=37.

7   My thanks to Muhammad Addakhakhny for reminding me of this point.

8   See Vitalis (1995) for a crucial analysis of this period and some of the individuals I mention.

9   Abdel-Khalek, October 10, 2011, email communication with the author.

10   In these paragraphs on Bonaparte, finance, and the Saint-Simonians, I draw heavily from Mastnak (2021) and his analysis of "Bonapartism."

11 On the Mandates, see a classic analysis by Antony Anghie (2002) and his claim that "examination of the Mandate System reveals issues of enduring theoretical and practical significance about sovereignty, international institutions, and the management of relations between European and non-European peoples. This is because it is in the Mandate System that these three broad themes first come into relationship with each other" (516). See also Anghie (2012), Seikaly (2019), and Cyrus Schayegh and Andrew Arsan's (2015) edited volume, *The Routledge Handbook of the History of the Middle East Mandates*, particularly Schayegh's "Mandates and/as Decolonization" (412–19) and Natasha Wheatley's "Mandate System as a Style of Reasoning" (106–22).

12 The most important communications channel for the British Empire in Egypt was the Suez Canal. The Suez Canal was then, as now, a hub and potential chokepoint of global commerce and imperial communications. "Security of communications" also referred to Britain's extensive network of trains and underwater cables winding around the vast stretches of the British Empire, with Egypt in general and the Suez Canal in particular as a hub where, to this day, wires and cables and channels converge underwater through the Suez Canal, just like massive container ships pile up on the surface.

13 Also see Genell (2019) for detailed analysis of the process leading up to declaration of the Mandates and the Veiled Protectorate in Egypt in the context of the dissolution of the Ottoman Empire. For other relevant sources on the Mandates, see Abou-Hodeib (2020), Pursley (2019), and Schayegh and Arsan (2015).

14 The notion of bonds as a safe haven would itself become problematic by late 2022's dramatic decline in global bond markets, starting in the UK, Egypt's former colonizer. In a joke/not joke coming out of the Egyptian IMF negotiations on social media in October 2022, Egyptians were told not to worry about their bonds because they were in so much better shape than the new emerging market economy, the United Kingdom. See Kassab, al-Naggar, and Mamdouh (2022).

15 Timothy E. Kaldas, "85% of Egypt's reserves are made up of deposits from 3 Gulf allies," Twitter, November 8, 2022, 8:14 a.m., https://twitter.com/tekaldas/status/1589984712424321027?s=20&t=rNCog-9GRf-D7h6sjkDleQ).

16 See the Central Bank of Egypt, *External Situation Report of the Egyptian Economy*, 2022/2023, vols. 79–82, https://www.cbe.org.eg/ar/EconomicResearch/Publications/Pages/ExternalPosition.aspx. Accessed November 14, 2022, thanks to a tweet from Ziad Daoud.

17 Lively histories of the Eastern Telegraph Company can be found on the websites of corporations and trade journals concerned with telegraphs

and cables and communications. One example is C&W Communications, a very modern corporation that traces its history back to 1856 and a man named John Bender who, over the course of his life, was a cotton merchant, member of the British Parliament, and chairman of the largest submarine telegraph-operating company in the world. See C&W Communications, "Our Story," accessed July 16, 2024, https://www.cwc.com /live/past-present/our-history.html. For more on Egyptian telecom history, see Rachty (1999); on Ottoman telegraphs, imperialism, and territoriality, see Minawi (2016). On telegraph lines and the Mixed Courts in Egypt, see Hoyle (1987). On telegraphs and temporality, see Barak (2013). On the business and politics of British "underwater telegraph cables" as they pertain to Egypt and India, see Glover (2020) and Headrick and Griset (2001). On industrial research and innovation at Eastern Telegraph Company, see Noakes (2014).

18   See such cases discussed in multiple places in the *Gazettes of the Proceedings of Mixed Courts*, edited by Phillipe Gelat Bey. For cases about telegraphs and the Mixed Courts, see Hoyle (1987, 368–69).

19   These strategic companies that made the infrastructure and shipping materials for moving through the canal included Timsah Shipbuilding Company, Canal Harbor and Great Projects Company, Canal Mooring and Lights Company, Canal Naval Constructions Company, Canal Company for Ropes and Fiber projects, Suez Shipyard Company, Port Said Engineering Works Company, and Canal Company for the Nile Arsenal. See Kassab, al-Naggar, and Mamdouh (2022).

20   Huxley finished his Masters of Arts degree in anthropology at Harvard the year he returned from the Syrian Expedition in 1902, with a thesis on a "physical anthropology study of Levantine populations" he had examined during the expedition (Browman and Williams 2013). He published a report of his findings in *American Anthropologist* in 1902, as well as an article in the *Journal of the American Oriental Society* that same year, on "Syrian Songs, Proverbs, and Stories."

Chapter 3. Sorting Things Out

1   At its founding, the Mixed Courts had thirty-two judges (Wilner 1975, 411fn20). By the 1930s, seventy judges served on the Mixed Courts; they were drawn from countries that had signed capitulatory treaties with the Ottoman Empire and the founding Charter of the Mixed Courts: Germany, Austria, Belgium, Denmark, Spain, the United States, France, Great Britain, Greece, Italy, Norway, Holland, Portugal, and Russia (409fn9).

2   See "Invention of the Typewriter," Online Typing.org, August 23, 2019, https://onlinetyping.org/blog/invention-of-the-typewriter.php.

3   As early as 1093, Amalfi maintained its own consular court at Naples in accordance with the provisions of its Tables. In the fifteenth century, both in England and the Netherlands, Italian consuls with judicial functions were to be found. In form and content alike, the grant of privileges to English merchants in 1555 by the emperor of Russia bears a striking resemblance to the Ottoman capitulations. See Thayer (1923, 208).

4   For a brilliant ethnography of *waqf* in Beirut, see Moumtaz (2021).

5   The two terms are often used as synonyms, but *wakala* could include customs offices as well (AlSayyad 2011, 143).

6   On the Mamluks in Cairo and the transition to Ottoman rule, drawing on extensive sources from pious trusts or waqf (*awqaf*), architecture, and Islamic courts, see Behrens-Abouseif (1994). For analysis of gifts and diplomacy in the Mamluk Sultanate and inter-imperial worlds in a fashion that would illuminate anthropological analyses of gift exchange, see Behrens-Abouseif (2014).

7   Like so many of these institutions of hospitality, the *rab* is linked to a Roman institution: the Roman *insulae*, which was "located along the main streets or their immediate vicinity between the main bazaars. Rarely does it have a courtyard" (Raymond 2000, 57, citing Clerget 1934, 1:316–17).

8   See Constable (2003). Here we can see the Ottoman Empire as the continuity of the Western Roman Empire being overthrown farther west.

9   This process is part of what Banaji (2020) analyzes as commercial capitalism.

10   For a classic analysis of establishment of the Mixed Courts in the context of a dynamic and shifting field of power between Cairo and Istanbul, where the brilliant maneuvers of Khedive Ismail for more independence also land Egypt in the grip of structural indebtedness to Europe, see Marsot (1975).

11   Making the *indigène* in Egypt was a different process than in other parts of North Africa colonized by the French. See Thénault (2014) and Davis (2022).

12   On the "accumulation" of power in the consular courts and the inexorable expansion of the dynamics of extraterritorial jurisdiction within the Ottoman Empire, see Pal (2020).

13   See Hanley (2017, 293): "Protected imperial subjects able to substantiate standing were channeled into the legal status of Western nationality and (crucially) citizenship."

14   Sorting out became even more consequential in the decades to come, culminating in Egypt with the wave of financial sector nationalizations, when Abdel Nasser expropriated the wealth of remaining Egyptian "extraterritorials," stamping some Egyptian passports with a one-way *laissez-passez* with the words "never to return" (Tignor 2010, 269).

15 See Rusty Greaves, "Egypt Khedivate Judge's Badge Question," Gentleman's Military Interest Club, June 4, 2018, https://gmic.co.uk/topic/69749-egypt -khedivate-judges-badge-question/page/2/.

Chapter 4. Commons Goods

1 "The common is a long-running story that precedes, traverses, and extends beyond the Industrial Revolution and modernity with a strong and unexpected resurgence in contemporary capitalism. It is therefore useful to [review] . . . the key developments of this historical journey and the questions it raised to better understand the origin, meaning, and issues at stake in the current debate" (Brancaccio and Vercellone 2019, 699). See also a review of commons literature claiming a new field of "communology" that would contribute to renewal of progressive politics after 2010 (Mattei and Mancall 2019).

2 For some other important treatments of space, time, the body, gender, and the commons, see El-Tamami (2013), Elsadda (2010), Nassar and Moodley (2020), and Seikaly and Scalanghe (2022).

3 Hugo Grotius ([1609] 2004) formed these arguments to defend the position of the Dutch and the Dutch East India Company against the Portuguese, and their claims to a monopoly over commerce across the oceans to their vast network of imperial forts and factories in India, Africa, and the Americas. Grotius claimed these channels for commerce as a common, in the sense that no one nation or sovereign power should control it.

4 Maine's theory of the commons also laid out an intellectual framework for what became British social anthropology. See Kuper (2009) and Kockelman (2007).

5 My argument here is specific to urban commons.

6 Kockelman's concept of semiotic community builds, first, on Leonard Bloomfield's 1933 definition of speech community as "a group of people who interact by means of speech" or a "system of speech-signals" (Bloomfield [1933] 1984, 29, 42, as cited in Kockelman 2005, 261–62). Thirty-five years later, John Grumperz ([1968] 2001) shifted attention to the "sociolinguistic study of speech communities." Where Bloomfield's speech community emphasized commonality within a community with shared communicative resources, Grumperz looked at both differences and similarities among "speech varieties" in one social field. Kockelman's semiotic community brings together Bloomfield and Grumperz and makes a crucial move: he shifts emphasis from linguistic code in particular to nonlinguistic signs more generally.

7   For the rest of Mead's quote: "Only in terms of gestures as significant symbols is the existence of mind or intelligence possible; for only in terms of gestures which are significant symbols can thinking—which is simply an internalized or implicit conversation of the individual with himself by means of such gestures—take place" ([1934] 1967, 47). Leroi-Gourhan (1993), by contrast, rejected the notion of a clear distinction between gesture and linguistic form. Gesture is not antithetical to linguistic code, and there is a long history of thinking about the relation. Gesture was long seen as more primitive than spoken language, as in John Locke's ([1690] 1975) theory of natural language; Mandeville's *The Fable of the Bees* ([1732] 1988); Condillac ([1756] 2001); and Rousseau ([1755] 2004).

8   For ethnographic analysis of electricity and water infrastructures in the Global South, see Anand (2017); Anand, Gupta, and Appel (2018); Larkin (2008, 2013); Nucho (2016); and Schnitzler (2016).

Chapter 5. Phatic Labor and Channels of Commerce

1   For a beautiful analysis of coffeehouses and other essential social institutions of Cairo through the literature written in and about them, see Mehrez (2008).

2   By the time I finished this long period of fieldwork, there was one other, much-smaller coffeehouse that carried the basics: coffee, tea, and *shisha*. Over the years, more coffeehouses reopened.

3   See Nucho (2016) on such practices in Beirut.

4   This is similar to the language of the "sinews of trade," which Laleh Khalili (2020) deployed to brilliant effect.

Chapter 6. Across the *Barzakh*

1   The move from raised fist to "taking a knee" on the ground in Black resistance movements and sports since Colin Kaepernick's 2016 protest also shifts attention to body in relation to ground.

2   See the "Overview" at Citystars Properties' website, http://www.citystars .com.eg/about_us.php?active=page_overview: "With the government opening up Egypt's property sector to the international market, the country has seen a boom in real estate. This has seen the development of major new communities for people who wanted and could afford a quieter life away from the city centre. . . . With this in mind, Citystars Properties filled the gap with Citystars Heliopolis, Cairo. The integrated mixed-use nature of Citystars Heliopolis made it an automatic choice for business, leisure, shopping and entertainment. Citystars Properties was able to combine the best

elements of work and play into one location that became an instant hit as the city's favoured destination."

3   The following by Ibn ʿArabi (1911, 3:274.28) is also often cited in relation to *barzakh*: "The Real is sheer Light and the impossible is sheer darkness. Darkness never turns into Light, and Light never turns into darkness. The created realm is the *barzakh* between Light and darkness. In its essence it is qualified neither by darkness nor by Light, since it is the *barzakh* and the middle, having a property from each of its two sides. That is why He 'appointed' for man 'two eyes and guided him on the two highways' (Koran 90:8–10), for man exists between the two paths. Through one eye and one path he accepts Light and looks upon it in the measure of his preparedness. Through the other eye and the other path he looks upon darkness and turns toward it." There are vast literatures on Ibn ʿArabi. For English-language sources, Chittick (2020) is widely cited and a good starting point. On Ibn ʿArabi in relation to my argument, see also Bashier (2004) and El Shakry (2018). On Ibn ʿArabi and implications for debates about place, space, and time, see Winkel (2019). On the relation of Ibn ʿArabi to Andalusian mysticism and the Islamic West, see López-Anguita (2021).

4   Pandolfo (1997) draws on *barzakh* as a concept in relation to the world of dreams and the passage to life, as "sendings from elsewhere" that like dreams, are never one's own, "from the region of death and the beyond," or "an intermediate imaginal realm, an entre-deux between absence and presence, spiritual and bodily existence, between self and other, the living and the dead" (9).

5   For the first definition, see "Isthmus," in *Encyclopedia Britannica*, accessed September 10, 2024, https://www.britannica.com/science/isthmus. For the second, see "Isthmus," in *Cambridge Dictionary*, accessed September 10, 2024, https://dictionary.cambridge.org/us/dictionary/english/isthmus.

6   An interview with Abou El Fetouh called "The Time Is Out of Joint" (Bailey 2016) offers other pathways to think with this concept in relation to disjointed space and time in the global urban.

7   For one discussion of the twentieth-century literature on proprioception, see Proske and Gandevia (2012). For references to literature on proprioception up to 2010, see Berthoz (2000) and Nicolelis (2011).

8   Sherrington studied the spinal cord using experimental physiology and neuroanatomical methods of his time (Burke 2007, 889). In the seventh edition of his *Textbook of Physiology*, Sherrington wrote chapters on the nervous system that "solved at a stroke the great question of the direction of the nerve currents in their travel through the brain and spinal cord," showing that nerve currents were unidirectional. In the reflex arc, he found, the "'wiring diagram' of the spinal reflexes, afferent (sensory) and efferent

(motor) elements were related at centres in the grey matter by synaptic contacts between the neurons" (Breathnach 2004).

9   A comparative history of thought in Great Britain and France on such issues is waiting to be written. Berthoz (2000) offers a good overview of research up to 2000. See also the work of his Laboratory of Physiology of Perception and Action.

10   William James studied physiology at Berlin University in 1867–1868, taught an undergraduate course in comparative physiology at Harvard in 1872, and established the first American psychology laboratory in 1874–1875. Théodule Ribot, author of *Diseases of the Personality*, was another interlocutor of William James (Ribot [1895] 2009). They exchanged letters for twenty years (Bixler 1945, 155, 157). James said that Alexander influenced him in his classic work on the theory of the self, which built on concepts of consciousness, space, and physiology (Bixler 1945, 155, 157; Morgan 2010, 2). In 1890, James described and sketched out a "neural circuit that anticipates the sensory consequences of movement" (Berthoz 2000, 9). For information about the Alexander Technique, including links to resources, see their institutional website, "The Complete Guide to the Alexander Technique," accessed July 20, 2024, https://alexandertechnique.com/.

11   On the related phenomenon of synesthesia, where input from one sense is experienced as another, see Cytowic (1995).

12   Freud was concerned that "progress in understanding the brain would be too slow for his taste" (LeDoux 2003, 39).

13   Jacques Lacan referred to Ibn 'Arabi on a number of occasions in his writings. Moustapha Safouan, a member of Lacan's inner circle, originally trained with Ibn 'Arabi scholar and translator Abu al-'Ala al-Afifi (El Shakry 2017, 8).

14   Franz Gall popularized cranioscopy as a method "for identifying fundamental character traits and mental skills through careful analysis of a person's skull. . . . Gall divided the brain into twenty-seven 'organs' (translated as skull bumps), nineteen of which he said were shared by all animals, up to and including humans. In addition to the organs dedicated to basic emotions such as the instinct of reproduction, the love of one's offspring, pride, arrogance, vanity, and ambition, there were organs specified to dictate a person's religion, poetic talent, and firmness of purpose and perseverance" (Nicolelis 2011, 35).

15   In his popular writings on neuroscience, Nicolelis (2011) draws on metaphors and stories from football and political mass events, like mass revolts. We need, he writes, to "investigate the physiological principles that underlie the dynamic interactions of large distributed populations of neurons that define a brain circuit" (16).

16   Here I have been inspired by work in the anthropology of dance, kines-
        thesia, and collective movement (Chin 2014; Cox 2015; Cox 2021; Kwan
        2013; Ness 1992; Samudra 2008), Indigenous theories and politics of col-
        lectivity and relationality (Estes 2019; Moreton-Robinson 2016; TallBear
        2016), rhythmanalysis of urban life and endurance (Lefebvre 2013; Simone
        2018), and scientific research into the multiple ways in which movement
        forward is inscribed in the pathways of receptors of the past.

17   On gift exchange between Queen Elizabeth and Sultan Murad, see Skilliter
        (1977).

18   "In Greek he is also called Hermes, that is, *ermeneuse*, which in Latin we
        call translating, for the reason that fluency in languages is needful to a
        trader. He is said to pass through both realms, the upper and the lower,
        because now he rushes aloft through the winds, now plunging down he
        seeks out the lower world through storms" (Fulgentius 1971, 59).

19   Urbicide involves attack on the urban form itself (Graham 2003; Coward
        2008). Cities and towns of the semicivilized became magnets for urbicide
        in Bosnia in the 1990s and in Gaza in 2023. Cities targeted from Sarajevo
        through to Baghdad, Falluja, Raqqa, Mosul, Damascus, Aleppo, and Beirut
        faced the decimation of lingering traces of inter-imperial infrastructures
        from the Ottoman era and those built up by the nonaligned movement,
        prominently Yugoslavia.

20   For one presentation, see Underground/On the Surface (trailer), uploaded
        to YouTube, April 12, 2012, https://www.youtube.com/watch?v=6C1dyAaf-
        CnM. On "Cairo Calling," see Metwaly (2014).

REFERENCES

Abaza, Mona. 2020. *Cairo Collages: Everyday Life Practices after the Event*. Manchester: Manchester University Press.

Abd el-Fattah, Alaa. 2022. *You Have Not Yet Been Defeated: Selected Works 2011–2021*. New York: Seven Stories.

Abdel-Malek, Talaat. 2002. "Exports: The Five-Piece Puzzle (2)." *Al-Ahram Weekly* 587, May 23–29, 2002.

Abou El Fetouh, Tarek. 2015. "Lest the Two Seas Meet." Universes in Universe, May 2015. https://universes.art/en/nafas/articles/2015/lest-the-two-seas-meet.

Abou-Hodeib, Toufoul. 2020. "Involuntary History: Writing Levantines into the Nation." *Contemporary Levant* 5 (1): 44–53. https://doi.org/10.1080/20581831.2020.1710674.

Addakhakhny, Muhammad. 2022. "Egypt: A Battle for the Heart and Soul of Cairo." Middle East Eye, January 14, 2022. https://www.middleeasteye.net/discover/egypt-cairo-downtown-gentrification-locals-concerns.

Adly, Amr. 2020. "Baladi Capitalism." In *Cleft Capitalism: The Social Origins of Failed Market Making in Egypt*, 177–207. Stanford, CA: Stanford University Press. https://doi.org/10.1515/9781503612211-012.

Alhassen, Maytha. 2015. "The 'Three Circles' Construction: Reading Black Atlantic Islam through Malcolm X's Words and Friendships." *Journal of Africana Religions* 3 (1): 1–17.

Al-Maqrīzī. [1270] 1854. *Al-Mawā ʿiẓ wa-al-Iʿtibār fī Dhikr al-Khiṭaṭ wa-al-Āthār*. Vol. 2. Cairo: Bulaq.

Al-Saleh, Danya, and Mohammed Rafi Arefin. 2020. "Introduction: A Roundtable on Engineers, Technopolitics, and the Environment." *Jadaliyya*, November 16, 2020. https://www.jadaliyya.com/Details/41992.

AlSayyad, Nezar. 2011. *Cairo: Histories of a City*. Cambridge, MA: Belknap.

Ambrust, Walter. 1996. *Mass Culture and Modernism in Egypt*. Cambridge: Cambridge University Press.

Ambrust, Walter. 2020. *Martyrs and Tricksters: An Ethnography of the Egyptian Revolution*. Princeton, NJ: Princeton University Press.

Amin, Shahira. 2021. "Curse or No Curse, Cairo's Mummy Parade Goes Smoothly." *Al-Monitor*, April 5, 2021. https://www.al-monitor.com/originals/2021/04/curse-or-no-curse-cairos-mummy-parade-goes-smoothly.

Anand, Nikhil. 2017. *Hydraulic City: Water and the Infrastructures of Citizenship in Mumbai*. Durham, NC: Duke University Press.

Anand, Nikhil, Akhil Gupta, and Hannah Appel, eds. 2018. *The Promise of Infrastructure*. Durham, NC: Duke University Press.

Anghie, Antony. 2002. "Colonialism and the Birth of International Institutions: Sovereignty, Economy, and the Mandate System of the League of Nations." *New York University Journal of International Law and Politics* 34 (3): 513–634.

Anghie, Antony. 2012. *Imperialism, Sovereignty, and the Making of International Law*. Cambridge: Cambridge University Press.

Antrim, Zayde. 2012. *Routes and Realms: The Power of Place in the Early Islamic World*. Oxford: Oxford University Press.

Antrim, Zayde. 2018. *Mapping the Middle East*. Chicago: Reaktion.

Aquinas, Saint Thomas. 1975. *Summa theologiae*. Vol. 38. Edited by Marcus Lefébure and T. Gilby. London: Eyre and Spottiswoode.

Arsan, Andrew. 2021. "Versailles: Arab Desires, Arab Futures." *Public Books*, January 25, 2021. https://www.publicbooks.org/versailles-arab-desires-arab-futures/.

Assaad, Ragui. 1993. "Formal and Informal Institutions in the Labor Market with Applications to the Construction Sector in Egypt." *World Development* 21 (6): 925–39.

Attalah, Lina. 2019. "On Power, Machines, and Departures: Running Mada Masr in Today's Egypt." *Funambulist*, no. 22, February 29, 2019. https://thefunambulist.net/magazine/22-publishing-struggle/power-machines-departures-running-mada-masr-todays-egypt-lina-attalah.

Bahoo, Salman, Ilan Alon, and Andrea Paltrinieri. 2020. "Sovereign Wealth Funds: Past, Present and Future." *International Review of Financial Analysis* 67. https://doi.org/10.1016/j.irfa.2019.101418.

Bailey, Stephanie. 2016. "The Time Is Out of Joint: Tarek Abou El Fetouh in Conversation with Stephanie Bailey." *Ibraaz Interviews*, May 6, 2016. http://www.ibraaz.org/interviews/193.

Balibar, Étienne. 2019. Lecture. Columbia University, November 2019.

Banaji, Jairus. 2020. *A Brief History of Commercial Capitalism*. Chicago: Haymarket.

Barak, On. 2013. *On Time: Technology and Temporality in Modern Egypt*. Berkeley: University of California Press.

Barakat, Nora Elizabeth. 2015. "Regulating Land Rights in Late Nineteenth-Century Salt: The Limits of Legal Pluralism in Ottoman Property Law." *Journal of the Ottoman and Turkish Studies Association* 2 (1): 101–19. https://doi.org /10.2979/jottturstuass.2.1.101.

Barakat, Nora Elizabeth. 2023. *Bedouin Bureaucrats: Mobility and Property in the Ottoman Empire*. Stanford, CA: Stanford University Press.

Barakat, Rana. 2018a. "Lifta, the Nakba, and the Museumification of Palestine's History." *Native American and Indigenous Studies* 5 (2): 1–15.

Barakat, Rana. 2018b. "Writing/Righting Palestine Studies: Settler Colonialism, Indigenous Sovereignty and Resisting the Ghost(s) of History." *Settler Colonial Studies* 8 (3): 349–63. https://doi.org/10.1080/2201473X.2017.1300048.

Bartelson, Jens. 2011. "On the Indivisibility of Sovereignty." *Republics of Letters* 2 (2): 85–94.

Bashier, Salman H. 2004. *Ibn al-'Arabī's Barzakh: The Concept of the Limit and the Relationship between God and the World*. Albany, NY: SUNY Press.

Bayat, Asef. 2013. *Life as Politics: How Ordinary People Change the Middle East*. Stanford, CA: Stanford University Press.

Behrens-Abouseif, Doris. 1994. *Egypt's Adjustment to Ottoman Rule: Institutions, Waqf and Architecture in Cairo (16th and 17th Centuries)*. Leiden: Brill.

Behrens-Abouseif, Doris. 2014. *Practising Diplomacy in the Mamluk Sultanate: Gifts and Material Culture in the Medieval Islamic World*. London: I. B. Tauris.

Bell, Christine. 2016. "Capitulations." In *The Law of Armed Conflict and the Use of Force: The Max Planck Encyclopedia of Public International Law*, edited by Frauke Lachenmann and Rüdiger Wolfrum, 169–72. Oxford: Oxford University Press.

Benton, Lauren A. 2002. *Law and Colonial Culture: Legal Regimes in World History, 1400–1900*. Cambridge: Cambridge University Press.

Benveniste, Émile. 1953. "Civilisation: Contribution à l'histoire du mot." In *Éventail de l'histoire vivante*. Vol. 1, *Hommage à Lucien Febvre*, edited by Fernand Braudel. Paris: Libraire Armand Colin.

Berenson, Ruth. 2002. *The Operatic State: Cultural Policy and the Opera House*. London: Routledge.

Bermúdez, José Luis. 2018. *The Bodily Self: Selected Essays on Self-Consciousness*. Cambridge, MA: MIT Press.

Berthoz, Alain. 2000. *The Brain's Sense of Movement*. Cambridge, MA: Harvard University Press.

Bhandar, Brenna. 2018. *Colonial Lives of Property: Law, Land, and Racial Regimes of Ownership*. Durham, NC: Duke University Press.

Birch, Kean, and Fabian Muniesa. 2020. "Introduction: Assetization and Techno-scientific Capitalism." In *Assetization: Turning Things into Assets in Technoscientific Capitalism*, edited by Kean Birch and Fabian Muniesa, 1–41. Cambridge, MA: MIT Press.

Bishara, Fahad Ahmad. 2017. *A Sea of Debt: Law and Economic Life in the Western Indian Ocean, 1780–1950*. Cambridge: Cambridge University Press.

Bixler, Julius Seelye. 1945. "Letters from William James to Théodule A. Ribot." *Colby Quarterly* 1 (10): 153–61.

Bloomfield, Leonard. [1933] 1984. *Language*. Chicago: University of Chicago Press.

Bobbio, Noberto. 1996. *Left and Right: The Significance of a Political Distinction*. Translated and introduced by Allan Cameron. Chicago: University of Chicago Press.

Bonilla, Yarimar. 2015. *Non-sovereign Futures: French Caribbean Politics in the Wake of Disenchantment*. Chicago: University of Chicago Press.

Bonilla, Yarimar. 2017. "Unsettling Sovereignty." *Cultural Anthropology* 32 (3): 330–39.

Bourdieu, Pierre. 1990. *The Logic of Practice*. Translated by Richard Nice. Stanford, CA: Stanford University Press.

Bourdieu, Pierre. 1993. "Concluding Remarks: For a Sociogenetic Understanding of Intellectual Works." In *Bourdieu: Critical Perspectives*, edited by Edward Lipuma, Moishe Postone, and Craig Calhoun, 263–75. Chicago: University of Chicago Press.

Bowker, Geoffrey C., Julia Elyachar, Martin Kornberger, Andrea Mennicken, Peter Miller, Joanne Randa Nucho, and Neil Pollock, eds. 2019. "Introduction to Thinking Infrastructures." In *Thinking Infrastructures*, 1–12. Bingley, UK: Emerald.

Brancaccio, Francesco, and Carlo Vercellone. 2019. "Birth, Death, and Resurrection of the Issue of the Common: A Historical and Theoretical Perspective." *South Atlantic Quarterly* 118 (4): 699–709.

Breathnach, Caoimhghin S. 2004. "Charles Scott Sherrington's Integrative Action: A Centenary Notice." *Journal of the Royal Society of Medicine* 97 (1): 34–36.

Brinton, Daniel G. 1885. "The Lineal Measures of the Semi-civilized Nations of Mexico and Central America." *Proceedings of the American Philosophical Society* 22 (118): 194–207.

Brinton, Jasper Y. 1926. "The Mixed Courts of Egypt." *American Journal of International Law* 20 (4): 670–88.

Browman, David L., and Stephen Williams. 2013. *Anthropology at Harvard: A Biographical History, 1790–1940*. Cambridge, MA: Peabody Museum Press.

Brown, Nathan J. 1993. "The Precarious Life and Slow Death of the Mixed Courts of Egypt." *International Journal of Middle Eastern Studies* 25 (1): 33–52.

Brown, Norman Oliver. 1990. *Hermes the Thief: The Evolution of a Myth*. Great Barrington, MA: Lindisfarne.

Brundage, James A. 1995. *Medieval Canon Law*. London: Longman.

Bsheer, Rosie. 2020. *Archive Wars: The Politics of History in Saudi Arabia*. Stanford, CA: Stanford University Press.

Burbank, Jane, and Frederick Cooper. 2011. *Empires in World History: Power and the Politics of Difference*. Princeton, NJ: Princeton University Press.

Burke, Robert E. 2007. "Sir Charles Sherrington's *The Integrative Action of the Nervous System*: A Centenary Appreciation." *Brain* 130 (4): 887–94.

Butler, Judith. 2011. "Bodies in Alliance and the Politics of the Street." *Transversal Texts* (blog), September 2011. https://transversal.at/transversal/1011/butler/en.

Camic, Charles. 2020. *Veblen: The Making of an Economist Who Unmade Economics.* Cambridge, MA: Harvard University Press.

Campos, Michelle U. 2010. *Ottoman Brothers: Muslims, Christians, and Jews in Early Twentieth-Century Palestine.* Stanford, CA: Stanford University Press.

Can, Lâle, and Aimee M. Genell. 2020. "On Empire and Exception: Genealogies of Sovereignty in the Ottoman World." *Comparative Studies of South Asia, Africa, and the Middle East* 40 (3): 468–73.

Can, Lâle, and Michael Christopher Low. 2016. "The 'Subjects' of Ottoman International Law." *Journal of the Ottoman and Turkish Studies Association* 3 (2): 223–34. https://doi.org/10.2979/jottturstuass.3.2.02.

Cascone, Sarah. 2021. "Egypt Just Held an Astonishing, Real-Life Mummy Parade through the Streets of Cairo to Celebrate the Opening of a New Museum." *Artnet News*, April 5, 2021. https://news.artnet.com/art-world/cairo-mummy-parade-1956993.

Çaykent, Özlem, and Derya Gürses Tarbuck. 2017. "Coffeehouse Sociability: Themes, Problems and Directions." *Osmanlı Araştırmaları/Journal of Ottoman Studies* 49: 203–29.

Chakrabarty, Dipesh. 2000. *Provincializing Europe: Postcolonial Thought and Historical Difference.* Princeton, NJ: Princeton University Press.

Chin, Elizabeth, ed. 2014. *Katherine Dunham: Recovering an Anthropological Legacy, Choreographing Ethnographic Futures.* Santa Fe, NM: School for Advanced Research.

Chittick, William. 2020. "Ibn 'Arabî." In *Stanford Encyclopedia of Philosophy*, edited by Edward N. Zalta and Uri Nodelman. https://plato.stanford.edu/archives/spr2020/entries/ibn-arabi/.

Clay, Christopher. 2000. *Gold for the Sultan: Western Bankers and Ottoman Finance, 1856–1881.* London: I. B. Tauris.

Clerget, Marcel. 1934. *Le Caire: Étude de géographie urbaine et d'histoire économique.* Paris: Geuthner.

Cohn, Bernard S. 1996. *Colonialism and Its Forms of Knowledge: The British in India.* Princeton, NJ: Princeton University Press.

Cole, Juan Ricardo. 2007. *Napoleon's Egypt: Invading the Middle East.* New York: Palgrave Macmillan.

Condillac, Étienne Bonnot de. [1756] 2001. *Essay on the Origin of Human Knowledge.* Translated and edited by Hans Aarsleff. Cambridge: Cambridge University Press.

Constable, Olivia Remie. 2003. *Housing the Stranger in the Mediterranean World: Lodging, Trade, and Travel in Late Antiquity and the Middle Ages.* Cambridge: Cambridge University Press.

Cooper, Frederick. 2005. *Colonialism in Question: Theory, Knowledge, History.* Berkeley: University of California Press.

Coward, Martin. 2008. *Urbicide: The Politics of Urban Destruction.* London: Routledge.

Cowen, Deborah. 2014. *The Deadly Life of Logistics: Mapping Violence in Global Trade.* Minneapolis: University of Minnesota Press.

Cox, Aimee Meredith. 2015. *Shapeshifters: Black Girls and the Choreography of Citizenship.* Durham, NC: Duke University Press.

Cox, Aimee Meredith. 2021. "Cosmic Cartographies: Black Women Remapping Cincinnati, Ohio." *CSPA Quarterly* 31: 54–67.

Culang, Jeffrey. 2019. "'Ordering the 'Land of Paradox': The Fashioning of Nationality, Religion, and Political Loyalty in Colonial Egypt." In *Beyond Versailles: Sovereignty, Legitimacy, and the Formation of New Politics after the Great War,* edited by Marcus M. Payk and Roberta Pergher, 99–123. Bloomington: Indiana University Press.

Cytowic, Richard E. 1995. "Synesthesia: Phenomenology and Neuropsychology: A Review of Current Knowledge." *Psyche: An Interdisciplinary Journal of Research on Consciousness* 2 (10), unpaginated.

Dallasheh, Leena. 2015. "Troubled Waters: Citizenship and Colonial Zionism in Nazareth." *International Journal of Middle East Studies* 47 (3): 467–87.

Davis, Muriam Haleh. 2022. *Markets of Civilization: Island and Racial Capitalism in Algeria.* Durham, NC: Duke University Press.

Derri, Aviv. 2021a. "Bonds of Obligation, Precarious Fortunes: Empire, Non-Muslim Bankers, and Peasants in Late Ottoman Damascus, 1820s–1890s." PhD diss., New York University.

Derri, Aviv. 2021b. "Imperial Creditors, 'Doubtful' Nationalities and Financial Obligations in Late Ottoman Syria: Rethinking Ottoman Subjecthood and Consular Protection." *International History Review* 43: 1060–79. https://doi.org/10.1080/07075332.2020.1774796.

Dolbee, Samuel. 2022. "Empire on the Edge: Desert, Nomads, and the Making of an Ottoman Provincial Border." *American Historical Review* 127 (1): 129–58.

Douglas, Carl. 2007. "Barricades and Boulevards: Material Transformations of Paris, 1795–1871." *Interstices* 8:31–42.

Douglas, Mary. 1996. *Natural Symbols.* 2nd ed. New York: Routledge.

Douglas, Mary. 1999. *Implicit Meanings: Selected Essays in Anthropology.* 2nd ed. New York: Routledge.

Douglas, Mary. 2002. *Purity and Danger: An Analysis of Concepts of Pollution and Taboo.* New York: Routledge.

Economist. 2015. "A Bigger Better Suez Canal." August 8, 2015, 46.

The Egyptian National Claims: A Memorandum Presented to the Peace Conference by the Egyptian Delegation Charged with the Defence of Egyptian Independence. 1919. Paris: Imprimerie artistique Lux.

Eldem, Edhem. 1999. *A History of the Ottoman Bank.* Istanbul: Osmanli Bankasi.

Eldem, Edhem. 2005. "Ottoman Financial Integration with Europe: Foreign Loans, the Ottoman Bank and the Ottoman Public Debt." *European Review* 13 (3): 431–45.

Elden, Stuart. 2013. *The Birth of Territory*. Chicago: University of Chicago Press.

El-Din, Gamal Essam. 2021. "Al-Mogamma: Phoenix from the Ashes." *Ahram Online*, December 8, 2021. https://english.ahram.org.eg/NewsContent/50/1201/446016/AlAhram-Weekly/Egypt/AlMogamma-Phoenix-from-the-ashes.aspx.

El Etreby, Mohamed Sobhy. 1968. *The Birth and Evolution of the Public Sector in the Egyptian Economy* [in Arabic]. Cairo: Al Ahram Press.

El-Ghobashy, Mona. 2021. *Bread and Freedom: Egypt's Revolutionary Situation*. Stanford, CA: Stanford University Press.

El-Messiri, Sawsan. 1978. *Ibn al-Balad: A Concept of Egyptian Identity*. Leiden: Brill.

El Rashidi, Yasmine. 2023. "See the Heartbreaking Destruction of Cairo's Iconic Gardens." *Washington Post*, August 1, 2023. https://www.washingtonpost.com/opinions/2023/08/01/cairo-gardens-disappearing-development-military/.

Elsadda, Hoda. 2010. "Arab Women Bloggers: The Emergence of Literary Counterpublics." *Middle East Journal of Culture and Communication* 3 (3): 312–32. https://doi.org/10.1163/187398610X538678.

Elshakry, Marwa. 2007. "Free Love, Funny Costumes, and a Canal at Suez: The Saint-Simonians in Egypt." *Bidoun: Technology Futuribles* , no. 10. https://www.bidoun.org/issues/10-technology.

Elshakry, Marwa. 2013. *Reading Darwin in Arabic, 1860–1950*. Chicago: University of Chicago Press.

El Shakry, Omnia. 2007. *The Great Social Laboratory: Subjects of Knowledge in Colonial and Postcolonial Egypt*. Stanford, CA: Stanford University Press.

El Shakry, Omnia. 2017. *The Arabic Freud: Psychoanalysis and Islam in Modern Egypt*. Stanford, CA: Stanford University Press.

El Shakry, Omnia. 2018. "Psychoanalysis and the Imaginary: Translating Freud in Postcolonial Egypt." *Psychoanalysis and History* 20 (3): 313–35.

El Shamsy, Ahmed. 2022. *Rediscovering the Islamic Classics: How Editors and Print Culture Transformed an Intellectual Tradition*. Princeton, NJ: Princeton University Press.

El-Tamami, Wiam. 2013. "To Willingly Enter the Circles, the Square." *Jadaliyya*, July 30, 2013. https://www.jadaliyya.com/Details/29207/To-Willingly-Enter-the-Circles,-the-Square.

El Wardany, Salma. 2022. "Egypt Farmers Cull Chicks as Poultry Feed Stranded in Ports." Bloomberg, October 17, 2022. https://www.bloomberg.com/news/articles/2022-10-17/egypt-farmers-cull-chicks-as-poultry-feed-stranded-in-ports?in_source=embedded-checkout-banner#xj4y7vzkg.

Elyachar, Julia. 2002. "Empowerment Money: The World Bank, Non-governmental Organizations, and the Value of Culture in Egypt." *Public Culture* 14 (3): 493–513.

Elyachar, Julia. 2005. *Markets of Dispossession: NGOs, Economic Development, and the State in Cairo*. Durham, NC: Duke University Press.

Elyachar, Julia. 2010. "Phatic Labor, Infrastructure, and the Question of Empowerment in Cairo." *American Ethnologist* 37 (3): 452–64.

Elyachar, Julia. 2011. "The Political Economy of Movement and Gesture in Cairo." *Journal of the Royal Anthropological Institute* 17 (1): 82–99.

Elyachar, Julia. 2012a. "Before (and after) Neoliberalism: Tacit Knowledge, Secrets of the Trade, and the Public Sector in Egypt." *Cultural Anthropology* 27 (1): 76–96.

Elyachar, Julia. 2012b. "*Jadaliyya*: A New Form of Producing and Presenting Knowledge in/of the Middle East (Interview with Bassam Haddad)." *Cultural Anthropology, Hot Spots: Revolution and Counter-Revolution in Egypt a Year after January 25*, February 8, 2012. https://www.jadaliyya.com/Details/25234.

Elyachar, Julia. 2012c. "Next Practices: Knowledge, Infrastructure, and Public Goods at the Bottom of the Pyramid." *Public Culture* 24 (1): 109–29.

Elyachar, Julia. 2014. "Upending Infrastructure: Tamarod, Resistance, and Agency after the January 25 Revolution." *History and Anthropology* 25 (4): 452–71.

Elyachar, Julia. 2020. "Neoliberalism, Rationality, and the Savage Slot." In *Mutant Neoliberalism: Market Rule and Political Rupture*, edited by William Callison and Zachary Manfredi, 177–95. New York: Fordham University Press.

Elyachar, Julia. 2021. "From Versailles to the War on Terror." *Public Books*, January 29, 2021. https://www.publicbooks.org/from-versailles-to-the-war-on-terror/.

Elyachar, Julia. 2022. "Anthropology of Proprioception: Endurance and Collectivity on Unstable Grounds in Postrevolutionary Cairo." *American Anthropologist* 124 (3): 525–35.

Elyachar, Julia. 2023. "Relational Finance: Ottoman Debt, Financialization, and the Problem of the Semi-civilized." *Journal of Cultural Economy* 16 (3): 323–36. https://doi.org/10.1080/17530350.2023.2189146.

Elyot, Thomas. 1538. *The Dictionary of syr Thomas Eliot knight*. London: Thomas Berthelet.

Elyot, Thomas. 1542. *Bibliotheca Eliotae: Eliotis librarie*. 2nd ed. London: Thomas Berthelet.

Emam, Amr. 2021. "Egypt to Turn Iconic Tahrir Square Building into Luxury Hotel." *Middle East Eye*, December 15, 2021. https://www.middleeasteye.net/news/egypt-turn-its-bureaucracy-icon-luxury-hotel.

Enfield, N. J., and Paul Kockelman, eds. 2017. *Distributed Agency*. Oxford: Oxford University Press.

Engels, Friedrich. [1845] 1987. *The Condition of the Working Class in England*. New York: Penguin Classics.

Engels, Friedrich. [1848] 1994. "The June Revolution: The Course of the Paris Uprising." *Neue Rheinische Zeitung*, no. 32, July 1, 1848. Translated by the Marx-Engels Institute. https://www.marxists.org/archive/marx/works/1848/07/01.htm.

Erkal, Namik. 2020. "Reserved Abundance: State Granaries of Early Modern Istanbul." *Journal of the Society of Architectural Historians* 79 (1): 17–38.

Esmeir, Samara. 2012. *Juridical Humanity: A Colonial History*. Stanford, CA: Stanford University Press.

Estes, Nick. 2019. *Our History Is the Future: Standing Rock versus the Dakota Access Pipeline, and the Long Tradition of Indigenous Resistance*. London: Verso.

Ezz, Mohamed, and Ahmed Medhat. 2022. "US$13 Billion in Gulf Deposits Allays Some Pressure on Egypt following Capital Flight from Emerging Markets." *MadaMasr*, September 14, 2022. https://www.madamasr.com/en/2022/09 /14/feature/economy/us13-billion-in-gulf-deposits-allays-some-pressure-on -egypt-following-capital-flight-from-emerging-markets/.

Fabian, Johannes. 2014. *Time and the Other: How Anthropology Makes Its Object*. New York: Columbia University Press.

Fahmy, Khaled. 2009. *Mehmed Ali: From Ottoman Governor to Ruler of Egypt*. Oxford: Oneworld.

Fahmy, Khaled. 2010. *All the Pasha's Men: Mehmed Ali, His Army, and the Making of Modern Egypt*. Cairo: American University in Cairo Press.

Febvre, Lucien. 1930. "Civilisation: Évolution d'un mot et d'un groupe d'idées." In *Civilisation: Le mot et l'idée*, edited by Lucien Febvre, Marcel Mauss, Émile Tonnelat, Alfredo Niceforo, and Louis Weber. Paris: La Renaissance du Livre.

Federici, Silvia. 2014. "From Commoning to Debt: Financialization, Microcredit, and the Changing Architecture of Capital Accumulation." *South Atlantic Quarterly* 113 (2): 231–44.

Ferguson, Adam. 1782. *An Essay on the History of Civil Society*. London: T. Cadell. https://oll.libertyfund.org/title/ferguson-an-essay-on-the-history-of -civil-society.

Fidler, David P. 2000. "A Kinder, Gentler System of Capitulations? International Law, Structural Adjustment Policies, and the Standard of Liberal, Globalized Civilization." *Texas International Law Journal* 35 (3): 387–413.

Fisch, Jörg. 1992. "Zivilisation, Kultur." In *Geschichtliche Grundbegriffe: Historisches Lexicon zur politisch-sozialen Sprache in Deutschland*. Vol. 7. Edited by Otto Brunner, Werner Conze, and Reinhardt Koselleck, 721. Stuttgart: Klett-Cotta.

Fuentes, Agustín. 2019. *Why We Believe: Evolution and the Human Way of Being*. New Haven, CT: Yale University Press.

Fulgentius, Fabius Planciades. 1971. *Fulgentius the Mythographer*. Translated by Leslie George Whitbread. Columbus: Ohio State University Press.

Gallagher, Shaun, and Zahavi, Dan. 2005. "Phenomenological Approaches to Self-Consciousness." In *Stanford Encyclopedia of Philosophy*, edited by Edward N. Zalta and Uri Nodelman. https://plato.stanford.edu/entries/self-consciousness -phenomenological/.

Gelvin, James L. 2015. "Was There a Mandates Period? Some Concluding Thoughts." In *The Routledge Handbook of the History of the Middle East Mandates*, edited by Cyrus Schayegh and Andrew Arsan, 420–32. London: Routledge.

Genell, Aimee M. 2013. "Empire by Law: Ottoman Sovereignty and the British Occupation of Egypt, 1882–1923." PhD diss., Columbia University.

Genell, Aimee M. 2016. "Autonomous Provinces and the Problem of 'Semi-sovereignty' in European International Law." *Journal of Balkan and Near Eastern Studies* 18 (6): 533–49.

Genell, Aimee M. 2019. "The End of Egypt's Occupation: Ottoman Sovereignty and the British Declaration of Protection." In *Beyond Versailles: Sovereignty, Legitimacy, and the Formation of New Politics after the Great War*, edited by Marcus M. Payk and Roberta Pergher, 77–98. Bloomington: Indiana University Press.

Gentili, Alberico. [1594] 1924. *De legantionibus libri tres*. Translated by Gordon J. Laing. Oxford: Oxford University Press.

Gentili, Alberico. [1612] 1933. *De jure belli libri tres*. Translated by John C. Rolfe. Oxford: Oxford University Press.

Gentili, Alberico. 1877. *De jure belli, libris tres*. Edited by Thomas Erskine Holland. Oxford: Clarendon Press.

Ghannam, Farha. 2002. *Remaking the Modern: Space, Relocation, and the Politics of Identity in a Global Cairo*. Los Angeles: University of California Press.

Ghannam, Farha. 2013. *Live and Die Like a Man: Gender Dynamics in Urban Egypt*. Stanford, CA: Stanford University Press.

Glover, Bill. 2020. "The Evolution of Cable and Wireless, Part 1." History of the Atlantic Cable and Undersea Communications. Accessed November 14, 2022. https://atlantic-cable.com/CableCos/CandW/Pender/.

Goswami, Manu. 2004. *Producing India: From Colonial Economy to National Space*. Chicago: University of Chicago Press.

Graham, Stephen. 2003. "Lessons in Urbicide." *New Left Review* 19:63–78.

Grant, Bruce. 2009. *The Captive and the Gift: Cultural Histories of Sovereignty in Russia and the Caucasus*. Ithaca, NY: Cornell University Press.

Grotius, Hugo. [1609] 2004. *The Free Sea (Mare Liberum)*. Edited by David Armitage. Indianapolis, IN: Liberty Fund. https://www.libertyfund.org/books/the-free-sea/.

Grotius, Hugo. [1625] 1925. *De jure belli ac pacis libri tres*. Translated by Francis Kelsey et al. Oxford: Clarendon Press.

Grumperz, John. [1968] 2001. "The Speech Community." In *Linguistic Anthropology: A Reader*, edited by Alesandro Duranti, 43–52. Malden, MA: Blackwell.

Hamera, Judith. 2007. *Dancing Communities: Performance, Difference, and Connection in the Global City*. New York: Palgrave Macmillan.

Handoussa, Heba. 1979. "Time for Reform: Egypt's Public Sector Industry." In *Cairo Papers in Social Science*, edited by H. Thompson, 101–24. Cairo: American University in Cairo Press.

Handy, Howard. 1998. "Modernizing Egypt's Financial Markets." In *Egypt: Beyond Stabilization, Toward a Dynamic Market Economy*. N.p.: International Monetary Fund. https://doi.org/10.5089/9781557757203.084.

Hanieh, Adam. 2018. *Money, Markets, and Monarchies: The Gulf Cooperation Council and the Political Economy of the Contemporary Middle East*. Cambridge: Cambridge University Press.

Hanley, Will. 2013. "When Did Egyptians Stop Being Ottomans? An Imperial Citizenship Case Study." In *Multilevel Citizenship*, edited by Willem Maas, 89–109. Philadelphia: University of Pennsylvania Press.

Hanley, Will. 2016. "What Ottoman Nationality Was and Was Not." *Journal of the Ottoman and Turkish Studies Association* 3 (2): 277–98.

Hanley, Will. 2017. *Identifying with Nationality: Europeans, Ottomans, and Egyptians in Alexandria*. New York: Columbia University Press.

Hann, Chris, and Keith Hart. 2011. *Economic Anthropology: History, Ethnography, Critique*. Cambridge: Polity.

Hardt, Michael, and Antonio Negri. 2011. *Commonwealth*. Cambridge, MA: Belknap.

Harney, Stefano, and Fred Moten. 2013. *The Undercommons: Fugitive Planning and Black Study*. Wivenhoe: Autonomedia.

Haroun, Moustafa. 2021. "Analysis of Managing and Transferring of Ownership of Land Public Assets in Egypt. 'The Sovereign Fund of Egypt." Paper presented at the Second Arab Land conference, Cairo, February 22–24, 2021.

Hawkins, Michael C. 2020. *Semi-civilized: The Moro Village at the Louisiana Purchase Exposition*. Ithaca, NY: Cornell University Press.

Hayek, Friedrich. A. 1944. *The Road to Serfdom*. Chicago: University of Chicago Press.

Headrick, Daniel R., and Pascal Griset. 2001. "Submarine Telegraph Cables: Business and Politics, 1838–1939." *Business History Review* 75 (3): 543–78.

Hindess, Barry. 2005. "Politics as Government: Michel Foucault's Analysis of Political Reason." *Alternatives: Global, Local, Political* 30 (4): 389–413.

Hinsley, Harry. 1966. *Sovereignty*. London: C. A. Watts.

Hont, Istvan, and Michael Ignatieff. 1983. "Needs and Justice in the *Wealth of Nations*: An Introductory Essay." In *Wealth and Virtue: The Shaping of Political Economy in the Scottish Enlightenment*, edited by Istvan Hont and Michael Ignatieff, 1–44. Cambridge: Cambridge University Press.

Hoyle, Mark S. W. 1987. "The Mixed Courts of Egypt 1926–1937." *Arab Law Quarterly* 2 (4): 357–89.

Huber, Valeska. 2012. "Connecting Colonial Seas: The 'International Colonisation' of Port Said and the Suez Canal during and after the First World War." *European Review of History / Revue européene d'histoire* 19 (1): 141–61.

Huber, Valeska. 2013. *Channelling Mobilities: Migration and Globalisation in the Suez Canal Region and Beyond, 1869–1914*. Cambridge: Cambridge University Press.

Hunter, F. Robert. 1999. *Egypt under the Khedives, 1805–1879: From Household Government to Modern Bureaucracy*. Cairo: American University in Cairo Press.

Husserl, Edmund. [1907] 1997. *Thing and Space: Lectures of 1907*. Translated by R. Rojcewicz. Dordrecht: Kluwer Academic.

Ibn 'Arabi, 1911. *Al-Futuhat Al-Makkiyyah.* Cairo: Bulaq.

Ismail, Salwa. 2006. *Political Life in Cairo's New Quarters: Encountering the Everyday State.* Minneapolis: University of Minnesota Press.

Jakes, Aaron G. 2020. *Egypt's Occupation: Colonial Economism and the Crises of Capitalism.* Stanford, CA: Stanford University Press.

Jakes, Aaron G. 2021. "The World the Suez Canal Made." *Mada Masr*, April 4, 2021. https://www.madamasr.com/en/2021/04/04/opinion/u/the-world-the -suez-canal-made/.

Jakobson, Roman. [1960] 1990. "The Speech Event and the Function of Language." In *On Language*, edited by Linda R. Waugh and Monique Monville-Burston, 69–79. Cambridge, MA: Harvard University Press.

Jaser, Zahira. 2021. "The Real Value of Middle Managers." *Harvard Business Review*, June 7, 2021. https://hbr.org/2021/06/the-real-value-of-middle-managers.

Jezernik, Božidar. 2004. *Wild Europe: The Balkans in the Gaze of Western Travellers.* London: Saqi.

Jones, Peter E. 2018. "Karl Marx and the Language Sciences—Critical Encounters: Introduction to the Special Issue." *Language Sciences* 70:1–15.

Joseph, Suad. 1993. "Gender and Relationality among Arab Families in Lebanon." *Feminist Studies* 19 (3): 465–86.

Kafadar, Cemal. 1986. "When Coins Turned into Drops of Dew and Bankers Became Robbers of Shadow: The Boundaries of Ottoman Economic Imagination at the End of the Sixteenth Century." PhD diss., McGill University.

Kafadar, Cemal. 1995. *Between Two Worlds: The Construction of the Ottoman State.* Berkeley: University of California Press.

Kafadar, Cemal. 2002. "A History of Coffee." Rethinking Global Cities. Accessed July 30, 2023. https://sites.duke.edu/rethinkingglobalcities/files/2014/09 /64Kafadar16-coffeehistory.pdf.

Karabell, Zachary. 2003. *Parting the Desert: The Creation of the Suez Canal.* New York: Alfred A. Knopf.

Kassab, Beesan. 2019. "The New Administrative Capital: Outside the State Budget or Outside Public Accountability?" *Mada Masr*, May 25, 2019. https://www .madamasr.com/en/2019/05/25/feature/economy/the-new-administrative -capital-outside-the-state-budget-or-outside-public-accountability/.

Kassab, Beesan, Ehab al-Naggar, and Rana Mamdouh. 2022. "Egypt to Seek LE1.5 Trillion in Borrowing as Debt Servicing Consumes 50 percent of 2022/23 Expenditures." *Mada Masr*, May 11, 2022. https://www.madamasr.com/en/2022 /05/11/feature/economy/egypt-to-seek-le1-5-trillion-in-borrowing-as-debt -servicing-consumes-50-of-2022-23-expenditures/.

Kayaoğlu, Turan. 2010. *Legal Imperialism: Sovereignty and Extraterritoriality in Japan, the Ottoman Empire, and China.* Cambridge: Cambridge University Press.

Keene, Edward. 2004. *Beyond the Anarchical Society: Grotius, Colonialism, and Order in World Politics.* Cambridge: Cambridge University Press.

Kennedy, David. 1997. "International Law and the Nineteenth Century: History of an Illusion." *Quinnipiac Law Review* 17 (1): 99–138.

Khalidi, Rashid. 2020. *The Hundred Years' War on Palestine: A History of Settler Colonialism and Resistance, 1917–2017.* New York: Metropolitan.

Khalil, Osamah F. 2016. *America's Dream Palace: Middle East Expertise and the Rise of the National Security State.* Cambridge, MA: Harvard University Press.

Khalili, Laleh. 2020. *Sinews of War and Trade: Shipping and Capitalism in the Arabian Peninsula.* London: Verso.

Khalili, Laleh. 2021. "The Suez Canal Is a Lifeline for Global Capitalism." *Jacobin,* March 30, 2021. https://jacobin.com/2021/03/suez-canal-blockage-economy-global-capitalism.

King, Tiffany Lethabo. 2019. *The Black Shoals: Offshore Formations of Black and Native Studies.* Durham, NC: Duke University Press.

Kingsbury, Benedict. 1998. "Confronting Difference: The Puzzling Durability of Gentili's Combination of Pragmatic Pluralism and Normative Judgment." *American Journal of International Law* 92 (4): 713–23.

Kingsbury, Benedict, and Benjamin Straumann, eds. 2010. *The Roman Foundations of the Law of Nations: Alberico Gentili and the Justice of Empire.* Oxford: Oxford University Press.

Knight, Will. 2004. "Anthropologists to Beat Gadget Rage." *New Scientist,* December 19, 2004. http://www.newscientist.com/article/dn6803.

Kockelman, Paul. 2005. "The Semiotic Stance." *Semiotica* 157: 233–304.

Kockelman, Paul. 2006. "A Semiotic Ontology of the Commodity." *Journal of Linguistic Anthropology* 16 (1): 76–102.

Kockelman, Paul. 2007. "From Status to Contract Revisited: Value, Temporality, Circulation and Subjectivity." *Anthropological Theory* 7 (2): 151–76.

Kockelman, Paul. 2010. "Enemies, Parasites, and Noise: How to Take Up Residence in a System without Becoming a Term in It." *Journal of Linguistic Anthropology* 20 (2): 406–21.

Kockelman, Paul. 2012. "The Ground, the Ground, the Ground: Or, Why Archeology Is so 'Hard.'" *Yearbook of Comparative Literature* 58: 176–84.

Koh, Choon Hwee. 2021. "The Ottoman Postmaster: Contractors, Communication and Early Modern State Formation." *Past and Present,* 251 (1): 113–52.

Koselleck, Reinhart. [1975] 2004. "The Historical-Political Semantics of Asymmetric Counterconcepts." In *Futures Past: On the Semantics of Historical Time,* translated by Keith Tribe, 155–91. New York: Columbia University Press.

Kuper, Adam. 2009. "The Rise and Fall of Maine's Patriarchal Society." In *The Victorian Achievement of Sir Henry Maine: A Centennial Reappraisal,* edited by Alan Diamond, 99–110. Cambridge: Cambridge University Press.

Kwan, SanSan. 2013. *Kinesthetic City: Dance and Movement in Chinese Urban Spaces.* Oxford: Oxford University Press.

Lacouture, Jean, and Simone Lacouture. 2002. "The Night Nasser Nationalized the Suez Canal." *Le Monde diplomatique*, July 2002. Translated by Luke Sandford. https://mondediplo.com/2002/07/12canal.

Larkin, Brian. 2008. *Signal and Noise: Media, Urban Infrastructure, and Urban Culture in Nigeria*. Durham, NC: Duke University Press.

Larkin, Brian. 2013. "The Poetics and Politics of Infrastructure." *Annual Review of Anthropology* 42:327–43.

LeDoux, Joseph. 2003. *Synaptic Self: How Our Brains Become Who We Are*. New York: Penguin.

Lefebvre, Henri. 2003. "Space and the State." In *State/Space: A Reader*, edited by Neil Brenner, Bob Jessop, Martin Jones, and Gordon MacLeod, 84–100. London: Blackwell.

Lefebvre, Henri. 2013. *Rhythmanalysis: Space, Time and Everyday Life*. London: Bloomsbury.

Le Père, J. M. 1809. "Mémoire sur la communication de la mer des Indes à la Mediterranée par la mer Rouge et l'Istme de Soueys. " In *Description de l'Egypte, Etat moderne*, vol. 1, 21–186. Paris: Imprimerie Impériale.

Leroi-Gourhan, André. 1993. *Gesture and Speech*. Translated by A. B. Berger. Cambridge, MA: MIT Press.

Li, Tania Murray. 2014. "What Is Land? Assembling a Resource for Global Investment." *Transactions of the Institute of British Geographers* 39 (4): 589–602.

Liu, Shih Shun. 1925. *Extraterritoriality: Its Rise and Decline*. New York: Columbia University.

Locke, John. [1690] 1975. *Essay Concerning Human Understanding*. Oxford: Clarendon.

Locke, John. 1960. *Two Treatises of Government*. Edited by Peter Laslett. Cambridge: Cambridge University Press.

López-Anguita, Gracia. 2021. "Ibn ʿArabī's Metaphysics in the Context of Andalusian Mysticism: Some Akbarian Concepts in the Light of Ibn Masarra and Ibn Barrajān." *Religions* 12 (1): 40. https://doi.org/10.3390/rel12010040.

Lorimer, James. 1883. *The Institutes of the Law of Nations: A Treatise of the Jural Relations of Separate Political Communities*. Vol 2. Edinburgh: William Blackwood and Sons.

Lotze, Rudolf Hermann. 1852. *Medizinische Psychologie oder Physiologie der Seele*. Leipzig: Weidemann.

Luxemburg, Rosa. [1913] 1951. *The Accumulation of Capital*. London: Routledge.

Magdy, Mirette. 2022. "Qatar in Talks to Invest $2.5 Billion in Egypt as Ties Mend." Bloomberg, October 19, 2022. https://www.bloomberg.com/news/articles/2022-10-19/qatar-in-talks-to-invest-2-5-billion-in-egypt-to-expand-support#xj4y7vzkg.

Magdy, Mirette, and Takek El-Tablawy. 2023. "Egypt Tries to Coax Dollars Back with Higher Savings Returns." Bloomberg, July 25, 2023. https://www.bloomberg.com/news/articles/2023-07-25/egypt-seeks-to-lure-dollars-with-new-deposit-certificates#xj4y7vzkg.

Mahmood, Saba. 2005. *Politics of Piety: The Islamic Revival and the Feminist Subject*. Princeton, NJ: Princeton University Press.

Maine, Henry Sumner. 1915. *International Law: The Whewell Lectures of 1887*. 2nd ed. London: John Murray.

Maine, Henry Sumner. 1986. *Ancient Law: Its Connection with the Early History of Society, and Its Relation to Modern Ideas*. Tucson: University of Arizona Press.

Maitland, James, Earl of Lauderdale. 1804. *An Inquiry into the Nature and Origin of Public Wealth and into the Means and Causes of its Increase*. Edinburgh: A. Constable and Co.

Malabou, Catherine. 2008. *What Shall We Do with Our Brains?* Translated by Sebastian Rand. New York: Fordham University Press.

Maldonado-Torres, Nelson. 2007. "On the Coloniality of Being: Contributions to the Development of a Concept." *Cultural Studies* 21 (2–3): 240–70. https://doi.org/10.1080/09502380601162548.

Malinowski, Bronisław. [1922] 1999. *Argonauts of the Western Pacific: An Account of Native Enterprise and Adventure in the Archipelagoes of Melanesian New Guinea*. London: Routledge.

Malinowski, Bronisław. [1923] 1936. "The Problem of Meaning in Primitive Languages." In *The Meaning of Meaning*, edited by C. K. Ogden and I. A. Richards, 296–336. New York: Harcourt, Brace.

Mandeville, Bernard. [1732] 1988. *The Fable of the Bees or Private Vices, Publick Benefits*. Vol. 2. Indianapolis: Liberty Fund.

Manning, Paul. 2012. *Semiotics of Drinking and Eating*. New York: Continuum.

Mantena, Karuna. 2010. *Alibis of Empire: Henry Maine and the Ends of Liberal Imperialism*. Princeton, NJ: Princeton University Press.

Margolies, Daniel S., Umut Özsu, Maïa Pal, and Ntina Tzouvala, eds. 2019. *The Extraterritoriality of Law: History, Theory, Politics*. London: Routledge.

Marsot, Afaf Lutfi al-Sayyid. 1975. "The Porte and Ismail Pasha's Quest for Autonomy." *Journal of the American Research Center in Egypt* 12: 89–96.

Martin, Randy. 2006. "Toward a Kinesthetics of Protest." *Social Identities* 12 (6): 791–801.

Marx, Karl. [1885] 1956. *Capital: A Critique of Political Economy*. Vol. 2. Edited by Friedrich Engels. Translated by I. Lasker. Moscow: Progress.

Massey, Doreen. 2005. *For Space*. London: Sage.

Mastnak, Tomaž. 2008. "Barbarians to the Balkans." Paper presented at the Exclusion in and on the Borders of Europe conference, Paris, April 2008. https://www.medievalists.net/2013/03/barbarians-to-the-balkans/.

Mastnak, Tomaž. 2021. *Bonapartizem: Prolegomena za študij fašizma*. Ljubljana: Založba.

Mastnak, Tomaž, Julia Elyachar, and Tom Boellstorff. 2014. "Botanical Decolonization: Rethinking Native Plants." *Environment and Planning D: Society and Space* 32 (2): 363–80. https://doi.org/10.1068/d13006p.

Mattei, Ugo, and Mark Mancall. 2019. "Communology: The Emergence of a Social Theory of the Commons." *South Atlantic Quarterly* 118 (4): 725–46.

Mattelart, Armand. 1996. *The Invention of Communication*. Translated by Susan Emanuel. Minneapolis: University of Minnesota Press.

Maurer, Bill. 2012. "Mobile Money: Communication, Consumption and Change in the Payments Space." *Journal of Development Studies* 48 (5): 589–604.

Mauss, Marcel. [1935] 1973. "Techniques of the Body." *Economy and Society* 2 (1): 70–88.

McDermott, Anthony. 1988. *Egypt from Nasser to Mubarak: A Flawed Revolution*. London: Croom Helm.

McPhee, John. 1999. *A Sense of Where You Are: A Profile of Bill Bradley at Princeton*. New York: Farrar, Straus and Giroux.

Mead, George Herbert. [1934] 1967. *Mind, Self, and Society: From the Standpoint of a Social Behaviorist*. Chicago: University of Chicago Press.

Mehrez, Samia. 2008. *Egypt's Culture Wars: Politics and Practice*. London: Routledge.

Mehrling, Perry. 2017. "Financialization and Its Discontents." *Finance and Society* 3 (1): 1–10.

Mestyan, Adam. 2014. "Arabic Theater in Early Khedivial Culture, 1868–72: James Sanua Revisited." *International Journal of Middle East Studies* 46 (1): 117–37.

Mestyan, Adam. 2017. *Arab Patriotism: The Ideology and Culture of Power in Late Ottoman Egypt*. Princeton, NJ: Princeton University Press.

Metwaly, Ali. 2014. "UK and Egypt Musicians Respond to 'Cairo Calling.'" *Ahram Online*, March 26, 2014. https://english.ahram.org.eg/News/97561.aspx.

Mignolo, Walter D. 2007. "Delinking: The Rhetoric of Modernity, the Logic of Coloniality and the Grammar of De-coloniality." *Cultural Studies* 21 (2–3): 449–514.

Minawi, Mostafa. 2016. "Telegraphs and Territoriality in Ottoman Arabia during the Age of High Imperialism." *Journal of Balkan and Near Eastern Studies* 18 (6): 567–87.

Mitchell, Timothy. 1991. *Colonising Egypt*. Berkeley: University of California Press.

Mitchell, Timothy. 2008. "Rethinking Economy." *Geoforum* 39 (3): 1116–21.

Mohammed, Bassant. 2022. "All We Know about Egypt's Biggest National Project in 2022: Al-Fustat Garden Restoration." *Daily News Egypt*, February 22, 2022. https://www.dailynewsegypt.com/2022/02/22/all-we-know-about-egypts-biggest-national-project-in-2022-al-fustat-garden-restoration/.

Moneim, Doaa A. 2020. "Cairo's Mogamma El-Tahrir Building among 7 State-Owned Assets Transferred to Egypt's Sovereign Wealth Fund." *Ahram Online*, September 3, 2020. https://english.ahram.org.eg/News/379271.aspx.

Moreton-Robinson, Aileen. 2016. "Relationality: A Key Presupposition of an Indigenous Social Research Paradigm." In *Sources and Methods in Indigenous Studies*, edited by Chris Andersen and Jean M. O'Brien, 69–77. London: Routledge.

Morgan, Kate Tarlow. 2010. "The Body Is a House." Paper presented at the Charles Olson 100 conference, Worcester, MA, March 27, 2010.

Morimoto, Ryo. 2012. "Shaking Grounds, Unearthing Palimpsests: Semiotic Anthropology of Disaster." *Semiotica* 192:263–74.

Moss, Sebastian. 2022. "The Colonial Roots of Egypt's Submarine Cable Routes." Data Center Dynamics, September 19, 2022. https://www.datacenterdynamics.com/en/analysis/the-colonial-roots-of-egypts-submarine-cable-routes/.

Moumtaz, Nadia. 2021. *God's Property: Islam, Charity, and the Modern State*. Oakland: University of California Press.

Mundt, Theodor. 1861. *Niccolò Machiavelli und das System der modernen Politik*. 3rd rev. ed. Berlin: Otto Janke.

Munn, Nancy. 1986. *The Fame of Gawa: A Symbolic Study of Value Transformation in a Massim (Papua New Guinea) Society*. Cambridge: Cambridge University Press.

Naff, Thomas. 1977. "Ottoman Diplomatic Relations with Europe in the Eighteenth Century: Patterns and Trends." In *Studies in Eighteenth Century Islamic History*, edited by Thomas Naff and Roger Owen, 88–107. Carbondale: Southern Illinois University.

Nagasawa, Eiji. 2014. "'An Autobiography as Case Study' of an Egyptian Sociologist: Sayyid 'Uways, *The History Which I Carry on My Back*." In *Modern Egypt through Japanese Eyes: A Study on Intellectual and Socio-economic Aspects of Egyptian Nationalism*, edited by Eiji Nagasawa and Kazushi Murase, 71–76. Cairo: Merit.

Naguib, Shahenda. 2021. "'Egypt with No Slums': Authorities Displace Residents for Mummies and Modernity." *Middle East Eye*, April 5, 2021. https://www.middleeasteye.net/news/egypt-mummies-parade-hundreds-families-evicted-make-way-regeneration.

Narotzky, Susana. 2008. "Reply: What's Changed (since 1975)?" *Dialectical Anthropology* 32 (1–2): 9–16.

Nassar, Aya. 2017. "Where the Dust Settles: Fieldwork, Subjectivity and Materiality in Cairo." *Contemporary Social Science* 13 (3–4): 412–28.

Nassar, Aya, and Roanne Moodley. 2020. "Cairo, Jan. 28, 2011: A View of the Revolution from the 6th of Oct. Bridge." *Funambulist*, no. 28, February 24, 2020. https://thefunambulist.net/magazine/28-our-battles/cairo-jan-28-2011-a-view-of-the-revolution-from-the-6th-of-oct-bridge-by-aya-nassar.

Nasser, Gamal Abdel. 1955. *Egypt's Liberation: The Philosophy of the Revolution*. Washington, DC: Public Affairs.

Negri, Antonio. 2000. *Kairos, Alma Venus, Multitude*. Paris: Calmann Levy.

Ness, Sally Ann. 1992. *Body, Movement, and Culture: Kinesthetic and Visual Symbolism in a Philippine Community*. Philadelphia: University of Pennsylvania Press.

Nicolelis, Miguel. 2011. *Beyond Boundaries: The New Neuroscience of Connecting Brains with Machines—and How It Will Change Our Lives*. New York: Times Books.

Nixon, Rob. 2019. "Fallen Martyrs, Felled Trees." *Conjunctions* 73:8–29.

Noakes, Richard. 2014. "Industrial Research at the Eastern Telegraph Company, 1872–1929." *British Journal of the History of Science* 47 (1): 119–46.

Nucho, Joanne Randa. 2016. *Everyday Sectarianism in Urban Lebanon: Infrastructures, Public Services, and Power*. Princeton, NJ: Princeton University Press.

Nucho, Joanne Randa. 2018. "Essential Readings: Infrastructure." *Jadaliyya*, August 4, 2018. https://www.jadaliyya.com/Details/37829.

Nye, E. M. 2023. "'A Bank of Trust': Legal Practices of Ottoman Finance between Empires." *Journal of Early Modern History* 27 (6): 502–25. https://doi.org/10.1163/15700658-bja10070.

Omar, Hussein. 2021. "Pharoahs on Parade." *London Review of Books* (blog), April 6, 2021. Accessed June 17, 2023. https://www.lrb.co.uk/blog/2021/april/pharaohs-on-parade.

Özsu, Umut. 2016a. "The Ottoman Empire, the Origins of Extraterritoriality, and International Legal Theory." In *The Oxford Handbook of the Theory of International Law*, edited by Anne Orford and Florian Hoffmann with Martin Clark, 123–37. Oxford: Oxford University Press.

Özsu, Umut. 2016b. "Ottoman International Law?" *Journal of the Ottoman and Turkish Studies Association* 3 (2): 369–76.

Pagden, Anthony. 2003. "Human Rights, Natural Rights, and Europe's Imperial Legacy." *Political Theory* 31 (2): 171–99.

Pagden, Anthony. 2015. *The Burdens of Empire: 1539 to the Present*. Cambridge: Cambridge University Press.

Pal, Maïa. 2020. *Jurisdictional Accumulation: An Early Modern History of Law, Empires, and Capital*. Cambridge: Cambridge University Press.

Pamuk, Sevket. 2000. *A Monetary History of the Ottoman Empire*. Cambridge: Cambridge University Press.

Pandolfo, Stefania. 1997. *Impasse of the Angels: Scenes from a Moroccan Space of Memory*. Chicago: University of Chicago Press.

Philpott, Daniel. 2020. "Sovereignty." In *The Stanford Encyclopedia of Philosophy Archive*, edited by Edward N. Zalta and Uri Nodelman. https://plato.stanford.edu/archives/fall2020/entries/sovereignty/.

Pocock, J. G. A. 2009. *Barbarism and Religion*. Vol. 4, *Barbarians, Savages and Empires*. Cambridge: Cambridge University Press.

Polanyi, Michael. 1966. *The Tacit Dimension*. Garden City, NY: Doubleday.

Poon, Martha, and Robert Wosnitzer. 2012. "Review Essay: Liquidating Corporate America: How Financial Leverage Has Changed the Fundamental Nature of What Is Valuable." *Journal of Cultural Economy* 5 (2): 247–25.

Popperl, Simone. 2018. "Geologies of Erasure: Sinkholes, Science, and Settler Colonialism at the Dead Sea." *International Journal of Middle East Studies* 50 (3): 427–48.

Powell, Eve M. Troutt. 2003. *A Different Shade of Colonialism: Egypt, Great Britain, and the Mastery of the Sudan*. Berkeley: University of California Press.

Power, Mike. 2019. "Modelling the Microfoundations of the Audit Society: Organizations and the Logic of the Audit Trail." *Academy of Management Review* 46 (1): 6–32.

Prahalad, C. K. 2010. "Column: Best Practices Get You Only So Far." *Harvard Business Review*, April 2020.

Proske, Uwe, and Simon C. Gandevia. 2012. "The Proprioceptive Senses: Their Roles in Signaling Body Shape, Body Position and Movement, and Muscle Force." *Physiological Review* 92 (4): 1651–97.

Pursley, Sara. 2019. *Familiar Futures: Time, Selfhood, and Sovereignty in Iraq*. Stanford, CA: Stanford University Press.

Quataert, Donald. 2000. *The Ottoman Empire, 1700–1922*. Cambridge: Cambridge University Press.

Quijano, Aníbal. 1992. "Colonialidad y modernidad/racionalidad." In *Los conquistados: 1492 y la población indígena de las Américas*, edited by Heraclio Bonilla, 437–48. Ecuador: Tercer Mundo Editores.

Quijano, Aníbal, and Michael Ennis. 2000. "Coloniality of Power, Eurocentrism, and Latin America." *Nepantla: Views of South* 1 (3): 533–80.

Rabbat, Nasser. 2011. "Circling the Square: Architecture and Revolution in Cairo." *Artforum* 49 (8). https://www.artforum.com/print/201104/circling-the-square -architecture-and-revolution-in-cairo-27827.

Rabie, Kareem. 2021. *Palestine Is Throwing a Party and the Whole World Is Invited: Capital and State Building in the West Bank*. Durham, NC: Duke University Press.

Rachty, Gehan. 1999. "History of Telecommunications in Egypt." In *Telecommunications in Africa*, edited by Eli M. Noam, 39–50. New York: Oxford University Press.

Rancière, Jacques. 2004. *The Politics of Aesthetics*. London: Continuum.

Rancière, Jacques. 2010. *Dissensus: On Politics and Aesthetics*. Edited and translated by Steve Corcoran. London: Bloomsbury Academic.

Ravndal, G. Bie. 1921. *The Origin of the Capitulations and of the Consular Institution*. Washington, DC: Government Printing Office. https://babel.hathitrust .org/cgi/pt?id=hvd.32044057506354&seq=5.

Raymond, André. 2000. *Cairo*. Translated by Willard Wood. Cambridge, MA: Harvard University Press.

Reid, Donald Malcolm. 1990. *Cairo University and the Making of Modern Egypt*. Cambridge: Cambridge University Press.

Ribot, Théodule. [1895] 2009. *The Diseases of Personality*. Ithaca, NY: Cornell University Library.

Ribot, Théodule. 1897. *The Psychology of the Emotions*. London: W. Scott.

Roelvink, Gerda. 2010. "Collective Action and the Politics of Affect." *Emotion, Space and Society* 3 (2): 111–18.

Rohrer, Tim. 2007. "The Body in Space: Dimensions of Embodiment." In *Body, Language and Mind*. Vol. 1, *Embodiment*, edited by Dirk Geeraerts, René Dirven, and John R. Taylor, 339–78. Berlin: De Gruyter Mouton.

Roitman, Janet. 2013. *Anti-crisis*. Durham, NC: Duke University Press.

Roitman, Janet. 2020. "Crisis in History or Crisis Historiography." *Finance and Society* 6 (2): 136–40.

Rosenberg, Emily S. 2003. *Financial Missionaries to the World: The Politics and Culture of Dollar Diplomacy, 1900–1930*. Durham, NC: Duke University Press.

Rothman, E. Natalie. 2012. *Brokering Empire: Trans-imperial Subjects between Venice and Istanbul*. Ithaca, NY: Cornell University Press.

Rousseau, Jean-Jacques. [1755] 2004. *A Discourse upon the Origin and Foundation of Inequality among Mankind*. Project Gutenberg. https://www.gutenberg.org/ebooks/11136.

Rozanov, Andrew. 2005. "Who Holds the Wealth of Nations?" *Central Banking*, May 20, 2005. https://www.centralbanking.com/central-banks/financial-stability/2072255/who-holds-the-wealth-of-nations.

Rutherford, Danilyn. Forthcoming. "Beautiful Mystery: Living in a Worldless World." Durham, NC: Duke University Press.

Saad, Sadek. 2020. "The Myth of Nasser's Arabism: Cairo (1956–1970), a Political-Urban Paradox." *International Journal of Engineering Applied Sciences and Technology* 5 (5): 37–45.

Sabea, Hanan. 2013. "A 'Time out of Time': Tahrir, the Political and the Imaginary in the Context of the January 25th Revolution in Egypt." Hot Spots, *Fieldsights*, May 9, 2013. https://culanth.org/fieldsights/a-time-out-of-time-tahrir-the-political-and-the-imaginary-in-the-context-of-the-january-25th-revolution-in-egypt.

Said, Edward. 1987. "The Imperial Spectacle." *Grand Street* 6 (2): 82–104.

Said, Edward. 1993. *Culture and Imperialism*. London: Chatto and Windus.

Sakr, Laila Shereen. 2023. *Arabic Glitch: Technoculture, Data Bodies, and Archives*. Stanford, CA: Stanford University Press.

Salamanca, Omar Jabary, Mezna Qato, Kareem Rabie, and Sobhi Samour. 2012. "Past Is Present: Settler Colonialism in Palestine." *Settler Colonial Studies* 2 (1): 1–8.

Salem, Sara. 2020. *Anticolonial Afterlives in Egypt: The Politics of Hegemony*. Cambridge: Cambridge University Press.

Samir, Nehal. 2021. "Culture, Tourism Ministers Honour Royal Mummies Parade Line-Up." *Daily News Egypt*, April 14, 2021. https://www.dailynewsegypt.com/2021/04/14/culture-tourism-ministers-honour-royal-mummies-parade-line-up/.

Samudra, Jaida Kim. 2008. "Memory in Our Body: Thick Participation and the Translation of Kinesthetic Experience." *American Ethnologist* 35 (4): 665–81.

Sayigh, Yezid. 2019. *Owners of the Republic: An Anatomy of Egypt's Military Economy*. Washington, DC: Carnegie Endowment for International Peace.

Sayigh, Yezid. 2022. *Retain, Restructure, or Divest? Policy Options for Egypt's Military Economy*. Washington, DC: Carnegie Endowment for International Peace.

Scham, Sandra A. 2013. "The Making and Unmaking of European Cairo." *Journal of Eastern Mediterranean Archaeology and Heritage Studies* 1 (4): 313–18.

Schayegh, Cyrus, and Andrew Arsan, eds. 2015. *The Routledge Handbook of the History of the Middle East Mandates*. New York: Routledge.

Schmitthoff, M. 1939. "The Origin of the Joint-Stock Company." *University of Toronto Law Journal* 3 (1): 74–94.

Schnitzler, Antina von. 2016. *Democracy's Infrastructure: Techno-politics and Protest after Apartheid*. Princeton, NJ: Princeton University Press.

Sedgwick, Eve Kosofsky. 2008. *Epistemology of the Closet*. Berkeley: University of California Press.

Seikaly, Sherene. 2015. *Men of Capital: Scarcity and Economy in Mandate Palestine*. Stanford, CA: Stanford University Press.

Seikaly, Sherene. 2019. "The Matter of Time." *American Historical Review* 124 (5): 1681–88.

Seikaly, Sherene, and Sara Scalanghe. 2022. "The Body and Revolution in the Middle East." In *Routledge Handbook on Women in the Middle East*, edited by Suad Joseph and Zeina Zaatari. London: Routledge.

Serres, Michel. [1980] 2007. *The Parasite*. Translated by Lawrence Schehr. Minneapolis: University of Minnesota Press.

Serres, Michel. 2003. "The Science of Relations: An Interview." *Angelaki* 8 (2): 227–38. https://doi.org/10.1080/0969725032000162675.

Shannon, C. E. 1948. "A Mathematical Theory of Communication." *Bell System Technical Journal* 27 (3–4): 379–423; 623–56.

Sharkey, Heather J. 2017. *A History of Muslims, Christians, and Jews in the Middle East*. Cambridge: Cambridge University Press.

Shell, Jacob. 2019. "*Verkehr*, or Subversive Mobility: Recovering Radical Transportation Geographies from Language." *Human Geography* 11 (3): 11–29.

Sherrington, Charles Scott. 1906. *The Integrative Action of the Nervous System*. New Haven, CT: Yale University Press.

Shlala, Elizabeth H. 2018. *The Late Ottoman Empire and Egypt: Hybridity, Law, and Gender*. London: Routledge.

Sikainga, Ahmad Alawad. 1996. *Slaves into Workers: Emancipation and Labor in Colonial Sudan*. Austin: University of Texas Press.

Simmel, Georg. 2011. *The Philosophy of Money*. Edited by David Frisby. Translated by Tom Bottomore. New York: Routledge.

Simone, AbdouMaliq. 2004. *For the City Yet to Come: Changing African Life in Four Cities*. Durham, NC: Duke University Press.

Simone, AbdouMaliq. 2013. "Cities of Uncertainty: Jakarta, the Urban Majority, and Inventive Political Technologies." *Theory, Culture and Society*, 30 (7–8): 243–63.

Simone, AbdouMaliq. 2018. *Improvised Lives: Rhythms of Endurance in an Urban South*. Cambridge: Polity.

Simone, AbdouMaliq. 2022. *The Surrounds: Urban Life within and beyond Capture*. Durham, NC: Duke University Press.

Simone, AbdouMaliq, and Edgar Pieterse. 2017. *New Urban Worlds: Inhabiting Dissonant Times*. Cambridge: Polity.

Simone, AbdouMaliq, and Vyjayanthi Rao. 2012. "Securing the Majority: Living through Uncertainty in Jakarta." *International Journal of Urban and Regional Research* 36 (2): 315–35. https://doi.org/10.1111/j.1468-2427.2011.01028.x.

Simpson, Audra. 2014. *Mohawk Interruptus: Political Life across the Borders of Settler States*. Durham, NC: Duke University Press.

Skilliter, S. A. 1977. *William Harborne and the Trade with Turkey, 1578–1582: A Documentary Study of the First Anglo-Ottoman Relations*. Oxford: Oxford University Press.

Slys, Mariya Tait. 2014. *Exporting Legality: The Rise and Fall of Extraterritorial Jurisdiction in the Ottoman Empire and China*. Geneva: Graduate Institute.

Smith, Adam. [1796] 1982. *An Inquiry into the Nature and Causes of the Wealth of Nations*. Vol. 1. Edited by R. H. Campbell, A. S. Skinner, and William B. Todd. Indianapolis, IN: Liberty Fund.

Solomon, Richard. 2024. "Egyptian Leverage: The IMF Invests in the Egyptian Dictator's Structural Payments Imbalance," *Phenomenal World*, March 14, 2024. https://www.phenomenalworld.org/analysis/egyptian-leverage/.

Sorokin, Pitirim A. 1959. *Social and Cultural Mobility*. Glencoe, IL: Free Press.

Springborg, Robert. 2022. "Sisi Tries to Rebrand in the Face of Dissatisfaction in Egypt—and within His Regime." *Democracy in Exile, Egypt*, November 3, 2022. https://dawnmena.org/sisi-tries-to-rebrand-in-the-face-of-dissatisfaction-in-egypt-and-within-his-regime/.

Srnicek, Nick. 2016. *Platform Capitalism*. Cambridge: Polity.

Starobinski, Jean. 1990. "A Short History of Bodily Sensation." *Psychological Medicine* 20 (1): 23–33.

Stavrianakis, Anthony, and Gaymon Bennett. 2012. "On Concept Work." *Somatosphere: Science, Medicine, and Anthropology*, September 25, 2012. https://somatosphere.com/2012/on-concept-work.html/.

Steedman, Carolyn. 2002. *Dust: The Archive and Cultural History*. New Brunswick, NJ: Rutgers University Press.

Stein, Sarah Abrevaya. 2016. *Extraterritorial Dreams: European Citizenship, Sephardi Jews, and the Ottoman Twentieth Century*. Chicago: University of Chicago Press.

Stein, Sarah Abrevaya. 2019. *Family Papers: A Sephardic Journey through the Twentieth Century*. New York: Farrar, Straus and Giroux.

Stocking, George Jr. 1987. *Victorian Anthropology*. New York: Free Press.

Stroul, Dana. 2019. Talk given at the Center for Strategic and International Studies (CSIS), October 31, 2019. Twitter, accessed November 26, 2024. https://twitter.com/KevorkAlmassian/status/1633822562684661760/.

Svantesson, Dan Jerker B. 2015. "A Jurisprudential Justification for Extraterritoriality in (Private) International Law." *Santa Clara Journal of International Law* 13 (2): 517–71.

Sweigard, Lulu E. 1974. *Human Movement Potential: Its Ideokinetic Facilitation*. Chicago: Allegro.

Tabikha, Kamal. 2021. "Egypt's Mummies Parade: How to Listen to the Musical Soundtrack of This Unique Event." *National News*, April 7, 2021. https://www.thenationalnews.com/arts-culture/music/egypt-s-mummies-parade-how-to-listen-to-the-official-soundtrack-of-this-unique-event-1.1199163.

Tadiar, Neferti X. M. 2022. *Remaindered Life*. Durham, NC: Duke University Press.

TallBear, Kim. 2016. "Standing with and Speaking as Faith: A Feminist-Indigenous Approach to Inquiry." In *Sources and Methods in Indigenous Studies*, edited by Chris Andersen and Jean M. O'Brien, 69–77. London: Routledge.

Tarlo, Emma. 1996. *Clothing Matters: Dress and Identity in India*. Chicago: University of Chicago Press.

Taylor, Charles. 1991. "The Dialogic Self." In *The Interpretive Turn: Philosophy, Science, Culture*, edited by D. R. Hiley, 304–14. Ithaca, NY: Cornell University Press.

Taylor, Charles. 1993. "To Follow a Rule . . ." In *Bourdieu: Critical Perspectives*, edited by E. Lipuma, M. Postone, and C. J. Calhoun, 45–60. Chicago: University of Chicago Press.

Thayer, Lucius Ellsworth. 1923. "The Capitulations of the Ottoman Empire and the Question of Their Abrogation as It Affects the United States." *American Journal of International Law* 17 (2): 207–33.

Thénault, Sylvie. 2014. "Le 'code de l'indigénat.'" In *Histoire de l'Algérie à la période coloniale, 1830–1962*, edited by Abderrahmane Bouchène, Jean-Pierre Peyroulou, Ouanassa Siari Tengour, and Sylvie Thénault, 200–206. Paris: Éditions La Decouverte.

Thieme, Friedrich Wilhelm. 1859. *Neues vollständiges kritisches Wörterbuch der Englischen und Deutschen Sprache / A New and Complete Critical Dictionary of the English and German Languages*. 2 vols. Altona: Gustavus Mayer.

Thomas, Deborah A. 2022. "What the Caribbean Teaches Us: The Afterlives and New Lives of Coloniality." *Journal of Latin American and Caribbean Anthropology* 27 (3): 235–54. https://doi.org/10.1111/jlca.12578.

Thomas, Thomas. 1587. *Dictionarium linguae latinae et anglicanae*. London: Richard Boyle.

Thrift, Nigel. 1996. *Spatial Formations*. New York: SAGE.

Tignor, Robert L. 1998. *Capitalism and Nationalism at the End of Empire*. Princeton, NJ: Princeton University Press.

Tignor, Robert L. 2010. *Egypt: A Short History*. Princeton, NJ: Princeton University Press.

Tignor, Robert. 2022. "The Egyptian Private Sector: Historical Overview of a Delicate and Fragile Plant." Unpublished manuscript, last modified November 2022.

Todorova, Maria, 1997. *Imagining the Balkans*. New York: Oxford University Press.

Torpey, John C. 2018. *The Invention of the Passport: Surveillance, Citizenship and the State*. Cambridge: Cambridge University Press.

Tunçer, Ali Coşkun. 2015. *Sovereign Debt and International Financial Control: The Middle East and the Balkans 1870–1914*. London: Palgrave Macmillan.

Turner, Terence. 1980. "The Social Skin." In *Not Work Alone: A Cross-Cultural View of Activities Superfluous to Survival*, edited by Jeremy Cherfas and R. Lewin, 112–40. Beverly Hills, CA: Temple Smith.

Tzouvala, Ntina. 2020. *Capitalism as Civilisation: A History of International Law*. Cambridge: Cambridge University Press.

'Uways, Sayyid. 1989. *L'histoire que je porte sur mon dos: Mémoires*. Translated by Nashwa al-Azhari, Gilbert Delanoue, and Alain Roussillon. Cairo: CEDEJ.

van den Boogert, Maurits H. 2005. *The Capitulations and the Ottoman Legal System: Qadis, Consuls, and Beratlis in the Eighteenth Century*. Leiden: Brill.

Van Der Molen, Gezina H. J. [1937] 1968. *Alberico Gentili and the Development of International Law: His Life Work and Times*. Leyden: A. W. Sijthoff.

Vatikiotis, P. J. 1980. *The History of Egypt*. 2nd ed. Baltimore: Johns Hopkins University Press.

Vatikiotis, P. J. 1987. Review of *Egypt under the Khedives 1805–1879*, by F. Robert Hunter. *Journal of Middle Eastern Studies* 23 (4): 533–35.

Veblen, Thorstein, 1899. *The Theory of the Leisure Class: An Economic Study in the Evolution of Institutions*. New York: MacMillan.

Vitalis, Robert. 1995. *When Capitalists Collide: Business Conflict and the End of Empire in Egypt*. Berkeley: University of California Press.

Viviani, P. 1987. "Motor-Perceptual Interactions: The Evolution of an Idea." In *Cognitive Science in Europe: Issues and Trends*, edited by M. Imbert, P. Bertelson, R. Kempson, D. Osherson, H. Schnelle, N. Sreitz, A. Thomassen, and P. Viviani, 11–39. Heidelberg: Springer.

Vogt, Peter. 2015. "The Conceptual History of Barbarism: What Can We Learn from Koselleck and Pocock?" *Thamyris/Intersecting* 29:125–38.

von Mises, Ludwig. 1935. "Economic Calculation in the Socialist Commonwealth." In *Collectivist Economic Planning*, edited by F. A. Hayek, 87–130. London: Routledge and Kegan Paul, 1935.

Wagner, Andreas. 2012. "Lessons of Imperialism and the Law of Nations: Alberico Gentili's Early Modern Appeal to Roman Law." *European Journal of International Law* 23 (3): 873–86.

Wahba, Mourad Magdi. 1983. "The Egyptian Public Sector: The Control Structure and Efficiency Considerations." *Public Administration and Development* 3 (1): 27–37.

Wikan, Unni. 1996. *Tomorrow, God Willing: Self-Made Destinies in Cairo*. Chicago: University of Chicago Press.

Williams, John Alden. 1984. "Urbanization and Monument Construction in Mamluk Cairo." *Muqarnas* 2:33–45.

Wilner, Gabriel M. 1975. "The Mixed Courts of Egypt: A Study on the Use of Natural Law and Equity." *Georgia Journal of International and Comparative Law* 407 (5): 407–30.

Wilson, Eric. 2008. *The Savage Republic: "De Indis" of Hugo Grotius, Republicanism, and Dutch Hegemony within the Modern World-System (c. 1600–1619)*. Leiden: Brill.

Winkel, Eric. 2019. "Time Is Not Real: Time in Ibn 'Arabi, and from Parmenides (and Heraclitus) to Julian Barbour." *Journal of the Ibn 'Arabi Society* 51. https://ibnarabisociety.org/time-is-not-real-eric-winkel/.

Wolf, Eric R. 1999. *Envisioning Power: Ideologies of Dominance and Crisis*. Berkeley: University of California Press.

Wynter, Sylvia. 2003. "Unsettling the Coloniality of Being/Power/Truth/Freedom: Towards the Human, After Man, Its Overrepresentation—An Argument." CR: *The New Centennial Review* 3 (3): 257–337.

Yaycıoğlu, Ali. 2022. "Empire of Debt: Finance, Violence, and Accounting in the Ottoman Age of Crisis, 1770–1840." Talk given at the Department of Near Eastern Studies, Princeton University, March 16, 2022.

Zambrana, Rocío. 2021. *Colonial Debts: The Case of Puerto Rico*. Durham, NC: Duke University Press.

INDEX

Page numbers in italics refer to figures.

American Geographical Society, 83

American Journal of International Law, 105

American philosophical pragmatism, 159

American University in Cairo, 50, 60, 63, 68, 131

Americas, 13, 30, 180n8

Amir, Mr., 59–61, 63, 67, 69, 71, 116, 132, 185n1

Anatolia, 83–84, 90, 182n24

Anghie, Antony, 179n4, 186n11

Anglo-Egyptian Condominium Agreement, 76

anthropology, 5, 16, 77, 146, 158–59, 165, 188n6, 193n16; the commons in, 111; economic, 70; embodiment in, 120–21, 162–63; graduated development theory in, 73; historical, 6; physical, 84, 187n21; of postsocialism, 68; primitive concept in, 13–14, 141–42, 166; social, 189n4; unitary sovereignty in, 22

anthropometry, 84

anticolonialism, 65, 85, 118

anti-imperialism, 65

antimonopoly policies, 67

antisocialism, 67

Aquinas, Thomas, 111–12

Arab conquest of Cairo (646), 19

Arab regions, 74, 76, 165

Arabs, 1, 10, 44–45, 62, 83–84, 94, 101, 108, 161, 178, 182n26

Arab Spring, 166

Arab world, 1, 17, 20, 24, 86, 115, 155, 161, 171

archaeology, 42, 44–45, 83

"archives from the dust," 16–18, 24, 182n25

area studies, 8

Aristotle, 180n10

Armenia, 75, 83

Armenian genocide, 167

Artnet News, 42–43

Asia Minor, 20, 74

aspirational sovereignty, 177

assets, 31, 52, 57, 68, 79–81, 94, 184n12; assetification, 53–55

Aswan Dam, 62, 64

asymmetric counterconcepts, 13

atavism, 16

austerity, 31

Austria, 103–4, 187n1

Austro-Hungarian Empire, 23, 73–74, 102–3

Aztec Empire, 12

Badrawy, Mohamed, 77

baladi, 62, 147–48

baladi capitalism, 117

Balfour Declaration, 76

Balibar, Étienne, 108–9

Balkans, 13, 73, 102

banking/bankers, 1, 9, 30, 59–60, 61, 71, 145, 151; bank nationalization, 63, 65–67, 116; central banks, 53; and debt, 9, 70; and embodied archives, 18; history of, 86; and privatization, 68–69, 125; public-sector banking, 61, 79, 132; and valuation, 30. *See also individual banks and bankers*

Barakat, Nora Elizabeth, 47, 184n4

Barakat, Rana, 45

barbarian, category of, 7, 11–14, 23, 73, 83–84, 102, 115, 165, 175, 178, 180n8, 180n10

Barclays Bank, 66–67

Barrawi, Rashid al-, 64

barzakh, 155–58, 171–72, 177–78, 191nn3–4

bast, 38, 174

Baybars II (sultan), 94

beaten tracks, 139, 144

Bedouins, 27, 139

Belgium, 169, 187n1

Bender, John, 187n18

Benton, Lauren, 97

beratlis, 2, 5, 93, 114

Berthoz, Alain, 163, 192n9

Bey, Phillipe Gelat: *Gazettes of the Proceedings of Mixed Courts,* 87–88

Black, Eugene, 62, 64, 77

Black internationalism, 25, 173

Black resistance movements, 153, 190n1

Bloomfield, Leonard, 189n6

Boas, Franz, 84

Bodin, Jean, 21

Bolshevism, 73

Bonapartism, 71

bonds (financial), 30, 54, 74, 78, 95, 186n15. *See also* debt

Bonilla, Yarimar, 182n22

Book of the Dead, 42

Bosnia, 11, 14, 85, 193n19

Bosnia-Herzegovina, 102

extraterritoriality, 15, 23–24, 27–28, 33, 81, 180nn5–6, 181n20, 188n12; and capitulations, 5, 50, 65, 76, 82, 92, 97–98, 101, 179n4; channels of, 5, 22; and colonialism, 6–9; and the commons, 113–17; definition, 82; and Egyptian Mixed Courts, 25, 87–88, 91, 96–104; enabling commerce, 8, 18, 55, 82, 87–88, 92–93, 100, 111, 113, 122–23; and proprioception, 165; in private international law, 6; and semicivilized condition, 10–12

extraterritorials, 188n14; *vs.* commoners, 28, 34; *vs.* locals, 25, 33–34, 99, 101, 106, 113–15

Fabian, Johannes, 180n11

Facebook, 126

fahlawa, 61–63, 116

fallahi, 100, 115

family ethos, 147, 149

fascism, 160, 163

Fatimid Caliphate, 90–91

Fawzi, Essam, 15–138, 174, 177, 182n25, 185n1

Federal Reserve Bank, 87

Ferguson, Adam, 12

fictive kin, 138–39, 141

fields (Bourdieu), 120

finance, 60, 76, 111, 141, 144, 156, 174–75, 180n7, 181n17, 185n10; and debt, 29–32, 48–50, 55, 79, 86–87; and Egyptian Mixed Courts, 96; empowerment finance, 145, 151; and extraterritoriality, 5, 8–9, 181n20; and fahlawa, 61–63; and infrastructure, 48–50, 80, 82; microfinance, 146, 150; and mobility, 23, 27, 29–31; and national economy, 63–69; thick, 69–72

financialization, 24, 29, 55, 70, 78, 92, 150–51; militarized, 37, 53, 55, 169, 174, 177; of real estate, 37, 55, 154

fintech, 135, 146, 151

fixed-income capital market instruments, 54

food, 39–40, 59, 77, 134, 136, 167, 170

foreign currency reserves, 40, 78–79

foreigners, 65, 86, 93, 95, 98, 102–4, 115, 126, 137

foreign exchange–denominated bank capital (FOREX), 69

Foreign Office of Great Britain, 78

France, 12, 31, 47, 71, 87, 145, 160, 170, 184n11, 192n9; control of Egyptian finances, 49; credit from, 70; and Egyptian Mixed Courts, 96, 98, 101, 187n1; Paris, 39, 44, 75, 177; and Suez Canal, 2, 48, 50, 62, 64, 66, 156, 158. *See also* French colonialism

free market capitalism, 55, 63–64, 67, 113, 182n25

Free Officers Movement (1952), 19–20, 25, 37, 50, 60, 63–67, 105, 126

French Army, 131

French colonialism, 33, 36, 99, 101, 120, 177, 188n11. *See also* French Mandate

French Mandate, 74, 76, 99, 103, 105, 165

French occupation of Egypt, 33, 36, 101

French Revolution (1789), 71, 173

French Second Empire, 71

French University in Beirut, 1

Freud, Sigmund, 159–61, 192n12

futuwwah, 116, 123

gada', 116–17, 123, 139

Galata, Constantinople, 88–92

Gall, Franz, 192n14

Garden City, 131, 177

Garden of Eden, 111–12

Garozzo and Zaffarani, 184n11

Gaza: Israeli genocide in, 11, 14, 85, 167, 174–75, 193n19

Geertz, Clifford, 72

Gelvin, James, 69

gender, 88, 135–41, 179n3, 189n2

genocide, 7; Armenian, 167; in Bosnia, 11; in Gaza, 14, 85, 167, 174–75, 193n19. *See also* ethnic cleansing; urbicide

Gentili, Alberico, 27–29, 183nn31–32

gentrification, 125, 157

Germany, 57, 82, 153, 187n1

Gesr el-Suez, 43

gesture, 17, 110, 117, 119, 121–24, 127, 161, 164, 190n7; gestural commons, 19, 125, 162

Gharbiya, 52

gift economy, 70

gift of sovereignty, 23

Giza Zoo, 177

global capital, 49, 55, 180n7

global commerce, 5–6, 10, 28, 30, 44, 55, 87, 91, 93, 95, 105, 141, 186n13

globalization, 20
global legal order, 9
global nonaligned movement, 25, 65, 193n19
global order, 6, 8, 10, 104
Global South, 9, 110, 125, 147, 164, 190n8
Global Ventures, 54
gossip, 110, 126–27, 134, 137–38, 142, 149, 151, 166
government *vs.* state, 60–61
GPS, 154–55, 168
Great Britain, 32, 47, 50, 78, 87, 137, 156, 186n12, 186n13, 189n4, 192n9; and Egyptian Mixed Courts, 95–96; financial revolution in, 55; London, 68, 72, 75, 80; occupation of Egypt, 18; at Paris Peace Conference, 74–76; and Suez Canal construction, 62; and Suez Canal funding, 48–49; in Tripartite Aggression/Suez Crisis, 2, 64. *See also* British colonialism; British Mandate; United Kingdom
Greater Cairo, 36
Greater Lebanon, 76
Greece, 98, 101, 103, 109, 145, 166
Greek Orthodox Church, 2, 70, 103
green initiatives, 56–58, 167, 169
Grotius, Hugo, 21, 27, 32, 111, 144, 150, 189n3
Grumperz, John, 189n6
Gulf Corporation Council (GCC), 79, 174
Gulf of Suez Petroleum Company (GUPCO), 152–53
Gulf States, 15, 24, 54, 56–57, 67, 76, 78–79, 138, 143, 169. *See also individual countries*
Gulf War (first), 171

habitus, 120, 163
Hanley, Will, 115, 188n13
Hanseatic League, 93
Hapsburg Empire, 92
Hardt, Michael, 109, 113
Harney, Stefano, 14
Harvard University, 64, 84, 187n21, 192n10
Hatshepsut (queen), 43
Hayek, Friedrich, 66–67, 160
Heidegger, Martin, 160
Heliopolis, 169–70, 190n2
hermeneutics, 160
Hermes, 145, 149, 166, 193n18

Higher Sectoral Councils, 66
Hijaz, 20, 75
hospitality, 94, 133, 188n7
"Houma min wa ihna min?," 116
Houris, Spyro, 2
House Planning and Budget Committee, 77
Hoyle, Judge, 103
Huda, 147–49
Husserl, Edmund, 160
Huxley, Henry Minor, 84, 187n21

Ibn Al-Aas, Amr, 44
ibn al-balad, 61–62, 100, 114, 116
ibn 'arab, 115
Ibn 'Arabi, 155–57, 161, 191n3, 192n13
Ibn Khaldun, 94, 161
ideology, 9
Imam, Sheikh, 116
Imari, Abd al-Galil al-, 64
imperialism, 34, 88, 118, 158, 186n13, 187n18, 188n13, 189n3; and capitulations, 5, 9, 94; and commerce, 30, 92; and debt, 47; and Egyptian Mixed Courts, 100–101; and extraterritoriality, 8, 18, 87, 111; and finance, 69–70; inter-, 8, 18, 26, 87, 111, 188n6, 193n19; liberal, 33, 112, 164–65, 173; post-, 25, 113, 120; and settler colonialism, 22; and sovereignty, 74–75, 97, 181n19; and Suez Canal, 2; trans-, 20. *See also* colonialism; *individual empires*
Imperial Ottoman Bank. *See* Ottoman Bank (Imperial Ottoman Bank)
improvement, 162, 183n34; debts of, 27–31
imtiyazat. See capitulations, Ottoman
independence, 9, 25, 27, 49, 53–54, 73–76, 83–84, 188n10
India, 144, 177, 186n12, 189n3; anticolonial revolts in, 49, 80, 112, 158, 165; British colonialism in, 22, 31, 118, 140
Indian Ocean, 70–71
indigène, category of, 87, 96, 99–100, 104, 188n11
indirect rule, 112
Industrial Bank of Egypt, 60, 65
infitah, 20, 68, 138
inflation, 38, 78
informal economy, 145–46, 150
informal institutions, 134

liberalism, 64, 71, 163, 178; liberal imperialism, 33, 112, 164–65, 173
Libya, 167
lingua franca, 26, 87
Liverpool F.C., 131
loans, 54, 59, 64, 70, 78, 109, 145, 151, 174.
See also credit; debt; multilateral
lenders
local, category of, 2, 9, 19, 25, 87, 111, 171;
and capitulations, 5, 65, 93; and the
commons, 113–17, 119, 121, 123–25; and
Egyptian Mixed Courts, 96–106; versus
extraterritorial, 25, 33–34; versus
Levantini, 26
Locke, John, 183n34, 190n7
locomotory practices, 116–21, 143, 157
Lorimer, James, 72–73
Lotze, Rudolf Hermann, 159
Luxemburg, Rosa, 9

Mada Masr (website), 109–10, 183n3
Madinat al-Hirifyeen, 154
Mahdist Revolt (1881), 88
Mahfouz, Naguib, 131
Mahmood, Saba, 163
Maine, Henry Sumner, 21–22, 112, 189n4
Maitland, James, 144
Malabou, Catherine, 161, 171
Malcolm X, 25, 182n26
Maldonado-Torres, Nelson, 180n8
Malinowski, Bronisław, 141–43, 145–46, 148
Mamluks, 94, 188n6
Mandate system, 13, 73, 75, 84, 179n4,
186n11, 186n14; British Mandate, 1–2,
11, 74, 76, 99, 100–101, 103, 165; French
Mandate, 74, 76, 99, 103, 105, 165
Mandatory Palestine, 1–2, 11, 74, 76,
100–101, 103
Manning, Paul, 132
Mansoura, 87
Martin, Randy, 164
Marvel Studios/Disney, 19
Marx, Karl, 71, 145
Marxism, 145, 175
Masrah al-Salam, 35
Massey, Doreen, 157
Mausoleum of Imam Shafi'i, 19
Mauss, Marcel, 121
Mayan Empire, 12

Mead, George Herbert, 122–24, 190n7
Mecca, 91
Mediterranean, 20, 25, 28, 48, 70, 94, 98,
103, 108–9, 122, 182n25; Eastern, 26
megaprojects, 36, 41, 44–45, 47, 56
Mehrling, Perry, 31, 71
Melanesia, 146
merchants, 18, 70, 92, 94–95, 97, 166,
187n18, 188n3
Merleau-Ponty, Maurice, 160
Mesopotamia, 74, 76
methodology of book, 6–11, 165. *See also*
ethnography
microfinance, 146, 150
Middle Ages, 12–13, 102
Middle Eastern studies, 7, 61, 103
migrant labor, 57, 143
militarization, 168; and financialization, 37,
53, 55, 169, 174, 177
military companies, 52–54, 80
military economy, 37, 183n2
misri, 115
mobile phones, 69, 125–27, 126, 137, 146,
154, 176
Mogamma, 51–52, 54–55, 80, 169
Mohammedan World (report), 83
Mohawk Nation, 181n17
money changers, 70
monopoly corporations, 93, 189n3
Moon Nights (film), 19
moral philosophy, 14, 111–12
Morsi, Mohamed, 36, 55, 80
Moten, Fred, 14
motor theory of perception, 159
Mubarak, Gamal, 68
Mubarak, Hosni, 37–38, 51, 62, 129–30,
147; financial policy of, 45, 55, 63, 68,
78–79; and informal sectors, 170; over-
throw of, 20, 59, 109, 125
Mughal Empire, 22–23, 118, 158
Muhammad (Prophet), 44
Muhammed, Abu, 134–35
Muhammed, 'Um, 134–35, 138, 140–41, 147,
149
multilateral lenders, 69
Muna, 43, 57
Munif, Abdelrahman, 167
Muqattam, 46
Musa, Salama, 161

Ottoman Public Debt Administration, 87
Ottoman Public Debt Administration
    (OPDA), 30, 87, 144
Oxford Capital Group, 54
Oxford University, 28

Palestine, 5–6, 25, 27, 76, 82, 84, 87–88, 92,
    115, 178, 183n29; Bethlehem, 1; British
    Occupied Enemy Territory Admin-
    istration in, 4; Gaza, 11, 14, 85, 167,
    174–75, 193n19; Jaffa, 132; Jericho, 31;
    Jerusalem (al-Quds al-Sherif), 1, 134;
    Mandatory Palestine, 1–2, 11, 74, 76,
    100–101, 103
pan-Arabism, 25
Pandolfo, Stefania, 191n4
Papal States, 103
Parade of the Mummies (Pharoahs' Golden
    Parade), 41–47, 49–50, 161
Paris Peace Conference (1919–20), 9, 23,
    73, 74–76, 82, 83, 84, 182n24. See also
    Treaty of Versailles.
Pasha, Abbate, 161
Pasha, Ismail. See Ismail (Khedive)
Pasha, Mehmet (Mohamed) Ali. See Ali
    Pasha, Mehmet (Mohamed)
Pasha, Mariette, 184n11
Pasha, Nubar, 95
passports, 5, 9, 20–21, 23, 51, 93, 104, 106,
    117, 182n23, 188n14
payments space, 146
Péreire, Émile, 71
Persia, 12, 115
personality of law, 5, 82
personal law, 5, 7, 9–11, 15, 18, 22, 24, 50, 92,
    97, 110–14, 165
phatic communion, 142–43, 146
phatic labor, 25, 145–46, 148–49, 166
phenomenology, 160
Philippines, 12, 143
physiology, 83, 156–63, 172, 191n8, 192n15,
    192nn9–10
Poland, 70, 141
political economy, 5–9, 18, 23, 26, 33–34, 55,
    78–79, 91, 95, 117, 120, 141, 144–46, 149,
    166–67, 173
political theory, 5–6, 10, 14, 21, 108–9, 111,
    113, 179n4, 180n8
politics of the commons, 11, 34

popular sovereignty, 37
Porte, 30, 70, 75
Portuguese colonialism, 32, 187n1, 189n3
postcolonialism, 6, 8, 21, 23, 34, 54, 63, 113,
    147, 165–66, 179n2, 183n36; postcolo-
    nial states, 14, 33, 65, 120, 175
postcolonial studies, 14, 120
postsocialism, 68
potentiation, 171–72
poverty, 39–41, 48, 59, 61–62, 102, 113, 116,
    126, 139, 146, 150–51
price shopping, 40
primitive, category of, 13–14, 84–85, 180n8,
    190n7; primitive/civilized binary, 7–8,
    13–14, 141–42, 165–66
Princeton University, 83
private international law, 5–6, 72, 82, 91, 117
privatization, 54–55, 60, 63, 68–69, 80, 125,
    147, 174
property, 46, 54, 80, 110–11, 123, 144, 168,
    181n20, 183n29, 184n4, 190n2, 191n3;
    communal, 112–13; financialized, 24,
    154; informal, 45; private, 21, 112; prop-
    erty law, 94; property rights, 45, 61, 97,
    149; property speculation, 38
proprioception, 11, 19, 155–65, 171–72, 178,
    191n7
psychoanalysis, 160
public finance, 64
public goods, 24, 53–54, 109
public-private partnerships, 24, 46, 54–55,
    57, 80
public sector, 54–55, 59–60, 63–68, 79, 116,
    125, 132, 150, 169
public utilities, 68, 81, 170
Puerto Rico, 29, 174

qabd, 38, 40, 131, 173–74
Qasr el-Nil, 50
Qatar, 77–82
Qatar Investment Authority, 80
Quran, 134, 155–56

Rabaa Square massacre (2013), 41
racialization, 83–84, 97, 178. See also
    orientalism
racism, 162–63, 183, 183n33
ra'iya, 100, 115
Ramadan, 124, 131

Ramses II (pharaoh), 43
Rancière, Jacques, 39, 124
real estate, 17, 24, 41, 52, 56–58, 185n14, 190n2; financialized, 37, 55, 154; speculative, 18
Red Sea, 48, 81–82
Reil, Johann Christian, 159
relational finance, 72
relational self, 163
remaindered lives, 10, 14, 41
revaluation, 18, 30–31, 54, 151, 154. *See also* devaluation
Rhodes, 98
Ribot, Théodule A., 159, 192n10
rikaba, 36–37
Risgallah v. Zahar (1926), 104
Roman Empire, 5, 12–13, 28, 82, 92, 94, 114, 166, 188nn7–8
Roman law, 12, 28, 72, 82, 98
Royal African Company, 28
Rue el Khurunfich, 88–92, 96
Russia, *74*, 78, 82, 92, 102, 169, 187n1, 188n3

Sabea, Hanan, 109
Sadat, Anwar, 20, 55, 68, 138, 171
Safavid Empire, 23
Safouan, Moustapha, 192n13
Said, Edward, 47
Saint-Simon, Henri de, 66, 71, 156
Saint-Simonians, 31, 48–49, 71, 156, 185n10
Salah, Mo, 131–32
Sami-Ali, 161
San Remo Conference (1920), 76
Saudi Arabia, 45, 57, 77–82, 154, 167, 169
Sayyida Zeinab, 123, 131
Sedgwick, Eve, 179n3
self-determination, 9, 73–74
semicivilized, definition, 6–15
semiotics, 61, 113, 115–18, 145, 153, 161, 182n22; semiotic commons, 11, 122, 124–25, 140, 162; semiotic community, 122–25, 143, 148–49, 173, 189n6
Sepoy Rebellion (1857), 80, 158
September 11, 2021 attacks, 11
Serbia, 73. *See also* Kingdom of Serbia
Serres, Michel, 145, 166
settler colonialism, 1, 22, 27, 29, 97
sex work, 137–40, 149
shabab, 59, 123, 138

sha'bi, 19, 60–61, 107, 114, 125, 136, 173
shaken grounds, 11, 14, 23, 34, 157, 166
Shannon, C. E., 140–41
shared grounds, 117
Sherrington, Charles Scott, 156–60, 162, 164–65, 191n8
Shubra, 57
Shura Council, 36
Sidqi, Aziz, 64
Simone, AbdouMaliq, 14
Simpson, Audra, 181n17
Sinai Peninsula, 174
Sisi, Abdel Fatah, 36, 41–42, 44, 46–47, 53, 55–56, 131, 143, 168, 170, 184n6, 185n3
slavery, 88, 91, 99, 180n10
Slavic nations, 73
Slavs, 102
Slovenia, 11; Ljubljana, 28
slow death, 57
social infrastructure, 7, 17, 19, 25, 31–33, 110–11, 123–24, 126, 137, 140, 146, 148, 150–51
social infrastructures of communicative channels, 19, 25, 32–33, 110–11, 124, 126, 146
socialism, 9, 20, 48, 54, 63–65, 67–68, 153
social science, 6, 10, 19, 21, 30, 161, 163
social theory, 5, 7–9, 21, 23, 113, 140, 158–59, 166
sociology, 13, 18, 123, 160–61, 163
Sohag, 43
sojourners, 5, 18, 82, 94, 97–98, 111, 114, 143, 166
Somalia: Bosaso, 81
Somaliland: Berbera, 81
Sorokin, Pitirim, 139, 144
sorting, 18, 31, 33, 85–107, 178
sovereign affiliation, 2, 5, 102–3, 111, 113
Sovereign Fund of Egypt, The (TSFE), 50, 53–54, 80, 184n13
sovereign wealth funds, 24, 50, 52–55, 81, 184nn12–13
Soviet Union, 51, 65, 78
Spain, 12, 28, 187n1
Spencer, Herbert, 161
stadial theory, 12–14, 73
State of Slovenes, Croats, and Serbs, 73
state space, 47, 184n4
state versus government, 60–61